More Praise for Co
Poetics, Property, Polit ⸺, ⸺⸺ **ri**o**b**erek

*A 2015 Eisner Award nominee for
Best Scholarly/Academic Work*

"Even a thoroughly lauded and canonized work like *Watchmen* rests on more or less untrampled snow, and setting foot on it takes considerable nerve. Andrew Hoberek is to be commended for taking on such a daunting task."
—*Cinema Journal*

"Hoberek examines [*Watchmen*] from a variety of angles, crafting a well-written and well-argued series of interlocking theses. The focus on one work and dedication to formal discourse will appeal greatly to students of literature and philosophy as well as fans of serious deconstructions of popular culture."
—*Library Journal*

"Hoberek offers a scholarly approach to Alan Moore and David Gibson's *Watchmen* as a graphic novel, looking at elements most are aware of on an almost subconscious level. The author focuses on how *Watchmen* reached iconic status and on how it can be used as a touchstone for applying techniques from cultural studies, art studies, and literary studies to the emergent genre of the graphic novel. Overall, Hoberek does an outstanding job of injecting these fields, in addition to economics and history, into this slim overview of *Watchmen*. Detailed endnotes and a useful bibliography are the icing on the cake. Recommended."
—*Choice*

"*Considering Watchmen* takes its title seriously, presenting a thoughtful and multifaceted consideration of Alan Moore and Dave Gibbons' 12-issue comic book series."
—*American Literary History Online*

"*Considering Watchmen* provides a series of excellent readings of its subject, a thoughtful contribution to the study of contemporary American fiction, and an admirable demonstration of the best of contemporary comics criticism."

—*Postmodern Culture*

"Hoberek's book, for its wealth of fascinating details and compelling arguments alone, is a useful starting point for anyone interested in the work of Alan Moore and comic book studies. More interesting, I think, and one of its finest contributions to the study of comics and literature, is the refreshing methodology it offers, which sets the stage for a rigorous historicization of realism and its relations both to its own tradition and to genre fiction."

—*ImageTexT*

"When Hoberek studies *Watchmen*, he does not rest in the praise of the author or in the eternal debate between the prestige category of 'graphic novel' and the debased one of 'comic book' . . . *Considering Watchmen* bring[s] more perspectives to the work and thus seem[s] to confirm both the value of the originally published series and its existence as a postmodern text with multiple readings."

—*The Comics Grid*

"[*Considering Watchmen*] is appreciative but not reverent; [Hoberek]'s especially skeptical of the political stance in *Watchmen*."

—*Hooded Utilitarian*

"This is a smart, authoritative, and nuanced book, operating at a highly sophisticated level while still remaining accessible to a wide range of readers—a true knockout punch."

—Jared Gardner, author of *Projections: Comics and the History of 21st-century Storytelling*

CONSIDERING
WATCHMEN

EDITED BY COREY K. CREEKMUR, CRAIG FISCHER, CHARLES HATFIELD, JEET HEER, AND ANA MERINO

Volumes in the Comics Culture series explore the artistic, historical, social, and cultural significance of newspaper comic strips, comic books, and graphic novels, with individual titles devoted to focused studies of key titles, characters, writers, and artists throughout the history of comics; additional books in the series address major themes or topics in comics studies, including prominent genres, national traditions, and significant historical and theoretical issues. The series recognizes comics of all varieties, from mainstream comic books to graphic non-fiction, produced between the late 19th-century and the present. The books in the series are intended to contribute significantly to the rapidly expanding field of comics studies, but are also designed to appeal to comics fans and casual readers who seek smart critical engagement with the best examples of the form.

Bart Beaty, *Twelve-Cent Archie*

Noah Berlatsky, *Wonder Woman: Bondage and Feminism in the Marston/Peter Comics, 1941-1948*

Ian Gordon, *Superman: The Persistence of an American Icon*

Andrew Hoberek, *Considering Watchmen: Poetics, Property, Politics*

Paul Young, *Frank Miller's Daredevil and the Ends of Heroism*

CONSIDERING
WATCHMEN

POETICS,
PROPERTY,
POLITICS

Andrew
Hoberek

RUTGERS UNIVERSITY PRESS
NEW BRUNSWICK, CAMDEN, AND NEWARK, NEW JERSEY,
AND LONDON

LIBRARY OF CONGRESS CATALOGING-IN-PUBLICATION DATA
Hoberek, Andrew, 1967– author.
Considering Watchmen : Poetics, Property, Politics / Andrew Hoberek.
pages cm.—(Comics Culture)
Includes bibliographical references and index.
ISBN 978-0-8135-9037-0 (hardcover : alk. paper)—ISBN 978-0-8135-9036-3 (pbk. : alk.
paper)—ISBN 978-0-8135-9038-7 (e-book)
1. Moore, Alan, 1953– Watchmen. I. Title.
PN6728.W386H63 2014
741.5'973—dc23
2013046599

CONTENTS

ACKNOWLEDGMENTS

I read *Watchmen* in its initial serialized run, buying the issues at Fat Jack's Comicrypt in Philadelphia, where I walked every Friday after my classes at Penn to pick up that week's haul. I had been reading comics since, well, I learned how to read from comics, and beginning in junior high, I had bought a few titles regularly on the newsstand, especially Marv Wolfman and George Perez's *New Teen Titans*. In college I met people with more developed tastes and by 1986 had begun catching up on back issues of series such as Alan Moore's *Swamp Thing* and Mike Baron and Steve Rude's *Nexus*. Still, *Watchmen* blew my mind, and it has been a huge pleasure to go back and visit with my earlier self in the process of writing this book. I am grateful to Corey Creekmur for inviting me to propose something for the Comics Culture series, to Corey and Leslie Mitchner and Lisa Boyajian at Rutgers University Press for shepherding this book to print, and to Andrew Katz for his thorough and sensitive copyediting.

I have learned a lot about comics from the written work of and informal conversations with such people as William Bradley, Hillary Chute, J. D. Connor, Jared Gardner, Joshua Lukin, Daniel Worden, Paul Young, and, especially, my colleague at the University of Missouri Brad Prager. Scott Bukatman's work, in particular the "Boys in the Hoods" chapter of *Matters of Gravity*, has been an inspiration. Craig Fischer and Jared Gardner offered incisive but generous comments that made this a better book. My PhD student Colin Beineke helped me edit the final manuscript and has also taught me many things about how one might approach the study of comics within and between disciplines. As my undergraduate research assistant during the summer of 2012, Ted Hart helped me begin to map out the origins and career of *Watchmen*. Besides these people, I also need to thank the University of Missouri Research Council (which generously provided me with leave time in which to write this book) and the University of Missouri Library's Comic Art Collection and Interlibrary Loan Department (which helped me track down some of my more obscure sources). Any faults with the finished product of course remain my own. This also seems like the appropriate place for a shout-out to Rock Bottom Comics in Columbia, which while not directly involved in this project has fed my comics habit for the past fifteen years.

I wrote much of this book on Sheri Harrison's sofa and liked it so much I decided to stay.

CONSIDERING
WATCHMEN

IS IT LITERATURE?

Time magazine's October 24, 2005, issue included a one-page feature titled "10 of *Time's* Hundred Best Novels." This piece consisted of "surprises" from an online list of the one hundred best English-language novels published since the magazine began its run in 1923.[1] The first item on the list was indeed a surprise: Alan Moore and Dave Gibbons's 1987 graphic novel *Watchmen*, which beat out such prestigious works as Art Spiegelman's *Maus* (whose first volume was published in 1986) and Chris Ware's *Jimmy Corrigan, the Smartest Kid on Earth* (2000) to become the only graphic narrative on a list including literary heavy-hitters such as Virginia Woolf's *Mrs. Dalloway* (1925), Vladimir Nabokov's *Lolita* (1955), and Thomas Pynchon's *Gravity's Rainbow* (1973).[2] Lev Grossman, who compiled the list with his fellow *Time* critic Richard Lacayo, wrote that Moore and Gibbons's "story of a ragbag of bizarre, damaged, retired superheroes reunited by the murder of a former teammate . . . is told in fugal, overlapping plotlines and gorgeous panels rich with cinematic leitmotifs. A work of ruthless psychological realism, it's a landmark in the graphic novel medium. It would be a masterpiece in any."[3] A cynical reader might note that *Watchmen*, which was first published serially between September 1986 and October 1987 and then collected as a twelve-chapter volume in 1987, was then as now owned by DC Comics, a subsidiary since 1989 (when Time Inc. and Warner Communications merged) of Time Warner and that Grossman was simply cross-promoting another product in his company's portfolio. But there is something more interesting going on here, and I begin with *Time's* 2005 list in order to ask what we might learn by taking *Watchmen*'s inclusion seriously and treating it as a work of literature.

By this I do not mean that we should simply extend the designation of the literary to *Watchmen* and then proceed to analyze it on this basis. This is the approach taken by a number of critics, including Sara J. Van Ness (as her title suggests) in the book *"Watchmen" as Literature: A Critical Study of the Graphic Novel*. Van Ness's chapters variously address the history of *Watchmen*'s critical and scholarly reception, discuss the self-consciously complicated relationship between text and image within it, use the work of Gérard Genette to unpack its narrative structure, talk about the role of the narrator in the context of its nonlinear storytelling mode, employ the semiotician A. J. Greimas's concept of the semiotic rectangle to map characters' relationships to the concept of heroism, discuss the tension between two major characters' public personae and private motivations, measure the characters against Joseph Campbell's account of the universal myth of the hero's journey, and discuss the reception of director Zack Snyder's 2009 film version of Moore and Gibbons's book. As this overview suggests, *"Watchmen" as Literature* approaches its titular object from a range of angles, subjecting it to a variety of methodological approaches to see what each will yield. In the process Van Ness presents a great deal of useful information and a number of compelling insights.

But Van Ness never really interrogates the concept of literature itself, or what it might mean to apply it to a work such as *Watchmen*. She does not ask, for instance, how the nonverbal elements of the graphic novel complicate a definition of literature formulated with reference to print fiction, or how popular or journalistic accounts of *Watchmen* as literature might differ from academic ones. These are precisely the questions that interest me, and that is why I replace Van Ness's self-confident assertion of *Watchmen* "as literature" with the question, "Is it literature?" The purpose of posing this question is not to confer on Moore and Gibbons's work the prestige of an unexamined literary status but on the contrary to explore if a work such as *Watchmen* can help us to ask more interesting questions about what we mean when we call something literature.

This question can, of course, only be a starting point, since *Watchmen* is not a work of literature to the extent that that term purports to describe a certain aesthetically accomplished minority of purely verbal artworks. From this perspective, Grossman's inclusion of Moore and Gibbons's work on *Time*'s list of the best novels since 1923 is a category mistake. *Watchmen* is, to be sure, a "graphic novel," not only in the loose sense of a bound comic (many of which are, as Hillary Chute reminds us, works of nonfiction, making "graphic narrative" a preferable term)[4] but in the strict sense of being a fictional narrative. And this fictional narrative gives Moore and Gibbons's work more in common with the other novels on the list, from one perspective, than a work of poetry or print nonfiction might have. On the other hand, imagine if the list included a single movie, say *Citizen Kane* or *À bout de souffle* or *Chinatown*. All of these films are narrative based; all are fictional; all are considered accomplished works of art. But any one of them on a list otherwise composed of print novels would strike us as strange, since we instantly recognize that they belong to a different medium. Yet this insight fails us when we apply the term "literary" to the similarly word-and-image-based medium of graphic narrative.

Bart Beaty offers a useful counterapproach when he declares, in his 2012 study *Comics versus Art*, that he approaches the study of comic books from the perspective of the sociology of art in order to challenge "the prevailing orthodoxy in much of contemporary North American comics scholarship that suggests comics are best understood as a literary and fannish phenomenon, and, further, that scholarly approaches derived from the study of literature are the most appropriate tools for analysing comics as an art form."[5] If Beaty is on one hand interested in shifting the terrain of comics study from the literary to the art historical, he is on the other committed to challenging rather than simply replicating the terms within which we call something art. As he is well aware, comics are no more fine art than they are literature—no more at home in "the auction house and the museum"[6] than in the library and the English department—and so approaches derived from art history are no more inherently useful for the study of comics than are those derived from literary criticism.

Beaty's book, which addresses comics in the context of their historical dismissal by high-art worlds, thus tells us a great deal not only about comics but about visual art as well. I take a similar approach in starting from *Watchmen*'s complicated relationship to the category of literature. Here I also follow Charles Hatfield, who has likewise written about comics as literature and who argues that the study of comics must be truly multidisciplinary, in the sense that it brings different disciplines into dialogue and thus requires their practitioners to confront their most basic assumptions. Noting that "the heterogeneous nature of comics means that, in practice, comics study has to be at the intersection of various disciplines (art, literature, communications, etc.)," Hatfield nonetheless rejects the standard umbrella term of cultural studies because, he contends, cultural studies fails to address "the aesthetic and formal dimensions of comic art" and thus leaves the category of literature unchallenged. Bearing these "aesthetic and formal dimensions" in mind is important because, as Hatfield notes with reference to his own 2005 book *Alternative Comics: An Emerging Literature*, "*Alternative Comics* insists on framing comics in literary terms, not in a mere bid for status, but . . . as an incipient attack from within on hidebound ideas of what literature itself is or should be."[7] Following Hatfield, I stress the formal dimensions of *Watchmen* in a way that self-consciously interrogates—rather than taking for granted—the concept of literature. Part of this project will involve, of course, addressing the elements of the book that do not fit into conceptions of the literary, whether they need to be addressed with the tools of other disciplines, as Beaty and Hatfield in their different ways suggest, or from the perspective of the comic book as its own distinct medium, as Jared Gardner does in his 2012 study of comics and their relationships to other media *Projections: Comics and the History of Twenty-First-Century Storytelling*.[8]

Thus, part of *Watchmen*'s appeal is that—unlike works such as *Maus* or *Fun Home*—it immediately complicates this project thanks to its participation in the superhero genre. The story begins with the discovery of the dead body of Edward Blake, the former-superhero-turned-government-operative named the Comedian. The crime scene is investigated by Rorschach (born Walter Joseph Kovacs), another superhero who unlike his comrades did not either retire or become a government agent following the passage of the 1977 Keene Act that outlawed costumed crime fighting. Suspecting that someone might be killing former costumed heroes, Rorschach visits a series of them: Daniel Dreiberg, who fought crime (and for a while partnered with

Rorschach) as Nite Owl and is now living in melancholy retirement; Adrian Veidt, the former Ozymandias, who retired before the Keene Act and made a fortune by selling electric-car chargers and, later, toys based on his former exploits; Dr. Manhattan, a physicist named Jon Osterman who received tremendous powers (thus making him the only "super" hero in the story) following an accident and who like the Comedian works for the government; and Laurie Juspeczyk, a second-generation crime fighter who became the second Silk Spectre to please her mother and now lives with Dr. Manhattan on a government base as his lover. Subsequent chapters alternate between contemporary events set in motion by Rorschach's investigation and flashbacks to the origin stories of each of the major characters. Some force does seem to be systematically taking the former heroes out of play: Veidt is shot at in his corporate headquarters, Dr. Manhattan is accused of giving his closest associates cancer and leaves earth for Mars, Rorschach is set up for capture by the police and sent to jail. Dreiberg and Juspeczyk resume their costumed identities and break Rorschach out of prison. While Silk Spectre goes to Mars to speak with Manhattan, Nite Owl and Rorschach discover that the conspiracy has in fact been orchestrated by Veidt, who plans to fake an attack on New York City that will kill millions but will, he hopes, end the Cold War by convincing the United States and the USSR to join forces against a presumed extraterrestrial enemy. The various characters assemble at Veidt's Antarctic headquarters following the attack, and all but Rorschach agree to keep the conspiracy a secret. Manhattan kills Rorschach and then departs for another galaxy. In the first of two epilogues Dreiberg and Juspeczyk, now living under assumed identities, visit her mother and discuss a return to crime fighting. The second epilogue takes place at the *New Frontiersman*, the right-wing paper where Rorschach sent his journal before leaving for Antarctica, and concludes with a hapless editorial assistant named Seymour reaching for the pile of papers on which the journal sits.

As this description suggests, *Watchmen*'s elaborate genre elements— it also takes place in an alternate reality where America's superheroes helped the nation win the Vietnam War, and Richard Nixon went on to five terms as president—trouble its definition as literature, reinforcing the already existing "stigma attached to [comic books] as subliterate art."[9] In the years since *Watchmen*'s initial publication, however, this has become ironically less true of its relationship to fiction per se than of its place in the burgeoning canon of graphic narrative. *Watchmen* is one of three initially serialized works—the other two are Frank Miller's *The Dark Knight Returns* and the first volume of Art Spiegelman's *Maus*—frequently cited together in accounts of 1986 as the *annus mirabilis* of the so-called graphic novel, the year in which at least some comic books became something more serious.[10] Since the mid-eighties, however, critics have devoted far more attention to Spiegelman's book than the other two, for reasons that include but go beyond its assumption of the Holocaust as subject matter.

Specifically, *Maus* helps to found the autobiographical genre of graphic narrative that has been central to the comics medium's rise to aesthetic respectability, while *Watchmen*—despite having generated a great deal of academic and popular criticism—remains associated with the déclassé genre of the superhero story. As comics historian Paul Lopes details, the 1980s saw the rise of a "Heroic Age" in comics when changes in production and distribution enabled artists to begin challenging the medium's former limitations, either as "pulp rebels" such as Moore and Gibbons who worked within the dominant genres or as "alt rebels" who sought to distance themselves from these genres and in the process often "reproduce[ed] the same stigma found in official culture toward comic books more generally, that is, mainstream comic books as subliterate, childish art."[11] The popular critic Douglas Wolk, who writes sensitively about *Watchmen*'s form in his 2007 book *Reading Comics*, likewise notes that proponents of comics seek to establish their aesthetic seriousness not only by rightfully insisting on their status as a medium open to multiple genres but also by denigrating the superhero genre that remains their most mainstream and profitable face.[12] Drawing an analogy with another popular medium that had to fight its way into critical respect, Wolk criticizes "art-comics enthusiasts" on the basis that "reading only auteurist art comics is like being a filmgoer who watches only auteurist art cinema."[13]

This distinction goes beyond genre, however, to encompass conditions of production as well. As Wolk points out, the division between "art comics" and "mainstream comics" depends not only on the fact that the former "avoid genre" and "tend to be conceived as self-contained books" but also, crucially, on their status as single-authored works: art comics "are almost always written and drawn by a single cartoonist," while mainstream comics are "generally written and drawn by different people—sometimes by mid-sized committees."[14] Moreover, most superhero comics remain corporate products, published either by DC (which as I have already noted is a subsidiary of Time Warner) or Marvel (which in 2009 was acquired by Disney).[15] In this regard the association of the superhero genre with juvenile subject matter and presentation is redoubled by superhero comics' production in a context that violates longstanding Western prejudices about who creates art (individuals) under what conditions (independently and certainly not for large corporations) to further diminish the genre's status.

A preference for individually produced, independently published, nonsuperhero stories characterizes two of the best recent studies of comics, Gardner's *Projections* and Hillary Chute's *Graphic Women: Life Narrative and Contemporary Comics* (2010). Chute, who addresses the work of the female comics artists Aline Kominsky-Crumb, Phoebe Gloeckner, Lynda Barry, Marjane Satrapi, and Alison Bechdel, has specific reasons, feminist and otherwise, for focusing on these artists' autobiographical works, and she addresses their neglect both by cultural arbiters such as the *New York Times* (which, in an article she cites, ignores graphic narrative by women) and "feminist critics in the academy" (who do not see the comics' engagement with typically feminist concerns).[16] But it is worth noting that early in the book Chute slides from the claim that "some of today's most riveting feminist cultural production is in the form of accessible yet edgy graphic narratives"[17] to the much more sweeping (and canon-forming) claim that "the most riveting comics texts coming out right now—from men and women alike—are not novels at all" but are instead works of nonfiction.[18]

Gardner likewise has a larger goal, in his case providing a history of the comics medium beginning with late nineteenth-century newspaper comics. Yet after a chapter detailing the rise of comic books from the midthirties through the midfifties, Gardner sets aside the superhero genre and instead brings his story to the present day with two parallel chapters: one on the autobiographical strain running from the underground comix of the late sixties and early seventies through contemporary artists such as Spiegelman and Bechdel, and one on the equally prestigious line of artists, such as Ware and Daniel Clowes, who dedicate themselves to the historicist project of archiving previous mass culture. Gardner writes incisively about the influence of Marvel Comics' "vulnerable and masochistic superhero[es]"[19] of the early sixties on the former work, but otherwise the superhero disappears from his account—*Watchmen* returns briefly in his coda for a discussion of how its famous unadaptability to film in fact anticipates the newer medium of the DVD.

This is not to say that there is not brilliant academic criticism of the superhero genre: Geoff Klock's 2002 *How to Read Superhero Comics and Why*, the chapters on superheroes in Scott Bukatman's 2003 *Matters of Gravity: Special Effects and Supermen in the 20th Century*, and Charles Hatfield's 2012 *Hand of Fire: The Comics Art of Jack Kirby*, among others, offer wide-ranging, methodologically interdisciplinary, and formally sensitive accounts of the genre. But the fact that the 2006 special issue of *Modern Fiction Studies* on graphic narrative coedited by Chute and Marianne DeKoven addresses not a single superhero comic[20] or that Gardner can frame a history of the medium that all but ignores its most prominent genre suggests the extent to which Wolk's "art comics" have captured a lion's share of canonical prestige in academic criticism of the form. This is also true, albeit to a lesser extent, in popular criticism: *Comics Journal*'s 1999 list of the "100 Best Comics of the Century" included only seven superhero series, ranging from *Watchmen* at number 91 to Will Eisner's *The Spirit* (itself only marginally a superhero series) at number 15.[21]

Yet while *Watchmen*'s superhero narrative places it in tension with the generic biases of at least some contemporary comics criticism, it also gives it something in common with the works of print fiction on *Time*'s list—at least those chosen by Grossman. Grossman's fellow critic Richard Lacayo notes on the magazine's website that, after comparing notes, he and Grossman discovered eighty choices in common, then "more or less divided the remaining slots" between them, a procedure which would allow each of them "to include books that the other might not have chosen. Or might not even have read. (*Ubik*? What's an Ubik?)"[22] As Lacayo's faux-ignorant parenthetical joke about Philip K. Dick's 1969 novel suggests, Grossman does indeed champion genre fiction in his selections. While Lacayo's choices tend—if we can judge by which books the pair blurbs—toward either highbrow experimentalism (William Gaddis's *The Recognitions* [1955], John Barth's *The Sot-Weed Factor* [1960], two works by Pynchon) or the forgotten middlebrow (John O'Hara's *Appointment in Samarra* [1934], Jonathan Franzen favorite Christina Stead's *The Man Who Loved Children* [1940], Richard Yates's *Revolutionary Road* [1961]), Grossman's picks include not only *Watchmen* and *Ubik* but also Raymond Chandler's hard-boiled detective story *The Big Sleep* (1939), John LeCarré's espionage thriller *The Spy Who Came in from the Cold* (1963), and Judy Blume's young-adult novel *Are You There, God? It's Me, Margaret* (1970). Grossman, himself the author of genre novels such as the thriller *Codex* (2004) and the fantasy *The Magicians* (2009),[23] has more recently praised the increasing admixture of literary aspirations and genre motifs that characterizes much current fiction, arguing that "we're getting a revolution from below, coming up from the supermarket aisles. Genre fiction is the technology that will disrupt the literary novel as we know it."[24] In his selections for the *Time* list, we might say, Grossman offers a polemical prehistory for the phenomenon he notes in this more recent essay: the fact that respected authors such as Cormac McCarthy, Michael Chabon, Jennifer Egan, and Colson Whitehead have all more or less permanently moved into territory that blurs the line between literary and genre fiction, in ways that popular and academic critics of contemporary fiction have had to acknowledge.

This leads us to the first and most historically specific reason for discussing *Watchmen* as a work of literature: the fact that it anticipates a recent shift in the definition of what counts as mainstream literary fiction. *Watchmen* would have come nowhere near passing muster with the literary establishment in 1986, a time dominated by the domestic realism of the minimalist school, by the pseudominimalist writing of the Brat Pack, and, at the most nonrealistic end of the spectrum, by the magical realism of Toni Morrison and a few other authors. In the early twenty-first century this has changed, however, with literary fiction turning to genre fiction for its form as well as its content and the most prestigious authors citing genre works among their influences: Chabon's 2008 essay collection *Maps and Legends*, for instance, includes pieces on P. D. James, Philip Pullman's *His Dark Materials* trilogy (1995–2000), and a variety of comics artists, while in a recent interview with the *New York Times Sunday Book Review* Junot Díaz expresses his devotion to the science-fiction writers Octavia Butler and Samuel Delany and cites Moore's early *Miracleman* series (1982–1984; first published in the UK as *Marvelman*) along with Leslie Marmon Silko's *Ceremony* (1977) and Margaret Atwood's *The Handmaid's Tale* (1985) as "books that changed everything" for him.[25]

This change has been spearheaded by (although it is by no means limited to) a largely male cohort of authors born in the mid to late sixties who prior to or instead of formal training in MFA programs or other academic venues participated in the informal but dedicated taste cultures of science-fiction, comic-book, and other types of fandom. In the wake of the National Book Critics Circle Award given to Jonathan Lethem for his 1999 crime novel *Motherless Brooklyn* and the Pulitzer Prize awarded to Chabon for his 2000 *The Amazing Adventures of Kavalier & Clay*, which blended realism with disquisitions on comic book history and scenes from the title characters' own superhero comics, authors such as Lethem, Chabon, Díaz, and Whitehead could imagine their ambitions for literary greatness as not in conflict but continuous with the authorship of genre fiction. In the broadest terms *Watchmen* helped lay the groundwork for this shift by being among the first works of superhero fiction recognized by fans and mainstream commentators as aspiring to a kind of serious literary status. Indeed, *Watchmen* constitutes a direct influence in the case of Díaz, whose National Book Critics Circle Award– and Pulitzer Prize–winning 2007 novel *The Brief Wondrous Life of Oscar Wao* includes several direct references to *Watchmen* among other works in what the narrator calls "the Genres."[26]

The second reason for reading *Watchmen* as a work of literature derives from its historically significant role in this transition from serialized comics to the graphic novel. The cartoonist and critic R. C. Harvey attributes the term "graphic novel" to Richard Kyle, who Harvey claims used it in a 1964 newsletter of the Amateur Press Association,[27] and it was first employed as a marketing device by Baronet Press, the publisher of Will Eisner's 1978 volume of self-contained stories of New York tenement life *A Contract with God*.[28] In the early eighties Marvel Comics published a series of self-contained stories (beginning with 1982's *The Death of Captain Marvel* and *X-Men: God Loves, Man*

Kills) under the Marvel Graphic Novel imprint. DC soon thereafter followed suit. These volumes were sold, not as comic books traditionally had been, on racks at newsstands and other retail outlets but in new specialized comic book shops and, tentatively, in bookstores. Joe Queenan concisely outlined this shift in a 1989 piece for the *New York Times* on the changing comic book industry:

> By the 1980's, magazine distributors had long since lost interest in the thin profit margins they earned from comics. This encouraged a New Yorker, Phil Seuling, to set up a direct distribution network: selling comic books to specialty shops on a non-returnable basis. Today, at least two-thirds of comic books are sold in 3,500 specialty shops by owners who order three months in advance, and who, unlike newsstand and convenience-store operators, must keep every title they buy. The owners are constantly apprised of future plot lines, and are told far in advance who will be writing, drawing and inking stories, all of which are major concerns to comic-book readers and collectors.[29]

Historically, this shift in the distribution of graphic narrative, from the places where magazines were traditionally sold to dedicated specialty stores, is referred to as the rise of the "direct market."[30]

As Joshua Lukin points out, the transformation of the comic book industry in the early eighties made possible a book like *Watchmen*: the rise of specialty shops encouraged at least some comics creators to publish independently rather than working for DC and Marvel; in response the big two gave "their writers and artists new freedom" and sought out new talent—including the British writer Moore, whom DC editor Len Wein hired to take over DC's struggling horror comic *The Saga of the Swamp Thing*.[31] Lopes notes that this investment in talent not only enabled "artists to see comic books as a medium of self-expression" but also paid off for both the two major companies and independent publishers, insofar as it provided "a bridge to the outside world." Following the "critical success" of *The Dark Knight*, *Watchmen*, and *Maus*, "trade publishers, bookstores, and the press began to take comic books seriously in the form of graphic novels," and "trade publishers like Pantheon, Penguin, and Doubleday" joined comics publishers in releasing trade editions of comics, whether new works designed as self-contained books or collections of previously serialized material.[32]

The category of the graphic novel clearly raises important questions about the literary status of the thing it denotes, especially when that thing was, like *Watchmen*, previously serialized in a traditional comic book format.[33] On one hand the label "graphic novel" confers a new, more privileged aesthetic status on the narrative in question, which demands to be taken more seriously when it appears as a bound volume rather than a series of stapled pamphlets. At the same time the advent of the graphic novel also constitutes an economic transformation, since it allows publishers to sell their products in a different venue, the bookstore, and, in the case of previously serialized stories, to sell the same material twice, first in comics shops and then again in bookstores. Of course as Fredric Jameson noted long ago, with reference to the print novel itself, such material transformations are not distinct from aesthetic form but in fact help shape it: Jameson writes that "there seems, for instance, to have been an unquestionable causal relationship between the admittedly extrinsic fact of the crisis in late nineteenth-century publishing, during which the dominant three-decker lending library novel was replaced by a cheaper one-volume format, and the modification of the 'inner form' of the novel itself."[34] Part of the interest of *Watchmen*, then—like that of the novels of George Gissing, whose career overlaps for Jameson with the rise of the one-volume novel—is the fact that it appears at the moment of transformation and remains poised between an earlier status as mass cultural trash and a new status as art.

Grossman correctly gauges the two major formal aspects of *Watchmen*'s aesthetic aspirations when he refers to its "ruthless psychological realism" and its "fugal, overlapping plotlines and gorgeous panels rich with cinematic leitmotifs." *Watchmen*'s self-conscious relationships to the literary traditions of realist representation and the formal experimentation celebrated by modernism constitute the third reason for reading it as a work of literature. *Watchmen* and *Dark Knight* are jointly famous for bringing a darker, putatively more realistic tone to the superhero genre: unlike previous superheroes the protagonists of these series age, have sex, and commit morally questionable acts. In

fact this was not an unprecedented breakthrough so much as an extension of earlier movements in this direction. The Marvel Comics titles
that Stan Lee produced with the artists Jack Kirby and Steve Ditko
in the early sixties, such as *Fantastic Four* and *Spider-Man*, featured
heroes who were vexed about their powers and missions. And in the
early seventies the writer Denny O'Neill and the artist Neal Adams
brought this sensibility from Marvel to DC and ramped it up even
further for famous runs on *Batman* (which eschewed the campy sensibility inherited from the sixties television show in favor of returning the hero to his roots as a dark obsessive) and *Green Lantern and
Green Arrow* (whose heroes tackled contemporary social issues such
as drug use). Still, Miller and Moore and Gibbons took this trend even
further—their ability to do so in large part a product of the way that
direct sales had shifted the comic book market from a mostly juvenile
mass readership to a more adult niche audience. The growth of this
new niche audience increasingly allowed companies to publish work
outside the strictures of the Comics Code Authority that the industry
had put in place as a self-policing response to the anti-comic-book
movement of the 1950s.[35]

The increasing prevalence of such adult content invariably preoc-
cupied early journalistic accounts of the transformation of the comics
industry and the rise of the graphic novel. In a 1988 piece for *Newsweek*, for instance, Peter S. Prescott declared, "If the '40s comics were
an escapist remedy for the discontents of childhood, a comic book's
cover in the '80s may declare that it's for 'Adults Only.' The warning
has less to do with casual nudity and pornography of the frat-house
persuasion—though some of both has survived from the underground
comics of the '60s—than with a mood of unease, of anxiety, even of
paranoia. Today's comic books are getting ambitious."[36] No longer
strictly for children, Prescott suggests, the content of comic books has
grown more adult both in its representation of sex and violence and in
an uncertain affective palette that registers greater moral and aesthetic
ambition. In a brief 1986 piece for the trade journal *Advertising Age*,
Len Strazewski likewise cited DC's move from "the fantasyland tradition of comics" to "a series of highly literate and very realistic comics
that focus on social issues": the charity project "Heroes Against Hun-
ger"; a spin-off of DC's mainstream superhero title *Teen Titans* dealing

with South African apartheid and a Lois Lane miniseries about missing children; and, of course, *The Dark Knight* and *Watchmen*.[37]

For observers such as Prescott and Strazewski, however, realism, topicality, and other elements of aesthetic maturity were disturbingly imbricated with what they saw as the superhero genre's newly pornographic strain. Citing *The Dark Knight* and *Watchmen* as examples of *opposition* to the "trend that drew comic books away from fantasy and toward realism," Prescott notes that they "remain steeped in the fatigued conventions of the superheroes of the '40s, yet with a difference." This difference renders them, moreover, inappropriate for children: noting that "incredibly for a genre once directed at kids, these long tales deal with growing old," he writes that *Watchmen*'s "molting superheroes have been forced into retirement [because] society can no longer tolerate their sociopathy, their right-wing excesses," and that "the new 'Batman' reads like a story board for the Bernhard Goetz School of Social Work." Prescott's distaste for these series' content is so great that it shapes his account of their form: *Watchmen*, he contends, "has some glancing humor, but it runs to about 400 pages and soon sinks beneath the weight of its pretensions, its flashbacks and parallel plots."[38] Just as *Watchmen* violates the genre's implicit compact with the juvenile reader at the level of what it shows, he suggests, it is "overreaching" in how it shows it.

Queenan, whose title "Drawing on the Dark Side" suggests his critical animus, likewise locates this disturbing conjunction in comic books in general and *Watchmen* in particular. He begins his 1989 piece with a sensationalistic description that could easily have appeared in anti-comic-book crusader Fredric Wertham's 1954 *Seduction of the Innocent*: "The prostitute squats in the shadows, her leather-clad haunches poised atop black leather boots. Her cruel face is encased in a leather mask; in her left hand she clutches a leather whip. She has come for one purpose: to mete out punishment. Is this a dominant mistress working the wharves of Hamburg, a character in a porn film, or a Helmut Newton model?" Identifying this figure as "Batman's legendary rival, the Catwoman, appearing for the first time in her new comic-book role as a vigilante hooker," Queenan acknowledges that "recently, the avant-garde art press has been full of praise for the sophisticated graphics, and countless newspaper and magazine articles have cited the topicality of today's comic-book plot lines as a sign of the art form's maturity." He argues, however, that such accounts have ignored the fact "that over the last decade, comics have forsaken campy repartee and outlandishly byzantine plots for a steady diet of remorseless violence." *Watchmen*, while "well-written and elegantly drawn," becomes Queenan's key exhibit of "the vindictive, sadistic tone of comics of the 1980's." He notes that beside depicting the Comedian's attempt to rape the original Silk Spectre and his murder of his pregnant Vietnamese lover, it "also features a boy who laughs when he finds out that his mother committed suicide by drinking Drano, a heroine forced into early retirement because of lesbianism, and a child hacked to pieces and fed to German shepherds. This is all in the service of a sophisticated literary technique called 'foreshadowing' that prepares the reader for the riveting climax, in which half of New York City's population gets annihilated. (In the comic-book universe, anything Armageddon-like that takes place in New York is generally viewed as an improvement.)"[39] If for Prescott *Watchmen*'s formal innovations are just as inappropriate as its content, for Queenan these innovations take a backseat to the story's desire to wallow in sex and violence.

In these early responses to the transformation of the comic book industry, we see the seeds of the contemporary privileging of art comics over superhero comics. Prescott, for instance, cites the "comic-book naturalism" of Harvey Pekar's *American Splendor* series and also notes the counterrealistic but still aesthetically ambitious tendency of Art Spiegelman's *RAW*: "Because something about the comics form demands unreality, some of the most interesting artists have turned to surrealism, to primitivism, to an exaggerated black-and-white brand of expressionism—or a combination of all three."[40] Whereas autobiographical works by writers such as Spiegelman and Pekar can embrace realism and aspire to the status of art (especially if they eschew the pornographic excesses of the underground comix from which they sprang), however, realism in a superhero story is just grotesque. Who wants to see a Batman who, as Prescott notes, has "been drinking heavily," whose "teeth look flawed," and whose "private crusade is, of course, unbalanced"?[41] This grotesque content, moreover, both springs from and reinforces the overreaching ambition of the medium's corporate wing: noting that "most of the attention accorded comics as a serious art form . . . has been directed at the innovative independents like Spiegelman, the Hernandez brothers and Pekar—not the artists working for Marvel and DC," Queenan asserts that "comic books within the mainstream . . . want to have it both ways, enticing the reader with graphic visual renderings of the very depravity they supposedly deplore."[42] Mainstream graphic novels in the superhero medium can deliver only a stunted form of aesthetic ambition, their desire to escape the confines of a children's genre capable only of violence and pornography.

Yet while these popular accounts clearly indulge in oversimplification and hyperbole, they do not entirely misrepresent the mideighties transformation of the medium's corporate mainstream. Both Moore and Gibbons have expressed ambivalence about *Watchmen*'s role in ushering in a new wave of darker, more violent comics. In an interview for Mark Salisbury's 2002 volume *Artists on Comics Art*, Gibbons argued that the emphasis on *Watchmen* as "a grim and gritty kind of thing" ignored "the joy and romance" of the story, noting, "To me the series was a wonderful celebration of superheroes as much as anything else."[43] And when Tasha Robinson asked Moore, in a 2001 interview for the *Onion*'s *A.V. Club* entertainment site, "Is it true that you regret in some ways the effect that *Watchmen* had on the comics industry?" the writer bemoaned the manner in which subsequent creators picked up primarily on the series's dark and violent tone: "I think that what a lot of people saw when they read *Watchmen* was a high degree of violence, a bleaker and more pessimistic political perspective, perhaps a bit more sex, more swearing. And to some degree there has been, in the 15 years since *Watchmen*, an awful lot of the comics field devoted to these very grim, pessimistic, nasty, violent stories which kind of use *Watchmen* to validate what are, in effect, often just some very nasty stories that don't have a lot to recommend them." For Moore, too, the question of adult content and the repetitive nature of mass-produced art come together when he notes that "the gritty, deconstructivist postmodern superhero comic, as exemplified by *Watchmen*, also became a genre," although "it was meant to be one work on its own."[44] Moore, like Gibbons, argues that the comic books produced in *Watchmen*'s wake misread what the pair achieved in the series, an emphasis he later sought to correct with both his Superman tribute *Supreme* and his line of America's Best Comics. The latter especially offered smart but loving tributes to the history of superheroes and their high and pulp fictional antecedents, culminating in what Craig Fischer has aptly called the "charmageddon" of Moore and J. H. Williams III's 1999–2005 series *Promethea*.[45]

Geoff Klock's study *How to Read Superhero Comics and Why* describes a different line of comics influenced by Moore and Gibbons, one that allows us to see the realism of *Watchmen* in a different light. Klock identifies *The Dark Knight* and *Watchmen* as founding works of what he calls "the revisionary superhero narrative." Through this narrative the genre, responding "to the waning of the imaginative wave launched a quarter of a century earlier," takes on self-consciousness and thereby "becomes literature."[46] Klock's focus on revision (adapted from Harold Bloom's theory that great poets achieve their status by misreading previous strong models in the tradition) leads him to define realism not as the presentation of particular content but rather as a relationship to generic conventions. Thus, *The Dark Knight's* realism lies not only in Miller's characteristically "gritty, hard-boiled" tone but also in its depiction of an aged Batman "in a genre where characters persist for decades untouched by the passage of time" and in its clever synthesis of elements of the character's then nearly half-century history. Referring to the "eye-catching yellow Bat-Shield" that the character had acquired in 1967 and that seems odd "on a uniform meant to blend in with shadows," Klock notes that in Miller's work, "when Batman takes a rifle shot to the chest, which any reader assumes would kill him instantly, it reveals metal shielding. Batman says, 'Why do you think I wear a target on my chest—can't armor my head,' and with that one line a thirty-year mystery dissolves as every reader runs mentally through previous stories, understanding that plate as always having been there."[47]

Moore and Gibbons engage in a similar process of realist revisionism, but with a crucial difference in tone exemplified by the contrasting art styles of *The Dark Knight* and *Watchmen*: "Miller's moody shadows, reminiscent of film noir, are very romantic and invoke a world as tough and gritty as it is operatic. Gibbons's characters, on the other hand, all have a distinct sadness, and his frumpy characters stand in stark contrast to Miller's very 'cool' Batman."[48] Moore's script likewise cultivates this melancholy tone, with its persistent interest in the questions of "what would make a person dress up in a costume and fight crime"[49] and what it would look like if he or she did. In contrast to Miller, who gives *The Dark Knight* an air of realism by adopting the tropes of a different genre (crime fiction / film noir), Moore and Gibbons ground their realism in a kind of quotidian sadness. As I will argue, this tone has a great deal in common with the quotidian "naturalism" that Prescott praises in Pekar's work and that critics such as Chute and Gardner praise in fictional and nonfictional art comics.

Klock's discussion of this revisionist project, as well as the differences with which *The Dark Knight* and *Watchmen* approach it, makes clear that we can only fully understand *Watchmen*'s frequently cited realism in formal terms. Moore's earliest work for DC Comics, on the horror series *The Saga of the Swamp Thing*, suggests one way to do so. Moore's very first issue for the series shows him mixing traditional, if more writerly, third-person narration in his caption boxes ("Her name is *Lizabeth Tremayne*, and she's used to taking her sunlight a little more diluted")[50] with first-person narration from the point of view of characters ("I had to come, Arcane. I had to be sure").[51] This shift away from the omniscient narration that was standard in superhero comics through the early eighties ("Darting aside to dodge the Thing's blow, the blazing Torch accidentally touches off the automatic *sprinkler system. . .*")[52] has since become common in the genre. Moore's pioneering use of free-indirect discourse and first-person narration roughly condenses the similar transition in the history of the print novel from Henry James through Virginia Woolf and William Faulkner (albeit not in a linear fashion, since Moore is not inventing new techniques but adapting already existing ones from the history of prose fiction).

As in the late nineteenth- and early twentieth-century novel, greater realism here means the more realistic representation of subjectivity. In an interview with Moore done in 1983, the year he began writing *Swamp Thing*,[53] he addresses this issue with relation to an earlier (and to his mind still insufficient) technical innovation:

The thing with characterization is that it's important, but it's largely done wrong. When I started reading comics with Superman and Batman, they had no characterization whatsoever. . . .

Now what happened when Marvel came along in the sixties was that they thought, "Let's be realistic and give them human characters. We'll let them have one characteristic." They made Spider-Man neurotic, so that whereas Superman goes about being incredibly powerful and beating up villains, Spider-Man goes around being incredibly powerful, beating up villains, and then feeling guilty about it afterwards.[54]

Moore sees Marvel's innovation as a failure to adequately represent subjectivity—"[Characters] must be crippled, neurotic, or foreign, and [creators] don't bother to get anywhere near the complexity of human character"[55]—but one that, crucially, takes the form of a technical device rather than the representation of some particular content.

As my invocation of James et al. alongside Moore's commitment to technical innovation should suggest, what is at stake here is not simply realism but also the legacy of the modernist movement that took off in other media roughly a century before *Watchmen*'s publication. Moore's 2001 interview with Robinson makes clear his commitment to a brand of technical innovation that we can compare, not casually, to earlier forms of literary and visual modernism. Initially, Moore claims, he and Gibbons were planning a somewhat "more dark" and "naturalistic" version of the superhero story, but as he was writing the opening and drawing his customary thumbnail sketches for Gibbons to work with, he began to notice correspondences among the "two or three strains of narrative" he was juggling:

> I had a truculent newsvendor giving his fairly uninformed commentary on the political state of the world, the likelihood of a coming war. Across the street, in the background, we have two people fixing a radiation sign to a wall. Sitting with his back to a hydrant near the newsvendor, there's a small boy reading a comic, which is a pirate comic. And I think while I was doodling, I noticed that an extreme close-up of the radiation symbol, if you put the right sort of caption with it, could look almost like the black sail of a ship against a yellow sky. So I dropped in a caption in the comic that the child was reading about a hellbound

ship's black sails against a yellow Indies sky. And I have a word balloon coming from off-panel, which is actually the balloon of the newsvendor, which is talking about war. The narrative of the pirate comic is talking about a different sort of war. As we pull back, we realize that we're looking at a radiation symbol that's being tacked to the wall of a newly created fallout shelter. And finally, when we pull back into the beginning, into the foreground, we realize that these pirate captions that we've been reading are those in the comic that is being read by the small boy. This was exciting. There was something going on here. There was an interplay between the imagery, between the strands of narrative, the pirate narrative, the dialogue going on in the street. They were striking sparks off of each other, and they were doing something which I hadn't actually seen a comic do before.[56]

In contrast with his tendency elsewhere to describe his work in literary terms, Moore here displays a countervailing but equally important interest in the specificity of the comics medium. This latter interest, I argue, allows us to call Moore's work "modernist" in a very precise sense.

Specifically, Moore's account of this scene, which became the first page of chapter III in the finished graphic novel (figure 1),[57] is modernist in the strict sense defined by Clement Greenberg in his 1965 essay "Modernist Painting." In that essay, a revised version of a 1960 Voice of America lecture, Greenberg argued that the defining condition of modern art was the quest to discover and elaborate "that which was unique and irreducible not only in art in general, but also in each particular art," the drive of artists working in each art form "to determine, through the operations peculiar to [that form], the effects peculiar and exclusive to itself."[58] Thus, modernist painting, the form that most closely interests Greenberg, concerns itself primarily with the "flatness" that is "alone . . . unique and exclusive to that art."[59] Seeking to distinguish itself from other arts, on one hand it strives "to divest itself of everything it might share with sculpture,"[60] while on the other it abjures representation and "asks that a literary theme be translated into strictly optical, two-dimensional terms before becoming the subject of pictorial art—which means its being translated in such a way

FIGURE 1. The possibilities inherent in the medium
Source: Alan Moore and Dave Gibbons, *Watchmen* III.1

that it entirely loses its literary character."[61] Moore likewise begins with a more or less literary goal—the elaboration of a darker, more naturalistic version of the superhero narrative—and finds himself drawn to the purely technical aspects of what he can do within the comics medium. He builds on the way that visual puns can link his three narrative strands, for instance, or the way in which the words from one strand can overlay and thus comment on images from another.[62]

We can already see Moore's interest in the specificity of the comics medium qua medium in his pamphlet *Writing for Comics*, originally written for a British fanzine in 1985 and then republished, with a new afterword, by Avatar Press in 2003. In this long essay Moore seeks to distinguish comics from another medium with which they are frequently compared, film:

> While cinematic thinking has undoubtedly produced many of the finest comic works of the past 30 years, as a model to base our own medium upon I find it eventually to be limiting and restricting. For one thing, any emulation of film technique by the comics medium must inevitably suffer by the comparison. Sure, you can use cinematic panel progressions to make your work more involving and lively than that of comic artists who *haven't* mastered the trick yet, but in the final analysis you will be left with a film that has neither movement nor a soundtrack. The use of cinematic techniques can advance the standards of comic art and writing, but if those techniques are seen as the highest point to which comic art can aspire, then the medium is condemned forever to be a poor relative of the motion picture industry. That isn't good enough.[63]

Moore goes on to assert a parallel distinction from prose narrative, objecting to the principle behind the status-conferring label of graphic novel itself: "comic work of more than 40 pages is automatically equated with a novel, once more suffering badly from the comparison. . . . As opposed to films without movement or sound we get novels without scope, depth or purpose. That isn't good enough either."[64]

Despite this interest in the specificity of the comics medium, however, Moore elsewhere insists on describing his work in literary terms.

This leads to the fourth reason for discussing *Watchmen* as literature: as I will discuss at length in chapter 2, Moore frequently uses the literary as a way of modeling his own creative agency and ownership in an industry structured around the work-for-hire employment of creative talent.

Moore's reasons for adopting this strategy have been practical as well as intellectual. As Queenan pointed out in his 1989 *Times* piece, DC's and Marvel's efforts to woo new talent amid increasing competition for the direct sales market did not alter the fundamental ownership arrangements under which these companies produced the great mass of superhero comics: "Traditionally, comic books have been art by committee, with the companies calling the shots. Although that has changed to some extent in the last decade, with more and more creators bringing their own projects to the major publishers, most popular comic-book characters still belong to the companies, which exercise tight rein over what the artists can do with the characters."[65] Throughout Moore's career he has had a contentious, on-again-off-again relationship with DC, for which he wrote not only *Swamp Thing* and *Watchmen* but also the line of America's Best Comics that appeared under the company's WildStorm imprint between 1999 and 2007. Much of the tension between Moore and DC has centered on *Watchmen* and in particular DC's ownership of the rights to the series, which has allowed the company to profit from it more than Moore and Gibbons have and which gives it control over such projects as the 2009 Zack Snyder movie adaptation, which Moore has disavowed.

In the context of Moore's famous distaste for film adaptations of his work, his stress on the specificity of the comics medium and his interest in the literary dimensions of his work can be seen not as contradictory positions but as parallel strategies for resisting the cross-media fluidity that a corporation such as Time Warner exercises over the intellectual properties it controls. Discussing the then-ongoing efforts to make a *Watchmen* movie, for instance, Moore endorsed the former position, telling *Entertainment Weekly*, "My book is a comic book. Not a movie, not a novel. A comic book. It's been made in a certain way, and designed to be read a certain way: in an armchair, nice and cozy next to a fire, with a steaming cup of coffee. Personally, I think that would make for a lovely Saturday night."[66] Yet despite his insistence that *Watchmen* is "not a novel," in seeking to distinguish it from the industrially produced medium of film, he conjures a nostalgic scene that most people would in fact associate not with comics but with novels. Moreover, Moore describes not a comic book but what is clearly a graphic novel: the original series, after all, could not be read in one sitting because it appeared in more or less monthly installments over the course of a year.[67]

And in fact elsewhere Moore explicitly deploys the idea of *Watchmen* as a work of literature, sometimes in self-evidently contradictory ways, against the corporate control of stories and characters he has created: in a 2012 *New York Times* story on DC's plans to publish *Before Watchmen*, a series of prequels to *Watchmen* written and drawn by others, for instance, Moore declares, "As far as I know, . . . there weren't that many prequels or sequels to 'Moby–Dick.'"[68] Moore here ignores a tradition of literary sequels going back at least to the second book of *Don Quixote* (itself written, ironically, to assert Miguel de Cervantes's claims to his character over against Alonso Fernández de Avellaneda's unauthorized sequel).[69] In the context of *Before Watchmen*, however, Moore clearly poses his formulation against the corporate logic within which, as Noah Berlatsky notes in another piece on *Before Watchmen*, "creators are there to churn out marketable, exploitable properties . . . and then disappear." "Because the comics companies own the characters," Berlatsky further notes, "and because they have substantial marketing departments, they're in a position to make that disappearance stick."[70] In implicitly comparing *Watchmen* to a canonical work of literature such as *Moby-Dick*, Moore thus seeks to make the author reappear as the real owner of the work.

Of course *Watchmen* is not, in fact, literature. We can begin with the most basic feature distinguishing a work such as *Watchmen* from prose narrative (and the one responsible for the frequent comparison to cinema): the use of images as well as words. But Moore's use of the language of literature to describe *Watchmen* reminds us that the seemingly obvious distinction between comics and literature actually conflates a number of different propositions, not all of them equally true. Historically, the assertion that comics are not real literature (like the parallel notion that they are not real visual art) has been used not to uphold the specificity of particular media but to denigrate comics as a juvenile form not worthy of serious attention. The intransigence of this logic is suggested by the fact that even the British novelist Tom McCarthy, whose own fiction employs the material of popular genres in complicated ways, can fall back on it in his otherwise fascinating book *Tintin and the Secret of Literature*. Thus, after crediting the Belgian artist Hergé's series with a raft of literary features ("a bestiary of human types" on par with those of "Shakespeare and Chaucer," a Balzacian social tableau, "all the subtlety normally attributed to Jane Austen or Henry James," "Molière-style social comedy," "Dumas-style adventure," "Conradian boxed narratives," "Rabelaisian obscenities," "a huge symbolic register . . . worthy of a Faulkner or a Brontë," and the ability of "the best writers—Stendhal, George Eliot or Pynchon, for example"—to bring "a whole era . . . into focus"), McCarthy asks the same question that I have been pursuing here: "is it literature?"[71] His answer, crucially, hinges on the need to remember all the ways in which *Tintin* remains sub- or paraliterary: "In the last two decades of the twentieth century and the first of the twenty-first, writers of cartoons, hugely indebted to Hergé's work, have deliberately launched bids for literary status, producing 'graphic novels' that are often quite self-consciously highbrow and demanding. The huge irony is that the *Tintin* books remain both unrivalled in their complexity and depth *and* so simple, even after more than half a century, that a child can read them with the same involvement as an adult."[72] "Packed with significance, intensely associative, overwhelmingly suggestive," *Tintin* for McCarthy "still occupies a space below the radar of literature proper."[73]

Of course McCarthy asserts this not in a derogatory but in an honorific sense: the fact that Hergé was not a great writer *of literature* means that "the claim we should make for him is a more interesting one." "Wrapped up in a simple medium for children," McCarthy writes, "is a mastery of plot and symbol, theme and subtext far superior to that displayed by most 'real' novelists. [Hergé's story "The Castafiore Emerald"] holds all literature's formal keys, its trade secrets—and holds them at the vanishing point of plot, where nothing whatsoever happens."[74] Here I take McCarthy to be claiming that in *Tintin*'s pared-down simplicity, it exposes the molecular structure out of which narrative literature is built. Yet this claim remains more suggestive than anything else—McCarthy does not make entirely clear what he means by "the vanishing point of plot," for instance, or why this is important. Thanks to this lack of specificity, it is not always clear whether McCarthy is describing Hergé's series as a masterpiece in a different medium than print literature or a work of failed literature—something "below the radar of literature proper."

In stressing *Watchmen*'s difference from literature, then, we must remember that this is a difference not of achievement but of kind: the comic book is a medium with its own formal components, its own conditions of production, and its own history. These differences go well beyond the combination of images and text, although this combination provides a starting point for addressing them. In the case of *Watchmen*, for instance, it opens up the important issue of Moore's collaboration with the artist Gibbons. *Watchmen*'s visuals not only carry part of the burden of the narrative but also, as numerous commentators have noted, go beyond the confines of mere plot through a complex series of visual puns and symbols: as Wolk puts it, "almost every one of the tiny details Gibbons has somehow crammed into its panels signifies *something* of import to the story."[75] While Moore (who notoriously provides elaborate scripts, and sometimes even thumbnails, for the writers he works with) helps to shape the images as well as the prose, Gibbons also plays a key role in the finished product.

Nor are Moore and Gibbons the only figures responsible for the look of *Watchmen*, whose spine and title-page credits also include the colorist John Higgins. This brings us to another crucial difference between *Watchmen* and works of print fiction, as well as the sort of graphic narratives that most often attract critical praise: its status as a multiply and even corporately authored work. This element, which is not strictly specific to the medium of comics but distinguishes an ambitious mainstream superhero comic such as *Watchmen* from a single-authored work such as *Maus*, is another way in which Moore and Gibbons's series interestingly challenges our typical understanding of the work of literature—in this case as a product of individual genius.

Here we are reminded of Wolk's account of the hierarchy favoring individually created "art comics" over mainstream comics produced "by mid-sized committees."[76] This stress on the individual artist's vision actually undermines the specificity of the comics medium by valuing works whose conditions of production are more like those of traditional literature, while devaluing the collaborative and even in-dustrial labor process of mainstream comics. In this framework, Wolk notes, "The creator of a comic—the person who applies pen to draw-ing board or (lately) stylus to digital tablet—is its author, and comics produced under the sole or chief creative control of a single person of significant skill are more likely to be good (or at least novel enough to be compelling and resonant) than comics produced by a group of people assembly-line style—one writing, one penciling, one inking, one lettering, one coloring—under the aegis of an editor who hires them all individually."[77] Beaty, like Wolk, is suspicious of this model and draws on the sociologist Howard Becker's 1982 study of art worlds to argue for "an institutional definition of comics" whose "division of labour would include, just on the level of production and circula-tion, writers, pencillers, inkers, colourists, letterers, editors, assistant editors, publishers, marketing and circulation personnel, printers, dis-tributors, retailers, and retail employees."[78]

And as this reminds us, *Watchmen* is the product not just of a committee but of a corporation. Behind *Watchmen*'s assembly line, as behind most assembly lines, lies a corporate structure: the graphic novel's copyright page features a list of twenty-six names, from cur-rent DC Comics Senior VP–Executive Editor Dan Didio and Editors–Original Series Len Wein and Barbara Randall through VP–Publicity David Hyde and Senior VP–Business Development John Nee to VP–Sales Bob Wayne.[79] In seeking fully to understand Watchmen's aes-thetic qualities, we must not set this fact aside but rather confront it head-on, as critics such as Jerome Christensen, Derek Nystrom, and J. D. Connor have done for what Christensen describes as the quintes-sentially "corporate art" of film.[80]

My goal in this study is to consider *Watchmen* in ways that mu-tually illuminate both Moore and Gibbons's comic-book-series-cum-graphic-novel and the state of literature during the just under thirty years since it was published. This does not, as I hope I have made clear, mean ignoring all the nonliterary elements of the book: on the con-trary, a major advantage of the question "Is it literature?" is the way it forces us to attend to all the elements of *Watchmen*'s form, circum-stances of production, and institutional status that do not qualify as literary. When all is said and done, though, I still hope to make the case that Moore and Gibbons's story has been—both covertly and overtly—enormously influential on what has very recently become the newly genre-positive mainstream of contemporary literary fiction.

I divide the bulk of this book into three main chapters that address, in a recursive rather than a strictly linear fashion, what I consider to be the three most interesting aspects of *Watchmen* as a work produced jointly in England and America during the mid-1980s. The first of these chapters is titled "Poetics," and in it I address in more detail the blend of aspirational realism and formal experimentation that makes *Watchmen* a key participant in what we might call, with some degree of specificity, the modernist moment in comics history. We generally think of realism and modernism in mutually opposed terms—associating the former with content and the latter with form, or understanding the former as the dominant literary mode that the latter rises to challenge beginning in the late nineteenth century—but in fact Moore's approach participates in or parallels the blend of the two that has arguably been the dominant fictional mode of the twentieth century. For writers from Henry James and Virginia Woolf to late twentieth-century minimalists in the school of Raymond Carver and contemporary British neoimpressionists, the continual refinement of prose technique is by and large bent toward a more accurate representation of the world and especially of subjectivity—a correspondence that is in some ways more apparent in Moore and Gibbons's "revisionary superhero narrative" than in the more avant-garde wing of the graphic novel world discussed by critics such as Chute and Gardner.[81] In this respect we can understand Klock's model of comics revisionism, which he relates to Harold Bloom's reading of romantic poetry,[82] as also modernist, a "birth of self-consciousness in the superhero narrative"[83] that leads to and takes the shape of formal experimentation. While not the first creators to attempt to bring increased realism to the comic book medium and the superhero genre, Moore and Gibbons self-consciously understand this project as an explicit challenge to the conventions of the form in the interests of elevating it to the level of art.

Chapter 2, "Property," considers Moore's investment in the concept of literature as a function of his career-long struggle with DC over the rights to his work. This antagonism has certainly intensified as time has gone by, and DC has authorized films and comic books based on *Watchmen* and other works by Moore. In this context the category of literature serves the role of conferring on a work the status of a self-contained product of its creators, rather than a property owned by a corporation for which comic books themselves—as a 2001 *Forbes* piece noted—have value primarily as "a lucrative R&D tool": "Even if the books were bringing in paltry sales, hit films like Batman and Superman series have grossed $1 billion in the U.S., excluding video rentals and sales of an endless parade of merchandise."[84] But as Moore's initial pitch to DC about the series suggests, he already before his troubles with the company understood his nascent project as a self-contained work at odds with DC's standard approach to its characters: Moore and Gibbons created the series's original characters only after DC turned down Moore's initial proposal to use a set of characters DC had recently purchased from another company and thereby render them (thanks to the events of the story) unusable in other DC titles. *Watchmen* offers a metacommentary on this struggle between corporation and creator via the figures of Ozymandias (who profits from action figures and cartoon series based on his and others' adventures) and Rorschach (who becomes, via his connection to the comics artist Steve Ditko, a figure for the stubborn creator). Yet the values associated with these characters flip at the very end of the story, when Ozymandias becomes associated, through a conversation with another character, with the desire for narrative closure—a shift I read as evidence of an internal struggle between Moore's modernist notion of the autonomous literary work and his and Gibbons's understanding of comics as a collaborative, serial medium with its own history and aesthetic strategies.

In chapter 3, "Politics," I take up *Watchmen*'s story of the Cold War as a doubly displaced (since the story takes place not only in the United States but in an alternate United States) vision of the transformation of the United Kingdom under Margaret Thatcher. Ozymandias, as the villain of the piece, might seem to provide a poor figure for Thatcher insofar as he "solves" the problem of Cold War nuclear brinksmanship in a top-down, undemocratic fashion that resembles the totalitarian stereotypes of communism employed by Ronald Reagan and Thatcher to promote their policies. But as the historian Andrew Gamble argues, behind the Thatcher government's antistatist rhetoric it actually increased the power of the central state, undermining forms of local governance at odds with capital's interests and employing state power to deregulate industry and privatize services.[85] Moore, as his *V for Vendetta* series (1982–1989) makes clear, saw totalitarian implications in the Thatcher regime. Unfortunately, however, Moore's critique of Thatcherism from the point of view of his countercultural and anarchist politics actually shares the distrust of all institutions that was at the heart of eighties conservatism and a nascent neoliberalism. *Watchmen* ends with an impasse that Moore has described as a tribute to common people's agency but that ultimately renders such agency toothless, because it provides no social forms in which it can unfold.

My coda, "After *Watchmen*," considers the graphic novel's influence on contemporary American fiction. This influence was mostly indirect and has to do with Moore and Gibbons's role in bringing greater realism and formal sophistication not just to comic books but to the superhero genre in particular. This blend of superheroics and realism is central to a number of early twenty-first-century novels, beginning with Chabon's *Kavalier & Clay* and Lethem's 2003 *The Fortress of Solitude*, that transcend the limitations of minimalist realism by turning to superhero narratives—both indirectly, as things characters make or read, and directly, insofar as the novels incorporate actual bits of superhero narrative. Although Chabon and Lethem cite other comic books as their direct influences—Chabon, the books of the late thirties and early forties to which his protagonists contribute; Lethem, the Marvel comics of the seventies that his lead character reads as a boy—their novels share the melancholy tone that Klock attributes to Moore's script and Gibbons's drawings. Díaz's *Brief Wondrous Life of Oscar Wao* likewise shares this tone, although beyond this it directly cites *Watchmen* as one of its key intertexts.

All of these books are written by men of a certain age and with a certain relationship to the comics fandom that, up until the early nineties rise of the US manga market, remained by and large composed of "white heterosexual males from their teens to early thirties."[86] If these authors turn to comics fandom for an alternative intellectual culture that can be posed against the creative writing program, then, it is an alternative that remains—as they all more or less self-consciously recognize—problematically gendered. I close my coda, however, with Aimee Bender's 2010 *The Particular Sadness of Lemon Cake* and Rainbow Rowell's 2013 *Eleanor & Park*, two books that free the superhero narrative from its homosocial underpinnings. *The Particular Sadness of Lemon Cake* is a short, lyrical coming-of-age story with (as its title suggests) an investment in feminized domestic spaces; it is also a book in which characters just happen to have superpowers. And *Eleanor & Park* is a young-adult novel about two high-school misfits for whom *Watchmen*, like eighties postpunk, provides the basis for a bond of shared taste—one grounded, in *Watchmen*'s case, by both a commitment to realistic ugliness and an open-endedness that permits the possibility of change. By expanding the potential of the superhero story as both a literary adjunct of realism and an element of the coming-of-age tale, Bender and Rowell further develop the literary trajectory that *Watchmen* pioneers and that Chabon, Lethem, and Díaz take up in their various ways: the idea that the mass fantasy of superheroism that arose in the late 1930s and remained for a long time stigmatized as juvenile and preliterate now provides a storehouse of themes and tropes on which serious fiction can draw.

CHAPTER ONE

POETICS

In 1983 DC Comics editor Len Wein recruited Alan Moore, then primarily known in England for his work on series such as *Captain Britain* (a Captain America analog published by Marvel UK) and *Marvelman* (a 1950s British version of Captain Marvel revived for *Warrior* magazine) to take over the book *The Saga of the Swamp Thing*. This series, which featured a horror character created by Wein and artist Berni Wrightson in 1971, was at the time enjoying a renaissance thanks to a 1982 film adaptation by Wes Craven. Moore, jumping into the middle of a story begun by previous writer Martin Pasko, immediately remade the character entirely. Whereas Wein and Wrightson's original series told the story of a scientist who was turned into a swamp beast by ingesting a special formula prior to an explosion in the Louisiana swamps, Moore redescribed the character as an earth elemental who for a time had suffered the delusion that it was this scientist. Moore's run on *Swamp Thing* made his career and helped transform the mainstream comic book industry into one in which writers rather than artists were the stars.[1] The move of taking over a minor character (rather than, say, Batman or Spider-Man) and transforming him or her into a fan favorite—pioneered by Moore, who not only revived Swamp Thing but throughout his run on the title made it something of a specialty to revamp other obscure characters via guest appearances—became a typical auteurist star turn under this new regime.

In Moore's fifth issue of the series, however (*The Saga of the Swamp Thing* 24, May 1984), he brought in the big guns, framing the conclusion of a story pitting the Swamp Thing against a minor plant-themed villain named Jason Woodrue, the Floronic Man, around an appearance by the Justice League of America. The Justice League was DC's marquee team, featuring such perennial stars as Superman, Batman, and Wonder Woman alongside minor but still well-known characters such as the archer Green Arrow, the android Red Tornado, and Zatanna the female magician. In the story Moore employs the Justice League's appearance as a kind of metacommentary on Swamp Thing's minorness: the members of the team (referred to not by name but simply as "the over-people")[2] watch Woodrue's demands from their satellite headquarters; as the Swamp Thing confronts Woodrue, they debate if and how to intervene; the two most powerful members show up to take Woodrue into custody after he has already been defeated by the Swamp Thing.

But what was most compelling to me when I first read the issue in the eighties, and what remains, I think, its signal formal innovation, is the opening narration (figure 2), which (over a series of images that pan back to reveal the League's familiar satellite headquarters and an inset panel of the blurry members seen through one of its windows) reads,

> There is a house above the world, where the over-people gather. There is a man with wings like a bird . . . There is a man who can see across the planet and wring diamonds from anthracite. There is a man who moves so fast that his life is an endless gallery of statues . . . In the house above the world, the over-people gather . . . and *sit*. . . and *listen*. . .[3]

This passage bears the mark of Moore at his most self-consciously poetic, which here works to reinforce the Justice League members' contrast with the series's protagonist, the description's Olympian and Nietzschean resonances invoking both the League members' majesty and their detachment from the world below. The narration remains, moreover, in the omniscient third person that, as I noted in the introduction, Moore increasingly abandoned over the course of *Swamp Thing* in favor of more subjectively grounded free indirect discourse and first-person narration.

The descriptions of the three Justice League members in this passage move, however, in the direction of the concern with characters'

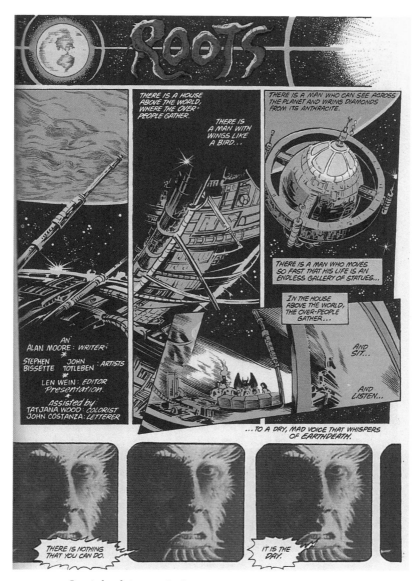

FIGURE 2. Comic book impressionism
Source: Alan Moore and Stephen Bissette, *The Saga of the Swamp Thing* 24 (May 1984): 1

subjectivity that became one of the hallmarks of Moore's work during the 1980s at DC. The first description, of the character Hawkman, is literal ("a man with wings like a bird"), while the second, of Superman, stresses the more mythic aspects of a character whose powers had become, by the early eighties, nearly unlimited.[4] But the third description, of the superfast hero the Flash, departs from the other two in that it offers not an external description of the character's powers but a subjective account of what it would be like to have those powers: if you moved near the speed of light, as the Flash did, then the world around you would actually appear to be perpetually standing still. Moore takes a lighthearted character from the 1960s—the protagonist, as he recalls in an interview, of "the first American comic [he] picked up"[5]—and adds a dimension of psychological realism that does not diminish but in fact enhances the character's larger-than-life status, hinting at the existential horror of being someone for whom the rest of the world seems to be frozen in place.

This is an old science-fiction device, employed by authors who represented the subjective reality and ironic downsides of telepathy (Theodore Sturgeon's 1953 *More than Human*), shrinking (Richard Matheson's 1956 *The Shrinking Man*), or teleportation (Alfred Bester's 1956 *The Stars My Destination*). All of these authors were working at a moment in the history of science fiction not unlike the one in comics history that produces *Watchmen*. Like the superhero narrative in the 1980s, science fiction in the 1950s attracted a range of accomplished creators who strove to confer a new seriousness on a genre whose origins lay in space opera and technophilic exposition. This new seriousness included, moreover, forms of direct or allegorical confrontation with the concerns raised by an earlier phase of the Cold War, and the fear of atomic destruction, that also preoccupies *Watchmen*. Stan Lee and his collaborators at Marvel Comics, beginning in the early sixties, translated mutation and radiation-induced superpowers into sources of fun and adventure, but in the science fiction of the 1950s these phenomena are more ambivalent. One way we can understand *Watchmen* is as going back and recovering this ambivalence in relation to the internal history of comic books: "Marooned," a story from the fictional *Tales of the Black Freighter* comic book that Moore and Gibbons incorporate into *Watchmen*, is a self-conscious nod to the more adult EC comics put out of business by the 1954 congressional hearings on comic books and the industry's subsequent imposition of the self-policing Comics Code. This is the aspect of *Watchmen*'s realism that Peter Paik gets at when, in his excellent account of Moore and Gibbons's series in his 2010 book *From Utopia to Apocalypse: Science Fiction and the Politics of Catastrophe*, he notes that it "investigates the [comics] medium by placing its costumed adventurers in a realistic world governed by power politics, rather than the juvenile, idealized universe of moral certitudes in which the upholders of truth and justice do battle against the forces of darkness."[6]

This chapter surveys *Watchmen*'s stylistic innovations, which from a literary point of view seem paradoxical because they involve both realism and modernism, two modes that have been understood to be in conflict with each other ever since the latter's emergence in the late nineteenth and early twentieth centuries. Modernism is generally (and not incorrectly) understood as a turn to formal innovation spurred by dissatisfaction with the conventions of an ossified realism. Moore and Gibbons, working in an essentially unrealistic genre, however, innovate by introducing greater realism. This goes beyond the usual—and, as we have seen, dissatisfying to Moore and Gibbons—identification of comics realism with a kind of nihilistic grittiness. *Watchmen* in particular devotes itself to fleshing out the subjectivities of its characters, and in this way we might see it as paralleling a literary tradition, exemplified by writers such as Henry James, E. M. Forster, and Virginia Woolf, in which modernist experimentation in fact serves the ends of a more precise psychological realism. *Watchmen* at its best registers its efforts at psychological realism in its very form, producing the sort of stylistic innovation that—more than any merely expanded content—makes it possible to understand the mideighties as the comic book's modernist era. At the same time, Moore and Gibbons reject, for obvious reasons, literary high modernism's typical disdain for mass culture, exploring the ways in which the comics medium and the superhero genre can expand rather than diminish our understanding of human subjectivity. In this way (as I will discuss at greater length in the coda) *Watchmen* anticipates recent works of literary fiction that turn to the superhero story and other genre models to move beyond the limitations of a now itself exhausted psychological realism.

But in order to see this we must first begin with *Watchmen*'s poetics, which emerge not out of some unified program but in response to a variety of at times competing factors. Moore, Paik argues, "turns the familiar comic book icon of Superman, the noble and indomitable hero who defends truth and justice, on its head with the premise that if superheroes really existed, their powers would be made to advance the interests of the state in its pursuit of geopolitical power, unless, of course, these superhuman beings were to turn on the ruling authorities and make themselves the masters of the world."[7] For Geoff Klock, as we have seen, this aspect of *Watchmen* makes it (along with Frank Miller's *The Dark Knight Returns*) both "the culmination of the silver age" of superhero stories[8] and the progenitor of subsequent "revisionary superhero narrative[s]" such as *The Authority* (which features a Justice League–like team of superheroes who engage in guilt-free sex, drug use, and revenge killing and who eventually make themselves the masters of the United States) and *Planetary* (in which Marvel's beloved Fantastic Four become a group of power-mad conspirators who destroyed an earlier generation of superpowered beings and now seek to block the emergence of a new order).[9]

Watchmen is, to be sure, deeply shaped by the question of how superheroes would alter the real world. This question in fact lies at the heart of the pitch that Moore made to DC when he still hoped to use the characters the company acquired in 1983 from the small and soon-to-go-out-of-business Connecticut comic book company Charlton. "What I'd like to try and do," Moore wrote in his pitch, "is to treat the world that the Charlton heroes live in exactly the same as our world, but to actually try to work out and follow through on the implications of the presence of super-heroes."[10] This leads to a story in which, perhaps most dramatically, Richard Nixon is serving his fifth term as president in 1985 because one particular superhero, the atomic-powered Dr. Manhattan, enabled the United States to win the Vietnam War. Of course, this aspect of the series ironically challenges the notion of realism, in ways that Moore recognizes elsewhere in the pitch: "For one thing, I'd like the world that the Charlton characters exist in to be at once far more realistic in conception than any super-heroes' world has been before, and at the same time far different to our own world than the worlds presented as Earth One, Earth Two or Marvel Earth.

To see what I'm trying to get at, you have to try and imagine what the presence of super-heroes would actually do to the world, both politically and psychologically."[11] In this passage Moore's invocation of realism and his concern with "what the presence of super-heroes would actually do to the world" exist in productive tension with the notion that the world he is writing about is "far different to our own world." *Watchmen* offers a fictional world that is "far more realistic" than one in which, say, Superman can crush coal into diamonds and fights evil as a private citizen. But it is nonetheless not a mimetic representation of the world we inhabit.

This distinction allows us to see that Moore understands realism at least implicitly in the terms that Erich Auerbach established in his landmark 1946 study *Mimesis*: not as a transparently mimetic representation of the world but as a set of formal practices designed to appear to so represent the world.[12] In the case of a baldly and dramatically unrealistic genre such as the superhero story circa 1986 this effect could be achieved via a minor violation of the genre's status quo. Superheroes under the Comics Code were not violent, so the increasing violence of non-Code comics in the 1980s appeared more realistic. The activities of superheroes did not fundamentally change the world, so the extrapolation of such changes in *Watchmen* appears more realistic. Earlier, at the start of the sixties, superheroes had not felt stress at balancing their crime-fighting activities with their everyday lives or angst about their ethical responsibilities, so when Stan Lee and his collaborators represented such stress and angst, their stories appeared more realistic—even as their realism primarily consisted of the importation of tropes from other genres, the soap opera and the romance comic, into the superheroic universe and even as it eventually became, as Moore recognized, its own sort of unrealistic conventional gesture.

Indeed, we might say it became unrealistic *because* it became conventional, in much the same way that Virginia Woolf in her 1924 essay "Mr. Bennett and Mrs. Brown" (famous for the statement that "on or about December 1910 human character changed")[13] criticizes the popular realist novel of her day for employing conventions that detract from rather than enhance the representation of reality: "This state of things is, I think, inevitable whenever from hoar old age or callow youth the convention ceases to be a means of communication between writer and reader, and becomes instead an obstacle and an impediment."[14] Woolf, making a case for the imperfect but necessary efforts of modernist authors such as James Joyce and T. S. Eliot (whom she calls the Georgians) to carve out new representational conventions, stresses the elaboration of character that the modernist moment and her own career helped make central to the twentieth-century novel's form. "I believe that all novels," she writes, "deal with character, and that it is to express character—not to preach doctrines, sing songs, or celebrate the glories of the British Empire, that the form of the novel . . . has been evolved."[15] For this reason she criticizes the Edwardians—H. G. Wells, Arnold Bennett, and John Galsworthy—for shying away from the actual mysteries of character and instead indulging in the description of environment conventionally understood to convey character.

Woolf's interest in novelistic character finds its counterpart in Moore's understanding of comic book characterization: Moore's critique of Marvel Comics writers' "one-dimensional characterization"[16]—their conventional assertion of neuroticism or some other characteristic[17]—parallels Woolf's critique of Bennett and his cohort. Moore here shares Woolf's understanding of realism not as faithfulness to external reality but as the elaboration of conventions designed to give the appearance of such faithfulness: "Great novels," Woolf contends, inevitably remind the reader of characters who seem "real," by which she "do[es] not mean . . . lifelike."[18] Woolf does not define real characters, except to slyly suggest that they subvert the very emphasis on character as the novel's true purpose, insofar as a real character "has the power to make you think not merely of it itself, but of all sorts of things through its eyes—of religion, of love, of war, of peace, of family life, of balls in county towns, of sunsets, moonrises, the immortality of the soul."[19]

Moore's interest in subjectivity, likewise parallel to Woolf's sense that the future of characterization lay in interiority, becomes even more apparent in the individual character sketches that accompanied his pitch for *Watchmen*. In his sketch for the Dr. Manhattan forerunner Captain Atom, for instance, Moore cites the "political" problems of Cold War destabilization and antisuperhero sentiment and then notes, "The personal problems that he has, on the other hand, are far more complex."[20] As with his brief description of the Flash in *Swamp*

Thing 24, Moore's account of these "personal problems" focuses on the character's perception of the world generated by his extrahuman powers:

> Try to imagine what it would be like to be Captain Atom. The desk you're sitting at and the chair you're sitting on give less of an impression of reality and solidity to you if you know that you can walk through them as if they weren't there at all. Everything around you is somehow more insubstantial and ghostly, including the people that you know and love. [Captain Atom] would experience the paradoxes of reality at a quantum scale of existence: that things can exist in two places at the same time, that certain particles can travel backwards through time and exhibit physical properties that are exactly the reverse of normal physical laws, that cause and effect does not seem to apply in the same way beneath a certain sub-microscopic level.[21]

Moore's interest in perception here is not too far from what Auerbach calls, in his chapter on Woolf's *To the Lighthouse* (1927), "the flow and the play of consciousness adrift in the current of changing impressions."[22] Or consider Woolf's *The Waves* (1931), with its detailed opening description of a sunrise at the seashore leading into the six main characters' accounts, framed as dialogue, of their first impressions upon waking up: "'I see a ring,' said Bernard, 'hanging above me. It quivers and hangs in a loop of light.'"[23] Moore thinks in a similarly impressionistic fashion, albeit starting from a character with a science-fictional reason for his idiosyncratic perceptions of the world.

Of course the fact that Moore's sketch is just a verbal outline, and not part of the finished graphic novel, should remind us of the main difference between his work and Woolf's. Whereas Woolf participates in print narrative's revolutionary early twentieth-century expansion into the representation of inner states, the dual image and text tracks of the graphic medium complicate such representation for Moore—a fact we can see by looking at the first panel of chapter IV of *Watchmen* (figure 3). This chapter relates the origin story of Dr. Manhattan, who gains his powers after an accident in the lab where he worked in his former identity as the physicist Jon Osterman. The chapter begins with Manhattan sitting on Mars and looking at a photograph, which he had retrieved before leaving Earth, of himself and a former lover. The first panel neatly epitomizes the image/text split: while the captions follow Manhattan's thoughts ("The photograph is in my hand"), the image, conventionally, focuses on him (in this case the hand holding the photo) and thus cannot be from his point of view.[24] There are a few images in the chapter that seem to function as subjective point-of-view shots: the panel at the center of the first page features a close-up of the photo that we can imagine to be from Manhattan's point of view; later in the story an image of Manhattan resurrected in midair after being disintegrated in a lab accident appears to take place from the point of view of one of his startled colleagues (figure 4).[25] But for the most part the images originate from some nonsubjective point in space focused, as in the first panel, on Manhattan/Osterman himself (or sometimes on things he does not himself witness). If Woolf thus seeks, in Auerbach's words, "a close approach to objective reality by means of numerous subjective impressions received by various individuals (and at various times),"[26] *Watchmen* is split between captions that can convey subjective impressions (as well as bits of found speech or writing) and images that are only infrequently bound to a subjective point of view.

Sara Van Ness suggests that the photograph in this sequence epitomizes Dr. Manhattan's ability to perceive, but not change, the future: "A photograph literally captures a moment in time, freezing it, and allows the keeper to revisit it in the future; however, once a photograph is taken, the event that has been recorded cannot be altered."[27] But insofar as the photo, with its white border, also looks very much like a comics panel, this image also emphasizes the way in which, as Mark Bernard and James Bucky Carter argue, Dr. Manhattan provides "a metaphor for the art of the graphic novel in and of itself as well as for the graphic novel experience."[28] Bernard and Carter contend that comics—because they combine words and images and make multiple images simultaneously viewable—are able to go beyond either literature or visual art alone in their representation of the sort of "simultaneous, multitudinous dimensionality deeply entwined in and part of individual experience" that was central to the work of early twentieth-century modernists such as Gertrude Stein and Pablo Picasso (and, we might add, Woolf).[29]

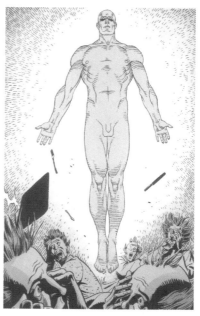

FIGURE 3. Words and images enacting different points of view
Source: Alan Moore and Dave Gibbons, *Watchmen* IV.1

FIGURE 4. A rare subjective point-of-view image
Source: Alan Moore and Dave Gibbons, *Watchmen* IV.10

Hence, Moore and Gibbons's finished series requires very little of the sort of verbal description that Moore gives in his character sketch for Captain Atom. The closest approach is a caption that reads, "It's February, 1960, and everything is frozen. I am starting to accept that I shall never feel cold or warm again."[30] And in fact this caption achieves its full resonance only in conjunction with the image accompanying it, of a camera in whose lens appears the inverted image of a publicity photo of Manhattan, the mechanically distorted image rhyming with the altered perceptions that the caption describes. Elsewhere Moore indicates Manhattan's complicated perceptions indirectly via the character's use of the present tense to refer to a range of dates that depart widely from the present moment of the scene on Mars ("It is 1985. I am on Mars. I am fifty-six years old").[31] While most of these dates are set in Manhattan's past, a few refer to the future (of both the character and *Watchmen*'s narrative). One reads, for instance, "Two hours into the future I observe meteorites from a glass balcony, thinking about my father,"[32] a reference to a scene that will appear in chapter IX of the graphic novel. The conceit here is that Manhattan's perceptions transcend linear time ("cause and effect does not seem to apply in the same way beneath a certain sub-microscopic level") and that he is not in fact remembering past events (hence, "reliving," which I used before, is incorrect) but experiencing every moment in his life, including ones set in the future of the novel's present, simultaneously: "I'm there *now*, in 1960, saying those words, watching that T.V. set . . .").[33]

It is tempting to say that *Watchmen* here strays far from Woolf's concern with ordinary subjectivity. Keeping in mind Auerbach's assertion that Woolf and the other modernists ground their representation of subjectivity in the conjunction of multiple, subjective time frames,[34] however, we might argue that the superhero genre allows Moore and Gibbons to extend that technique (in a paradoxically more realistic, because grounded in narrative events, fashion) to a character whose apprehension of time transcends the human.

But there is another subjectivity at stake in chapter IV of *Watchmen* besides Dr. Manhattan's. To return to the resemblance between Manhattan's photo and a comics panel, this resemblance slyly positions Manhattan as a comics reader. Van Ness suggests that "much like Dr. Manhattan's feelings of the lack of control over predetermined conditions (i.e., knowing the future, but not having the ability to change it), readers experience a similar feeling: they are presented with the knowledge of future negative events, but not enough information in order to fully understand."[35] Bernard and Carter agree that Manhattan is a stand-in for the reader, but they argue that he does in fact represent a form of agency specific to the medium. Manhattan, they contend, "is everywhere all the time as well as where he is presently. He is not most like any other character in the book, but most like the reader himself in that he transcends transience, simple being, via not displacement, but *multi*placement, of being many places at once, mentally and, in the storyline, physically as well."[36] Bernard and Carter's description here parallels the agentive role of the reader in Moore's account of the comics medium. While "with a film, you're being dragged through the experience at twenty-four frames a second," comics provide "complete control of the experience": "You wanna check out this panel there to see if there's any connection, you can just flick back. . . . And so it enables the comic book writer, the inventive writer, to utilize all those advantages and come up with really clever structures that would be lost in a film, but when they're frozen on the page where everyone can see how clever you are for all time, it works perfectly."[37] As this suggests, *Watchmen*, like the modernist fiction of an earlier period, not only associates "attempts to fathom a more genuine, a deeper, and indeed a more real reality"[38] with the more accurate representation of subjectivity but also does so in ways that self-consciously challenge and extend the medium's formal possibilities.

This relationship between characterization and formal innovation more generally is exemplified by a sequence in which Dr. Manhattan and his then-lover, Laurie Juspeczyk (the second superhero known as Silk Spectre), "buy a copy of *Time* magazine commemorating *Hiroshima week*" with a stopped watch on the cover.[39] The sequence transitions from the image of the cover to a panel featuring Dr. Manhattan's narration ". . . hands frozen" over a recurring close-up of his previous lover Jenny Slater handing him a glass of beer.[40] This image, which first appears on page 5 of chapter IV, works on three distinct levels. First, it constitutes a significant memory for the character, one that he recalls when, just prior to the accident that disintegrates him and transforms him into his superpowered state, he thinks, "I want very much for a beautiful woman to hand me a glass of very cold beer . . ."[41] Second, it exemplifies the cyclical rather than linear nature of time as Manhattan perceives it. Third and finally, however, it is a frame-breaking moment that calls attention to the nature of the medium itself, specifically its capacity to freeze time and thereby promote absorption. Unlike film, in which the viewer is, as Moore elsewhere remarks, "dragged along with the running speed of the projector," "with comics you can stare at the page for as long as you need in order to absorb all the little hints and suggestions going on in the background."[42] Yet even as Moore and Gibbons explore the formal possibilities of the medium, they remain committed to characterization. In one panel, for instance, the preaccident Osterman tells his soon-to-be-lover Slater why he finished his physics degree at an early age: "My *dad* sort of *pushed* me into it. That happens to me a *lot*. Other people make all my moves *for* me."[43] This

passage suggests a psychological predisposition toward the complicated relationship with time and causality that Osterman fully realizes
once he becomes Dr. Manhattan: "I can't prevent the future. To *me*, it's
already *happening*."[44]

Dr. Manhattan plays a special role in *Watchmen* insofar as he is the
only character with superhuman powers. But the other characters likewise exemplify a similar relationship between their subjectivity, as imagined by Moore in his character sketches, and the formal terms in which
that subjectivity is represented in the alternating chapters of *Watchmen*
that provide their backstories. As Moore told Christopher Sharrett in a
1988 interview, "We gave one issue to each of the characters, with a different method applied to each character's background."[45] For instance,
in his sketch for the Charlton character Thunderbolt, who became Ozymandias / Adrian Veidt, Moore writes, "The whole point behind the
way I think Thunderbolt should be treated is that we should try to make
the reader keenly aware of just what it would be like to be ten times
more intelligent than the most intelligent human being that ever lived."[46]
This capacity, as Moore was already aware in the sketch, would lead to
the role that the character plays in the final narrative, allowing him to
retire in advance of "the anti-super-hero backlash of the mid-seventies"
and to predict and seek to forestall nuclear apocalypse. But chapter XI,
which gives Ozymandias's backstory, offers something more formally
inventive than a representation of how the mind of the world's smartest
man works: "With Veidt, you'll notice that in his story, as he's recounting
his life, he's facing away from us. This distances the whole thing. All we
know is what he himself chooses to tell us."[47] If Dr. Manhattan on some
level represents the reader, then Ozymandias represents the story itself:
both in the generic sense that he lies at the end of the detective narrative
initiated in the opening pages by the discovery of the Comedian's body
and in the quasi-modernist sense that he creates an elaborate, obscure
structure designed to be autonomous from the world even as it interacts
with it. With Ozymandias as with Dr. Manhattan, though, the meta-
aesthetic resonances of the character exist alongside a commitment to
representing subjectivity in ways that go beyond the "one-dimensional"
model that Moore rejects. In Veidt's case, this takes the shape of hinting
at subjective depths negatively by pointedly denying the reader access
to them.

Moore takes a third tack with the character Rorschach / Walter Kovacs, who is based on a Charlton character named the Question. The Question was created by Steve Ditko, the cocreator of Spider-Man, and increasingly became a mouthpiece for Ditko's Ayn Rand–influenced philosophy. Thus, as Moore draws the character in his preliminary sketch, "The way I see the Question, he is such an extreme character that even hard-line right wingers would feel nervous about his attitudes and actions. The thing is, in order to present the character fairly, I will have to make those views completely logical and heartfelt so as not to present him as a parody of right-wing attitudes as seen by a left-winger."[48] Rorschach, we might say, embodies Moore's struggle with the one-dimensional model of character he associates with Marvel Comics. Like the Question, Rorschach at once functions as a rejection of that model (insofar as it is associated with neuroticism and other forms of self-doubt that he consciously eschews)[49] and its apotheosis (insofar as he derives all his actions from a single, inflexible moral code).

Rorschach, whom commentators frequently identify as the surprising (given his brutality, poor hygiene, and other negative qualities) focus of readerly identification in the series, exemplifies the complexities of Moore's approach to characterization. As Moore told Sharrett in their interview, he decided to take "a psychoanalytic approach" with Rorschach's origin story.[50] The word "approach" here is key, since the graphic novel does not (or does not solely) provide the character with a fleshed-out Freudian psychological history that makes sense of his adult behavior. It is true that Moore and Gibbons give Kovacs, in chapter VI, a traumatic backstory as the abused child of a prostitute, a story that the reader might conventionally take as explaining his subsequent turn to violent vigilantism. This is a standard motif in superhero origin narratives: Batman fights crime because he continually seeks to overcome the trauma of seeing his parents shot by a criminal when he was a child; Spider-Man because of the guilt he feels for letting the man who later killed his uncle flee a crime scene; and so forth. But Moore means "approach" literally, since we learn about Kovacs's past in conjunction with a series of interviews with Dr. Malcolm Long, the psychoanalyst assigned to the vigilante after his arrest.

The scenes of Long's sessions with Kovacs make clear that we should understand "psychoanalytic" in a methodological rather than an explanatory sense. We see Kovacs's childhood in a flashback triggered by a Rorschach blot test to which Long asks the captured crime-fighter to respond. After the flashback Kovacs tells Long that he sees "some nice flowers."[51] This flashback, in which Kovacs walks in on his prostitute mother having sex with a customer, verifies his traumatic childhood. But it is important to note that *Watchmen* represents another subjectivity in this scene, Long's, and that the disjunction between Rorschach's flashback and his statement also figures the psychiatrist's lack of knowledge about his patient. Hence, we distrust the optimistic reports about the sessions delivered in captions beginning, "From the Notes of Dr. Malcolm Long." This distrust comes to a head on page 11 of the chapter. Rorschach, who on the previous page claimed that he first put on a mask and started fighting crime after the murder of Kitty Genovese (which in popular lore was viewed by bystanders who did nothing to help her), accuses Long of being interested in him primarily for professional reasons and tells him, "You don't want to make me well. Just want to know what makes me sick." Then, as he is being escorted out of the interview room by his guards, he says, "You'll find out. Have patience, doctor. You'll find out." Here, as in Dr. Manhattan's origin, the disjunction between words and images does much of the work. The next three panels, at the bottom of the page (figure 5), show Long's dismayed reaction to Rorschach's response, while the captions return to his journal to offer a psychoanalytic account of Rorschach's origin: "Kovacs hated his mother. After her death, he needed somewhere to put the anger, and so he chose the criminal fraternity. The flimsy story about Kitty Genovese is obviously there to justify his behavior to himself. It's perfectly simple. Case solved."[52] The tension between the words and the images in these panels captures the complexity of Long's response to Rorschach: on one hand he believes his narrative about his patient, and on the other he feels its inadequacy; perhaps he even redoubles his belief in response to this feeling. We might thus take this sequence as a rebuke of what Moore describes as one-dimensional characterization. In this way the psychoanalyst Long, who might simply have served as a device for presenting Rorschach's origin story, both complicates our understanding of Rorschach's motivations and himself becomes a fleshed-out character—one with his

FIGURE 5. Malcolm Long's face belying his thoughts
Source: Alan Moore and Dave Gibbons, *Watchmen* VI.11

own motivations for pursuing his analysis and his own ambivalence about that process.

This ambivalence grows greater and greater as the chapter progresses, until Long finally falls fully under the sway of his patient's nihilistic worldview. Long's turn to Rorschach's way of thinking occurs after Rorschach tells the analyst what he claims is his true origin story, a horrific account of finding the remains of a six-year-old victim of a botched kidnapping who has been fed to dogs.[53] Here the graphic novel's concern with characterization once again provides a pushing-off point for complicating the form in which the story is being told. "It was Kovacs who said 'Mother' then, muffled under latex," Rorschach tells Long about splitting the first dog's head with a meat cleaver: "It was Kovacs who closed his eyes. It was Rorschach who opened them again."[54] With this new account of his (belated) origin Rorschach supplants his psychoanalytic origin story (he hated his mother and displaced his anger at her onto criminals) with a new one in which, long after he first put on a mask and started fighting crime, he realizes the true meaning of the name he had given himself: "Existence is random. Has no pattern save *what* we imagine after staring at it for too long. No meaning save what we choose to impose."[55]

Kovacs here transposes his origin from the psychoanalytic key into a Nietzschean one, a transposition to which Long himself proves susceptible when, sitting alone with an ink blot after he has ruined a dinner party by repeating Rorschach's story to guests fishing for salacious details, he muses,

> I tried to pretend it looked like a spreading tree, shadows pooled beneath it, but it didn't. It looked more like a dead cat I once found, the fat, glistening grubs writhing blindly, squirming over each other, frantically tunneling away from the light. But even that is avoiding the real horror. The horror is this: in the end, it is simply a picture of empty meaningless blackness. We are alone. There is nothing else.[56]

Beneath the pleasant story, that is, lies both a darker story and a darker one still. In terms of *Watchmen* itself, that is, the "grim, pessimistic, nasty, violent" narrative may function as a screen for the even darker assertion that there is no story save what humans impose on the meaningless of the universe. Yet we might in a further turn understand this existential logic as underlying the series's redemptive investment in its own formal possibilities. As Van Ness contends, the desire to impose patterns constitutes a major theme of the series, one present in Dr. Manhattan's encounter with the meaninglessness of nature, in Ozymandias's plot, in the deceased Comedian's worldview (as Manhattan puts it in a flashback, "I have never met anyone so deliberately amoral"), and in the *Tales of the Black Freighter* excerpts.[57] In each of these examples—most self-consciously in the final one—art emerges out of the effort to give order to a potentially random reality.

As I hope this account suggests, Dr. Manhattan, Ozymandias, and Rorschach are characters in the modernist sense with which we associate James, Forster, and Woolf: figures at the center of an effort to imagine new modes of characterization, who for this reason become both "rounded" in Forster's famous sense and the sites of formal innovation per se.[58] In the late nineteenth- and early twentieth-century moment emblematized by these writers, realism and modernist experimentalism are not as distinct as we have come to think of them. This rapprochement between realism and experimentalism in fact represents an ongoing strain in twentieth- and twenty-first-century literature, as exemplified, for example, by the "midfiction" Alan Wilde discusses in his 1987 book *Middle Grounds: Studies in Contemporary Fiction* and the "post-postmodern" fiction Robert McLaughlin describes in his 2004 article "Post-Postmodern Discontent: Contemporary Fiction and the Social World."[59] *Watchmen*, as I will discuss in the coda, influences an even more recent round of contemporary fiction in this regard, although as I have already suggested, it does so in a way complicated by its status as genre writing, a third mode lying until recently outside the realm of respectable fiction organized around the realist/experimentalist divide. Within the internal history of the comics medium, however, Moore and Gibbons's series takes up the task of formally innovative characterization out of dissatisfaction with conventional modes of characterization—a dissatisfaction strikingly similar to Woolf's own in the first decades of the twentieth century.

Of course Moore and Gibbons's project differs from Woolf's both because *Watchmen*'s creators have the history of modernist literary innovation to hand as a ready-made resource and because they work within a tradition not of clichéd realism but of irrealism. Dr. Manhattan, Ozymandias, Rorschach, and the Comedian are all, to use a perhaps outmoded phrase, "larger than life"—they all possess, that is, subjectivities that are at once more than human and less than fully rounded. To literary sensibilities trained by modernism this sounds like undiluted criticism, although we should perhaps recall that even Forster, in setting out his theory of rounded characters, reserves praise for what he calls the "types" of Charles Dickens. "Nearly every one [of Dickens's characters] can be summed up in a sentence," Forster writes, "and yet there is this wonderful feeling of human depth." While Dickens "ought to be bad, . . . his immense success with types suggests that there may be more in flatness than the severer critics admit."[60] Dickens provides an apt comparison here not least because he appears in Forster's genealogy as a residual figure from the era before modernism, which is to say from before the era when serious literature and genre fiction parted ways.

This is not the case, however, with the two remaining members of *Watchmen*'s central cast, the superheroes Nite Owl / Dan Dreiberg and Silk Spectre / Laurie Juspeczyk. As we have seen, Moore and Gibbons experiment with different formal means of representing different characters' subjectivities. Dreiberg and Juspeczyk not only differ from the other characters individually but also play a different role within the narrative than the larger-than-life characters en masse. Moore outlines this role in his character sketch for the Blue Beetle, the Charlton character who inspired Nite Owl. In contrast to Manhattan and Ozymandias, who "are both pretty weird psychologically speaking," the Blue Beetle

> is the most human of the entire bunch, and he will exist in this book as a standard against which the other characters are measured. If all the characters are weird and unusual, none of them will stand out. Thus, I see the Blue Beetle as being just an ordinary man who does extraordinary things, who sometimes makes mistakes or is uncertain about what's going on, and who sometimes feels afraid. He's not as remote and distant and godlike as Captain Atom, or as enigmatic, confident and cerebral as Thunderbolt, or as obsessed as The Question . . . , but he is nonetheless a hero. Maybe even more of hero in that blind courage does not come naturally to him.[61]

Watchmen follows through on this sketch in its depiction of Dreiberg / Nite Owl. Dreiberg is overweight, ambivalent about both his career as a superhero and his decision to retire, and an unabashed fan of such putatively childish subjects as birds (chapter VII is supplemented by an excerpt from his article on owls for the Fall 1983 issue of the *Journal of the American Ornithological Society*) and Arthurian legends. One panel in the first chapter, which departs from the series's usual nine-panel layout by taking up the entire bottom two-thirds of a page, shows Dreiberg, as Moore says in his sketch, "just sitting morosely in his underground hanger [*sic*]" (figure 6).[62] As Van Ness points out, the fundamental visual motif in this panel lies in the contrast between Dreiberg's erect, empty costume standing in a locker on the right, and his slumped and disheveled figure on the left.[63]

If the more psychologically weird characters function a bit like Dickensian types, then Dreiberg brings in something like what Auerbach describes as Woolf's emphasis on the minor and everyday, the "random moment which is comparatively independent of the controversial and unstable orders over which men fight and despair."[64] Auerbach here focuses, of course, on Woolf's formal innovations for capturing such moments, but in superhero comics the assertion of quotidian content as such carries its own revisionist charge. In Nite Owl's association with such content he has been perhaps the series's most influential character, his influence visible in a variety of mainstream super-

FIGURE 6. Man and Superman
Source: Alan Moore and Dave Gibbons, *Watchmen* I.13

hero stories that have appeared since. These range from Keith Giffen and J. M. DeMatteis's humorous 1986–1992 revamping of the Justice League, which featured Blue Beetle (the same character on whom Nite Owl was based) as a D-list, slightly out-of-shape adventurer, to Geoff Johns and Gary Frank's 2012 story *Batman: Earth One*, whose Bruce Wayne is an inexperienced vigilante whose weapons break and who gets beaten bloody by ordinary criminals and the police. In depicting this Batman as in at least some ways simply normal (something Frank Miller's Dark Knight was not), Johns exemplifies the technical trick that he and others have adopted from Moore and Gibbons's Nite Owl: the depiction of the superhero not as an operatic figure with grandiose flaws but, to paraphrase Moore, as an ordinary person who does extraordinary (we might just say strange) things.

Precedents for such deflationary characterization existed before *Watchmen*: one of Moore's telling details, for instance—a brief mention in the original Nite Owl's autobiography of a World War II–era comrade who is shot by bank robbers when "his cloak bec[omes] entangled in the bank's revolving door"[65]—seems borrowed from a 1974

Captain America story in which the hero adopts the new identity of Nomad and trips over the cape he is not used to wearing.[66] But Moore and Gibbons give their "frumpy characters," in Klock's words, "a distinct sadness" that is arguably the dominant tone of the art comics of creators such as Harvey Pekar, Daniel Clowes, and Chris Ware.[67] *Watchmen*'s realist exploration of the pathos and strangeness of what it might mean to put on a costume and fight crime is, in this respect, a forerunner of Ware's 2000 *Jimmy Corrigan: The Smartest Kid on Earth*, which plays with its comic book form by contrasting the smallness and sadness of the title character's life with his childhood fantasies about his absent father as a Superman-like hero.[68]

Moore acknowledges this aspect of *Watchmen* in the opening section of the original Nite Owl's book *Under the Hood*, in which the now retired Hollis Mason recounts the advice of his neighbor, an unpublished novelist: "Start off with the saddest thing you can think of and get the audience's sympathies on your side." For Mason this is Richard Wagner's *Ride of the Valkyries*, a choice he explains with a story about his father's employer Moe Vernon, a practical joker and opera buff who receives a Dear John letter from his wife while he is listening to Wagner and wearing a set of "lady's bosoms." Vernon announces this to his employees, and they begin laughing, even though they realize he has been crying; and later that night he commits suicide. Here, in the excerpt from *Under the Hood* that accompanies the first issue/chapter of *Watchmen*, we see all the complicated levels of mediation through which Moore and Gibbons are working: the heroic (and arguably protofascist) *Walküre* and the stilted language of Vernon's announcement ("Fred Motz has had carnal knowledge of my wife Beatrice for the past two years") signifying the comic book superhero narrative; the laughter exposing the ludicrousness of Vernon's costume, which as Mason notes is not too far from a superhero's ("I've stood there dressed in something just as strange"); the suicide and subsequent aura of sadness suggesting a layer of pathos subtending the laughter.[69]

Moore's fellow comics writer Grant Morrison and others have suggested that he drew the ideas for *Watchmen* and his other revisionist works from Robert Mayer's 1977 prose novel *Superfolks*, about a retired former superhero who is drawn back into action.[70] But the opening of *Under the Hood* suggests how Moore goes beyond Mayer's novel—which is by and large a postmodern pastiche committed to parody, in the style of Robert Coover's *The Public Burning* of the same year—by minimizing genre parody and stressing instead a broader range of emotions and motivations.

Silk Spectre / Laurie Juspeczyk, the final major cast member, also participates in this quotidianization of the superhero genre, in spite or perhaps even because of the dissatisfactory way that Moore describes her precursor, Nightshade, in his preliminary character sketch. In that sketch Moore acknowledges that Nightshade is the Charlton character he "know[s] least about and ha[s] the least ideas on." Moore notes that "as the only woman character she is obviously very important as well as being important to the story," though he grounds this importance in her role as "Captain Atom's only emotional link to the world" and suggests that "at least part of her purpose [will be] to expand upon the concept of super-hero sexuality."[71] But if Moore here recapitulates the superhero genre's longstanding difficulty with female characters, in the series proper he and Gibbons make Juspeczyk into a more complex character precisely by charting her growing dissatisfaction with and eventual break from her role as Dr. Manhattan's sexual partner. In the process of severing this link Juspeczyk also comes to terms with being forced into her superhero career at a young age by her mother, the first Silk Spectre, and with her anger at the Comedian, whom she knows as her mother's would-be rapist but who, she realizes at a climactic moment in the story, subsequently became her father.

In this way Silk Spectre joins Nite Owl (literally, insofar as they become a couple by the end of the series) in epitomizing another aspect of realist characterization, the developmental arc. Moore's character sketch for Nite Owl's inspiration, Blue Beetle, describes him as "the character who will go through the biggest changes in the course of the strip."[72] In the finished series this becomes true, in different ways, of both Nite Owl and Silk Spectre in contrast to the other, more static characters: Rorschach, who upholds his principles to the extent of dying for them; Dr. Manhattan, who leaves "this galaxy for one less *complicated*";[73] Ozymandias, who has carried out his plans and is last seen pondering their uncertain aftermath. Dreiberg and Juspeczyk alone appear after the main plot in the first of the series's two epilogues, living under assumed identities and considering a return to superheroics. It is this extension of realism beyond the genre plot that, I will argue in my final chapter, motivates Junot Díaz's citation of Dr. Manhattan's final words to Veidt—"*Nothing* ends, Adrian. Nothing *ever* ends"[74]—and Díaz's use of *Watchmen* as an intertext more generally.

Given Nite Owl and Silk Spectre's at least partial transcendence of the superhero genre, however, what are we to make of Moore's enigmatic suggestion, in his short character sketch for Nite Owl (written after he had given up on the original Charlton characters and begun imagining his new cast), that "this character is the nearest we get to a conventional superhero"?[75] The simple answer, by way of Paik, is that Nite Owl (along with Silk Spectre) comes closest to participating in straightforward acts of unambiguous do-gooding (in chapter VII saving people from a fire) rather than in state-sponsored power politics, brutal vigilantism, or elaborate, morally ambiguous conspiracies. But there is a more complicated answer that we can begin to unravel by considering the superhero archetypes on which, behind the Charlton characters, each of *Watchmen*'s protagonists is based.

Klock notes that part of Moore's revisionism lies in the way each of the characters refracts one or more archetypal figures from the 1940s: Ozymandias displays elements of both Superman (his "optimism, confidence, and Antarctic headquarters") and Batman ("his wealth, intelligence, birthday [1939], and perfected human physical prowess"); Nite Owl's "wealth, gadgets, costume, mode of transportation, and basement equipment room" also link him to Batman; "the Comedian . . . is a kind of Captain America if Captain America had gone to Vietnam"; Rorschach, with his "reactionary, violent, obsessive-loner personality and refusal to compromise" is yet another version of Batman; "Dr. Manhattan, as the only super-powered being, aloof, almost alien, and never aging, suggests Superman."[76] Setting aside the Comedian's role as patriotic superhero-manqué, the key distinction here is that between the all-powerful Superman (with Manhattan's ability to "control *atomic structure* itself" making him even more godlike than his predecessor)[77] and the various nonsuperpowered superheroes descended from Batman.

Moreover Rorschach, Ozymandias, and Nite Owl each stand in for different visions of the superhero genre's most famous nonsuperpowered character. Rorschach is the obsessed vigilante of Batman's earliest adventures, revived by Dennis O'Neill and Neal Adams for their early seventies run on the character and then carried to its logical extension by Frank Miller in *The Dark Knight Returns*. Ozymandias is Batman as corporate CEO (as Klock notes, "His role in his corporation suggests Bruce Wayne and Wayne Corp.")[78] and master strategist, a role that was perhaps nascent in the characters' pre-1986 appearances but has since become dominant through Grant Morrison's runs on both *Justice League* (in which he figured Batman as a kind of general) and the various Batman titles (including Morrison's *Batman Incorporated*, which sees the character forming an international team of Batman-like heroes to do battle with a global conspiracy). Nite Owl is, finally, the Batman that O'Neill and Adams replaced: the wealthy adventurer with lots of gadgets who starred in both the 1960s television series and the comic books that influenced and were influenced by it. Part of what Moore and Gibbons are drawn to in this last characterization is the faint whiff of ludicrousness, taken up by the TV series as camp but in which they find (as we have already noted) elements of pathos.

As this should suggest, Moore and Gibbons are also on some level interested in the way a serial character such as Batman complicates ideas of originality as such. Even more than Superman—whose creators, Jerry Siegel and Joe Shuster, drew on various sources (myth and folklore, science fiction, the circus) to create the modern superhero— Batman was an adaptation within the comic book medium of an existing type: the gentleman adventurer familiar from the Baroness Orczy's 1905 novel *The Scarlet Pimpernel*, Johnston McCulley's serialized pulp adventures of Zorro (which first saw print in 1919), and numerous radio characters including the Shadow (1930) and the Green Hornet (1936). Indeed, Batman was not even the first version of this character to appear in the comics but was preceded by the trench-coat-and-domino-mask-wearing Crimson Avenger, who debuted in *Detective Comics* 20 in October 1938, seven issues before Batman's first appearance in May 1939. If Bill Finger and Bob Kane's creation was ultimately the most successful comic book version of this figure, meanwhile, the mark of this fame was the numerous imitators that Batman himself spawned in the early 1940s and later. Indeed, Steve Ditko's 1966–1968 revamping of the Blue Beetle for Charlton passed the torch from the previous version of the character (an archaeologist given powers by a scarab he found in an Egyptian tomb) to an acrobatic inventor hero who was more or less Batman with neither the darkness nor the camp.

Moore recognizes this overdetermined aspect of the character in his brief sketch for Nite Owl, noting that he "substitutes for The Blue Beetle, and is a sort of composite of a certain type of super-hero, taking in Batman, Moon Knight, The Green Hornet and other notables along the way."[79] But already in his sketch for the Blue Beetle Moore had offered a realistic analog for this aspect of comic book form by stressing the character's relationship to his predecessor within the narrative: in the sketch Moore suggests that the second Beetle would seek out his predecessor in retirement "and by reading his book discover[] that many of the problems that the old man talks about are the ones that he is facing twenty years later."[80] Moore and Gibbons carry this motif over to *Watchmen* and in fact extend it to Silk Spectre once they are no longer tied to the original Charlton character Nightshade. The question of superheroic descent becomes, indeed, a major motif of the series, via the main characters' relation to an earlier generation of World War II–era heroes who fought crime together as the Minutemen. This motif allows Moore and Gibbons to thematize the history of the comic book superhero more generally, to create, as Moore notes in his sketch for the first Nite Owl, "a whole previous continuity for this world that will maybe only be alluded to in specific detail once or twice in passing."[81]

But beyond this metageneric play, the question of superheroic descent plays a central role in the realistic characterization of Nite Owl and Silk Spectre. Both are second-generation heroes: Nite Owl because he is inspired by and takes the name of his predecessor; Silk Spectre because her mother, the original Silk Spectre, trains her to follow in her footsteps. If, to return to the point with which we began, Nite Owl is "the nearest we get to a conventional superhero," this is true because to be a superhero is at least in part to exist in relation to previous superheroes. This is the case, notably, even for the original Nite Owl, Hollis Mason, whose autobiography recounts his experience, as a rookie policeman, of Superman's debut in the first issue of *Action Comics*:

For me, it all started in 1938, the year when they invented the super-hero. . . .

There was a lot of stuff in that first issue. There were detective yarns and stories about magicians whose names I can't remember, but from the moment I set eyes on it I only had eyes for the Superman story. Here was something that presented the basic morality of the pulps without all their darkness and ambiguity. The atmosphere of the horrific and faintly sinister that hung around the Shadow was nowhere to be seen in the bright primary colors of Superman's world, and there was no hint of the repressed sex-urge which had sometimes been apparent in the pulps, to my discomfort and embarrassment.[82]

With this passage, Moore elides the distinction between the influence of his characters on each other and the influence of mass culture on them (and, implicitly, on the reader).

The same elision characterizes a long sequence at the start of chapter VII, in which Dreiberg and Juspeczyk tour the former's underground headquarters and discuss their motivations for becoming superheroes. Dreiberg self-deprecatingly refers to his crime-fighting career as "a school kid's *fantasy* that got out of *hand*,"[83] and Juspeczyk replies, "At least you were living out your *own* fantasies. I was living out my *mother's*."[84] He notes that he "*idolized*" Mason as a child,[85] and when she asks him, "What got you *into* this business in the first place?" he responds that he wrote his hero, the retiring Mason, to ask if he "could carry on his *name*."[86] But even Dreiberg's relationship to Mason— "hanging out with a real *hero*, being his *friend* and everything"[87]—is to a certain degree prescripted by mass-cultural influences: "That's why I sort of regretted the *Crimebusters* [an abortive attempt to form a superhero group] falling through back in sixty-whenever-it-was. It would have been like joining the Knights of the Round Table; being part of a fellowship of *legendary beings. . .*"[88] Just as Mason himself was inspired by Superman, a fictional character in the world of *Watchmen*, Dreiberg's relationship to Mason is itself mediated by his encounter with mass-cultural versions of the Arthurian legends. (He names his owl-shaped airship "Archie" after Merlin's owl Archimedes in Disney's 1963 *The Sword in the Stone*.)

This split between personal and mass-cultural influences captures the distinction between the ordinariness of Dreiberg's decision, in his

world, to put on a costume and fight crime—"Well, I was *rich, bored,*
and there were enough *other* guys doing it so I didn't feel *ridicu-
lous. . ."*[89]—and the influences, at once idealistic in theory and embar-
rassing in practice, behind this decision. His ambivalence about these
influences continually surfaces in his apologies for his *"childish"*[90] or at
best "adolescent, *romantic"*[91] past and his self-deprecating description
of his crime-fighting equipment as both "mostly pretty *boring"* and
"pretty *kitsch* or *camp* or whatever . . ."[92] Moore's script also takes seriously the idea that Dreiberg's superhero career was simply a case of ar-
rested development: Dreiberg would have been eighteen, for instance,
when *The Sword in the Stone* premiered in 1963.

This aspect of Dreiberg's character is not shared by Juspeczyk,
whose own influences (and her ambivalence about them) are purely
personal. While *Watchmen* thus goes a long way toward correcting
Moore's inability, in his character sketch for Juspeczyk's precursor,
Nightshade, to see his female protagonist as more than a foil for male
characters or a vehicle to explore "the concept of super-hero sexuality,"
it nonetheless retains a clear gender distinction. If Nite Owl's character
arc requires him finally to own his superhero career in all its "adolescent, *romantic"* glory, Silk Spectre's involves reconciling herself to
her mother's displaced ambitions and to the fact, which she realizes in
chapter IX, that the Comedian is her father: in the first of the book's
two epilogues she reconciles with her mother and suggests to Dreiberg
that she may give up her *"girly"* Silk Spectre identity for a new one
modeled on the Comedian's.[93]

It is not entirely the case that *Watchmen* is unaware of this dynamic,
however. We can see Dreiberg's anxieties about his mass-cultural influences, for instance, as a metacommentary on the homosocial comic
book world, which (in the mideighties even more than today) was
dogged by fears of insufficient masculinity because of both its association with "feminized kitsch, or camp"[94] and its reputation "as childish junk not to be read or taken seriously by adults, and evidence of
some form of social deviance."[95] Juspeczyk's final words to her mother,
moreover, epitomize the affective core of *Watchmen*'s depiction of superheroes, which goes through and beyond shame to something like
an acceptance of the awkwardness and embarrassment inherent in a
range of human behavior. Juspeczyk's acknowledgment that the Co-

median is her father also requires her to admit that her mother, Sally Jupiter, the first Silk Spectre, forgave and slept with a man who tried to rape her when they were colleagues in the Minutemen. When Juspeczyk reveals to her mother at the end of the series that she knows who her father is, Jupiter replies, "I should have *told* you but . . . I don't know, I just felt *ashamed*, I felt *stupid*, and . . ." Juspeczyk responds, "People's *lives* take them strange *places*. They do strange *things*, and . . . well, sometimes they can't *talk* abut them. I know how that is."[96] It is Juspeczyk's own knowledge that she has done "strange," potentially shameful things, by choice and otherwise, which finally allows her to empathize with her mother's actions.

Once we have identified *Watchmen*'s melancholy tone, we can see hints of it in characters other than Dreiberg and Juspeczyk. In the supplemental materials to Rorschach's origin chapter, for instance, we learn that this character—the one most like Miller's Batman—constructed a heroic fantasy about his absent father while growing up in the Lillian Charlton Home for Problem Children in New Jersey. And in his final appearance we see the stoic character weeping openly while waiting for Dr. Manhattan to kill him in order to protect Ozymandias's scheme.[97] Ozymandias's own final panel, moreover, shows him looking hesitantly over his shoulder after Manhattan has cast doubt on his triumph. Indeed, Dreiberg and Juspeczyk are the only characters allowed a happy ending, shown smiling as they discuss a future crime-fighting career. But they are allowed this resolution in part because their sadness and ambivalence sets the tone for the series as a whole.

This tone, and the connection between subjectivity and mass culture that lies behind it, arguably constitutes *Watchmen*'s greatest legacy to contemporary culture. I have already suggested that Moore and Gibbons's story shares this tone with nonmainstream graphic novels more likely to be taken seriously as art. But it also characterizes recent literary fiction that actively draws on the conventions of superhero narratives to supplement its realist goals. Michael Chabon's 2000 *The Amazing Adventures of Kavalier & Clay*, Jonathan Lethem's 2003 *Fortress of Solitude*, and Junot Díaz's *The Brief Wondrous Life of Oscar Wao* all turn to the language (as their titles suggest) and devices of the superhero genre to provide their male coming-of-age stories with a blend of grandiosity and shame similar to the one that Moore and Gibbons give Dreiberg. And while these print novels spring from and focus on the same homosocial comic book world that *Watchmen* does, Aimee Bender's 2010 *The Particular Sadness of Lemon Cake* adapts the device of the realistic superhero story—Bender's protagonist discovers as a teen that she has the power to taste the emotions of whoever has prepared her food—to the female coming-of-age story and the lyric faux memoir.

While Moore and Gibbons seek to bring realism to the essentially irrealistic superhero genre, that is, and these fiction writers turn to that genre to enliven a played-out literary realism, they all arrive at essentially the same point. This recent wave of fiction also shares with *Watchmen* the insight that mass culture need not stand in opposition to psychological complexity—that its appearance need not signal, as it usually does for the works of high postmodernism, a parodic register of dehumanization but that it can in fact serve as a kind of prosthetic representation of subjectivity and even intersubjectivity. People relate to themselves and to others, that is, through generic templates (here I mean the adjective "generic" in both its most general sense and as a label for certain kinds of popular fiction), and in the hands of a sophisticated author such templates not only can serve as content for fiction but can also extend its formal resources.

Watchmen thematizes this understanding of mass culture as a space for exploring subjectivity in the career of the Tijuana Bible that appears briefly in chapter II and then again in chapter XII, in the epilogue featuring Dreiberg and Juspeczyk. In its first appearance, in the chapter organized around other characters' memories of the Comedian, Sally Jupiter hands her daughter "an item of *memorabilia*" sent by a fan she corresponds with, explaining, "It's a *Tijuana Bible*. . . a little eight-page *porno comic* they did in the '30s and '40s . . ." Juspeczyk is disgusted, but her mother explains that "those things are *valuable*, like *antiques*," and also notes that she finds it "*flattering*": a reminder of a time when "people used to *slobber* over me . . . Every day the future looks a little bit *darker*. But the *past*, even the *grimy* parts of it . . . well, it just keeps getting *brighter* all the *time*."[98]

This scene leads to Jupiter's flashback to a photo session for the Minutemen, after which the Comedian attempted to rape her, and another team member, Hooded Justice, intervened. This scene is complicated on a number of levels. The comic book, like the photo that seemingly prompts Jupiter's flashback, is a frozen artifact—recall the panel of "hands frozen" in Dr. Manhattan's origin chapter and the way that phrase echoes Moore's commentary about comics images "frozen on the page"—that simultaneously captures and misrepresents something from the past. In the case of the Tijuana Bible this is Jupiter's erstwhile status as a sex symbol. In that of the photograph it is the heroic public image of the Minutemen (their comic book image, one might say) belying their actual behavior following the session: Jupiter's vanity and denial of her Polish background, a character named Mothman's timidity (he will later be institutionalized), the sixteen-year-old Comedian's attempted rape, and Hooded Justice's disdainful attitude toward not only the attempted rapist but also his victim. By drawing a parallel between the comic book and the photo and juxtaposing them both to actual past events, *Watchmen* poses a contrast between the superhero genre's idealistic depiction of human motivations and realism's demand for a representation of character and action that is more accurate because more willing to expose flaws and weakness.

The transition out of the flashback, however, complicates this schematic contrast. Jupiter's reverie ends with an image of her kneeling, face bloody, in front of Hooded Justice while he tells her, "for God's sake, *cover* yourself"; it is followed by another image, set in the series's present, of Juspeczyk holding a page of the Tijuana Bible on which Jupiter tells a man, "Treat me rough, sugar," while she herself says, "Mother, this is *vile*" (figure 7).[99] This juxtaposition puts Juspeczyk in the same position of judging her mother as Hooded Justice, an obviously unflattering parallel insofar as the flashback implicitly criticizes Jupiter's rescuer for his puritanical inability to distinguish between rape and sexuality more generally and for his resultant cruelty to Jupiter. The sequence thus initially seems to confirm the contrast between the superhero genre and realism, insofar as Hooded Justice, who was the first superhero in *Watchmen*'s world, cannot acknowledge the full range of human behavior. Indeed, insofar as the series suggests he is himself a closeted homosexual, this scene implies a parallel between the costume and the closet as mechanisms of idealized misrepresentation.

The transition to the present day, however, pointedly shows Juspeczyk judging not simply her mother but, more specifically, a comic book representation of her mother. In part this serves as a commentary on the limiting conflation of the comic book medium with the superhero genre, reminding us that the medium also included other genres such as the pornographic Tijuana Bible. But Juspeczyk's scorn is also the more general scorn of non-comic-book readers, including such self-appointed experts as Fredric Wertham, for the medium as a whole, which they saw as awash in sex and violence rendered doubly objectionable by the medium's juvenile readership. The transition from Hooded Justice to Juspeczyk, then, in fact inverts the contrast between the comic book and realism, suggesting that it is not the medium but its critics who exclude whole realms of human behavior.

That said, Moore and Gibbons by no means present Jupiter as a model of self-awareness in contrast to her more repressed daughter. Indeed, the first Silk Spectre's own superhero identity is a kind of closet, insofar as she goes by the (publicly known) surname of Jupiter instead of the ethnically tinged one of which she is ashamed. In seemingly rejecting a secret identity, that is, she actually adopts a more effective one. Jupiter also remains confused about her reaction to and feelings for the Comedian for most of her life. But it is in fact because she is just as unself-aware, in different ways, as her daughter is—as most people are—

FIGURE 7. Laurie Juspeczyk judging her mother (and comic books)
Source: Alan Moore and Dave Gibbons, *Watchmen* II.8

that she needs the Tijuana Bible to express to herself and to others (the Hooded Justice she carries in memory, the daughter with whom she has a complex relationship) her lack of shame about her past.

This gesture is, moreover, accepted (if not explicitly understood) in the Tijuana Bible's return appearance in the first epilogue. Jupiter, casting about for a Christmas gift for her unexpected visitor, Dreiberg, sees that he is reading the comic book. She tells him, "Hope it hasn't *embarrassed* you," and he replies, "Oh *no*. Not at *all*. To tell the *truth*, I . . . well, in 1952, I *owned* a copy." She then makes a gift of it, jokingly telling him (since Juspeczyk is standing right there), "Take it. Just don't tell the wife."[100] This exchange once again uses the Tijuana Bible to conflate Jupiter's sexual past with comic books, although now in a more positive way that we can identify with the classic realist character arc: she has accepted her past, and her daughter has accepted it as well ("People's *lives* take them strange *places*, they do strange *things*"), just as Dreiberg has accepted his juvenile influences.

It is this expressive power of the comic book and other popular genres, their capacity for simultaneously courting and defusing shame, that will become central to the fiction of Chabon, Lethem, and Díaz. For Moore, as for these writers, this capacity is grounded not just in the characteristic plots devices of genre fiction but also in its characteristic use of a certain kind of florid, noneveryday language. *Watchmen*'s first words consist of such language, an excerpt from Rorschach's journal that appears over six panels that increasingly zoom out from the bloody site where the Comedian hit the sidewalk after being thrown out of his apartment by (as the reader later learns) Veidt:

Dog carcass in alley this morning, tire tread on burst stomach. This city is afraid of me. I have seen its true face. The streets are extended gutters and the gutters are full of blood and when the drains finally scab over, all the vermin with drown. The accumulated filth of all their sex and murder will foam up about their waists and all the whores and politicians will look up and shout "Save us!" . . . and I'll look down and whisper "No."[101]

Although Zack Snyder's 2009 movie transposes this scene with the comic book's second one, a discussion between the two detectives investigating the murder, and although it shows different images (Rorschach approaching the building and climbing its side, which is wordless in the comic book), it does repeat these lines almost verbatim in voice-over, only omitting the "I'll look down and" near the end. Yet the effect is almost entirely different. In the comic book these words are not yet tied to any particular figure; indeed, the panel which reads "I'll look down" in fact looks down on Rorschach himself, not in costume but in what the reader does not yet know is his secret identity of a man carrying a sign reading, "The end is nigh." Because the film uses the lines over the images of a costumed Rorschach, and because Jackie Earle Haley speaks them in the same guttural rasp employed by Christian Bale in Christopher Nolan's Batman movies, the effect is that of precisely the boilerplate superhero story that *Watchmen* seeks to complicate.[102]

The graphic novel also stylizes the presentation of Rorschach's dialogue, but to a completely different effect. In the graphic novel Gibbons letters Rorschach's journal in a different style, one that seems intended partially to replicate hand printing (as the movie recognizes in scenes showing the journal). But this may not be the key difference between the lettering Gibbons uses for Rorschach's journal and the one that he employs for the majority of the dialogue and captions (figure 8).[103] Alongside Gibbons's usual lettering style Rorschach's journal appears not more handwritten but simply more ornate. Whereas the presentation of these words in the movie thus seems intended to sound—as Klock says of Miller's *Dark Knight*—cool, their presentation in the comic book has exactly the opposite effect,

FIGURE 8. Lettering as expressive style I
Source: Alan Moore and Dave Gibbons, *Watchmen* I.1

echoing and reinforcing the awkwardly baroque nature of the language they embody.

The language of Rorschach's journal is not everyday language, nor is it the clipped, minimalist phrasing—sentence fragments, missing articles, sublinguistic vocalizations such as "Hurrm"[104]—that characterizes most of his dialogue. It is poetic but awkwardly so, as evidenced in the passage quoted earlier by the long mixed metaphor of streets as gutters full of blood scabbing over the drains and drowning verminous whores and politicians. Rorschach's journal plays a key role not only in the narration of *Watchmen* but also in its plot, insofar as he mails it to the right-wing newspaper the *New Frontiersman* prior to leaving for Ozymandias's Antarctic retreat, and the conclusion hints that because of this Ozymandias's plans may be revealed. Of course even if the plan does see the light of day, it will be in a manner easily discreditable as paranoid conspiracy theorizing. But this is apt insofar as the excerpts from the journal already suggest that Rorschach crafts it, intentionally or no, less as a piece of utilitarian communication than as a work of pseudoliterary expression.

Díaz's *Oscar Wao* likewise ends with three posthumous manuscripts (one of which in fact never arrives) mailed by the eponymous hero before his death. Given that Díaz's title character is a writer of popular genre fiction ("sci-fi monsterspieces")[105] that the narrator, a published writer of literary fiction, finds undisciplined but compelling, I take this as Díaz's reading of Rorschach as an analog for his title character: that is to say an unpublished writer of genre fiction. Moore acknowledges this aspect of the character in his 1988 interview with Sharrett, during which Sharrett notes that Rorschach is the series's "most demented character," but, he tells Moore, "you've obviously given him a poet's soul. He's capable of waxing lyrical." Moore replies, "It's a kind of black lyricism, but, yeah, I would agree. Of course my main inspiration for that character's voice was the notes that Son of Sam gave to the police."[106] Moore also notes that Rorschach was a combination of Steve Ditko's Mr. A, "this marvelously Ayn Randian character who was utterly merciless with any form of evil and was unable to see any shades of grey in terms of morality," and "the sort of mad crack poetry of the Son of Sam notes talking about the cracks in the sidewalk and the blood in the cracks and the ants that fed upon the blood."[107] As this contrast suggests, the "mad crack poetry" is the mark of the pure (literary) excess excluded by the ruthless logic practiced by Rand's characters and those that Ditko created under Rand's influence. Rorschach's writing, like his sudden outburst of violence when he is tormented by bullies as a child (he sticks a cigarette in one's eye and bites the other's cheek)[108] or like his murder of the dogs that have been fed the kidnapping victim Blair Roche, marks the violent excess that continually escapes his efforts to respond to a chaotic world solely with cold logic. In this respect his journal's very unliterary awkwardness—its awkward violations of the rules of good literary form—not only encodes the untutored protocols of genre fiction but also uses them to say something significant about Rorschach's character. The journal makes a claim, in this way, for the expressive capacities of bad genre form.

This claim for genre language is amplified—even as it is removed from the terrain of individual subjectivity—in the narration of the interpolated excerpts from "Marooned," the story-within-the-story from the fictional comic book *Tales of the Black Freighter*. "Marooned" offers first-person narration, yet it presents this narration, traditionally associated with a more accurate depiction of subjectivity, as explicitly fictional and diegetically present in the narrative only through the chance occurrence of a character named Bernie reading the comic book outside the newsstand that appears throughout the story. This narration is reproduced in captions that resemble the excerpts from Rorschach's journal, except that the edges of the caption boxes are not simply ragged but age stressed in a way meant to mimic old manuscripts, and the first letter of each caption is given a vaguely gothic design also intended to suggest a historical document (figure 9). These captions, from a story that first appeared in a 1960 DC comic book within the series's parallel universe (where the real-life presence of superheroes made that genre less dominant),[109] tell the story of a sailor whose boat is attacked by pirates and who goes insane during his effort to reach his hometown to warn it about the eponymous black freighter. Upon arriving he kills a couple on horseback and his own family under the delusion that they are pirates, only to finally discover that the haunted freighter's goal has been not the town but his own soul. This story provides an obvious analog not only for Veidt's plan to sacrifice millions in order to end the Cold War but also for all the moral compromises in the putative pursuit of good that Rorschach, Manhattan, and the other characters make throughout the book.

I am less interested in this thematic parallel, however, than I am in the way in which the *Black Freighter* excerpts serve as a figure for the relationship between popular forms and high art. The story is written by Max Shea, who appears briefly in the narrative as one of the writers and artists employed by Veidt as part of his plan. The supplemental material in chapter V, a prose chapter from the fictional *Treasure Island Treasury of Comics*, makes clear that Shea is a self-deprecatory analog for Moore

FIGURE 9. Lettering as expressive style II
Source: Alan Moore and Dave Gibbons, *Watchmen* V.9

himself. It notes that after Shea started receiving fan mail, he "began to see himself as the driving force of the book, becoming increasingly resentful of [artist Joe] Orlando's clearly important role and harassing the artist [in a manner similar to Moore's own often-cited procedure] with impossibly detailed panel descriptions and endless carping requests for revisions of artwork already drawn." It also contends that Shea's first script, "while sturdy enough, is clichéd and predictable in comparison with the work that Shea did later, and in that first issue was easily outshone by" Orlando's art—going on, however, to chart Shea's gradual improvement and point out that after the author left comics, he went "on to write such classic novels as the twice-filmed FOGDANCING."[110] A television news report about the missing Shea that appears in the background of the buildup to Dreiberg and Juspeczyk's first sexual encounter likewise notes that the author "wrote children's *pirate comics* before graduating to modern classics such as *The Hooded Basilisk* and *Fogdancing*."[111]

Shea, a writer who graduates from comic books to serious fiction, is clearly an aspirational figure for Moore. But it would be a mistake to too quickly conflate this aspiration with the news story's characterization of comic books as juvenile. The chapter from the *Treasure Island Treasury* argues that Shea's scripts "began to gradually improve in quality as the writer became used to the medium" and notes that "readers who came to the series expecting a good rousing tale of swashbuckling were either repulsed or fascinated by what were often perverse and blackly lingering comments upon the human condition."[112] Shea's "gradually developing skill as a writer,"[113] in other words, stems not from outgrowing the medium but from learning and adapting himself to its possibilities, and his writing disappoints those who expect a mere genre exercise. This is Bernie's reaction when after finishing his first issue he tells the newsstand owner Bernard, "*Hey* man, *I* ain't buyin' *this!* Ripoff story ain't got no *endin'!* Just left *hangin'* with that *ship* comin' in gonna *kill* everybody. Shee-it. I'm goin' *home*."[114] Even as this response criticizes the story's achievement as a work of entertainment, though, it refuses a distinction between modernism and genre, conflating the sort of irresolution associated with modernist difficulty with the suspense associated with genre fiction. And in fact Bernie does indeed return to read the subsequent issue. Here Moore suggests that there is a utopian underside to the very language used to dismiss genre fiction, if we understand genre writing as enacting not a subliterary failure to follow the rules of standard literature but a quasi-modernist refusal to be bound by these rules. The excerpt from the *Treasure Island Treasury* ends, following a reference to the now-respected Shea's comic book corpus, with the sentence fragment (the syntactical bad form here reinforcing the point), "Stories there to be rediscovered and reexamined, like so many of the fascinating sunken treasures lurking just beneath the surface of this fabulous and compelling genre."[115]

It is perhaps not surprising that Moore chooses for this exercise a style of comic book story associated with EC (Educational Comics), which, as Bart Beaty notes, was both pilloried by anti-comic-book crusaders for its sexual and violent content and lauded, at the time and since, for producing among the first comic book stories that might be considered art.[116] William Gaines took over EC after the death of his father, Max, in 1947, and under his leadership it became a premier publisher of crime, horror, war, and science-fiction stories until the anti-comic-book movement of 1954–1955 led to its lingering demise. (Although one of its comics, *MAD*, became even more successful when Gaines transformed it into a magazine at ambitious editor Harvey Kurtzman's insistence, a move that freed it from the restrictions of the new Comics Code.) *Watchmen* imagines a different trajectory for EC in its alternate reality:

> The brief surge of anti-comic book sentiment in the mid-fifties, while it could conceivably have damaged E.C. as a company, had instead come to nothing and left them stronger as a result. With the government of the day coming down squarely on the side of comic books in an effort to protect the image of certain comic book-inspired agents in their employ, it was as if the comic industry had suddenly been given the blessing of Uncle Sam himself—or at least J. Edgar Hoover.[117]

Although *Tales of the Black Freighter* is a DC publication and although EC was not associated with the pirate genre (it did publish a comic book called *Piracy* in 1954–1955), Moore and Gibbons's story bears the key formal marker of an EC narrative: "the surprise or twist ending, modelled on the short fiction of O. Henry (William Sydney Porter), which was often condemned as formulaic."[118]

EC thus provides a model for Moore and Gibbons of formulaic genre art that transcends its formulas. Beaty, concerned as I have noted with comics' relation to the visual art world, locates this transcendence in the stories' images—as does Moore, at least initially, with the *Treasure Island Treasury*'s praise of Orlando's drawings. But the development of Shea as both a genre writer and a writer more generally opens the possibility that the words too can transcend formula, as indeed they do in the excerpts from "Marooned."

Comparing these excerpts with Rorschach's journal makes clear how finely calibrated Moore's sense of literary levels can be. The captions putatively written by Shea for "Marooned" deal with the same grim subject matter as Rorschach's journal, and they too effect an exaggerated, baroque style; but in them Rorschach's "crack poetry" gives way to a much more finely disciplined imitation of premodernist Victorian genre fiction of the sort—written by immensely skilled writers such as Bram Stoker and Robert Louis Stevenson—that Moore was subsequently to draw on for the *League of Extraordinary Gentlemen* series he began with artist Kevin O'Neill in 1999. In one series of panels, for instance, the protagonist/narrator recalls his past life with his wife and children, migrating from there to the dead bodies of his shipmates that he has dug up to use as floats for his raft (itself a brilliant, spare image) to a shark he has killed and then back to the family, slaughtered in his imagination by the pirates:

> I remembered her waving goodbye from the verandah shadows, sunlight illuminating one cheek bone. Dead? Those glorious days; that innocence . . . *dead? Dead:* I imagine my shipmates' bloated corpses, carrying my raft on fisheaten backs . . . *Dead:* the putrefying shark, its snarl no longer *convincing. . . Dead:* I hear her *pleading;* see their yellowed *smiles,* their cutlasses carving relentlessly until all her *personality,* all her subtleties of *posture* and *expression* are *obliterated,* reduced to *meat. . .* dead. Finally, faced with horrors both *intolerable* and *unavoidable,* I chose *madness.*[119]

This passage remains genre fiction at the level of both form and content, but it is undeniably better writing than the mixed metaphor from Rorschach's journal that I quoted earlier. Eschewing metaphor altogether, it proceeds through a series of concrete images all echoing the series's overarching theme of a materialist universe that both solicits and defies human attempts to impute meaning. As the narrator moves from a nostalgic image of his family to the dead bodies of his shipmates employed as parts of his raft, from the sharks whose (imputed, merely anthropomorphizing) expressions are "no longer convincing" in death to his wife "reduced to *meat,*" he finally "ch[ooses] *madness*"—a formulation that raises the question, as Rorschach's story also does, of the relationship between choice and madness.

"Marooned," putatively written by Shea at a late high point of his work on the *Tales of the Black Freighter* series, serves as Moore and Gibbons's showcase for the artistic and literary merit of the comic book medium and of genre productions more generally. This is fitting since it was, as I noted in the introduction, Moore's discovery of the potential resonances between the overarching narrative and the comic book being read by Bernie that pushed him beyond questions of plot—the idea of doing a more "naturalistic" superhero story—and into the concern with the formal potential of the medium that makes *Watchmen* a landmark of the comic book's modernist moment. As I have been suggesting here, comic book modernism necessarily works differently from early twentieth-century literary modernism, insofar as the former is not a revolt against an ossified realism but rather a revolt that employs realism in the service of remaking a medium known for irrealistic genres. Yet insofar as much of Moore's thinking about the limitations of the comics medium revolved around questions of character, he drew for this revolt on some of the same technical innovations in the representation of subjectivity that characterized one major strain of modernist writing. Within *Watchmen*, as in the novels of James, Forster, and Woolf, psychological realism is not at odds but in fact continuous with formal innovation.

"Marooned" serves as a parallel to and diegetic example of the formal potentials of genre writing—potentials that, as *Watchmen* suggests and more recent works of prose fiction systematically explore, go beyond those of psychological realism and realism more generally. Moore's interest in the nonsuperhero genre productions of EC, that is to say, stems from a desire to see the company's reputation for aesthetic excellence within the comic book world, and the denigration of its products as simultaneously juvenile and obscene outside that world, as mutually constitutive registers of aesthetic possibilities not yet recognized within the mainstream. EC's comics provide another model for *Watchmen*, one that successfully anticipates the series's eventual celebration in a literary world more willing to admit the merits of genre fiction.

But as I will argue in the next chapter, Moore turns to EC for another reason as well, one that has to do not with his investment in the comic book medium but rather with his reservations about it—or, more precisely, about the industry that produces it. This aspect of

EC, as Beaty points out, is not unrelated to its artistic ambitions, or at least its efforts to diversify the medium. "Lacking ongoing characters in their titles like Superman or Batman that would spur repeat purchases," Beaty writes, "EC used a clubhouse strategy in their titles to generate fan identification with the small company. Crediting individual artists was one strategy that would humanize the creators and make them seem approachable to readers, encouraging reader identification with EC as a small, outsider publisher striving to raise the level of the form."[120] The notion of "ongoing characters" here links aesthetics and economics in complicated ways. Such characters were not solely a function of the superhero genre, of course: Disney, owner of the most profitable comic book characters of the early postwar period, achieved the same effect with Mickey Mouse and Uncle Scrooge. But recurring characters—whether superheroes, funny animals, or celebrities from other media, such as Roy Rogers or Dean Martin and Jerry Lewis—anticipated the economics of the film franchise (as Hollywood has recently rediscovered with specific reference to superheroes), providing a selling point to some degree independent of the producers or quality of a series of works.

This is not to say that there were not great aesthetic achievements within such genres, although, as Beaty notes, perhaps the greatest— Carl Barks's work from the early 1940s to the late 1960s on Disney's Donald Duck family of comics (published by Dell and Western Publishing)—was economically independent of Barks's name: Barks worked in complete anonymity, his stories credited to Walt Disney, until assiduous fans ferreted out his identity in the 1960s.[121] Nor, of course, are the superhero and other character-based genres necessarily incompatible with artistic credit: Marvel employed the same "clubhouse strategy" to build a fan base for its superhero titles in the 1960s and 1970s, and since the 1980s both Marvel and DC have oriented themselves around the promotion of popular creators as well as characters. But EC, in a period before writer and artist credits were common, gave such credits as a way of cultivating readers' ongoing identification with, if not characters, then creators. While EC still paid its artists on a work-for-hire basis (albeit at higher rates than other companies), it also made the names of artists such as Wally Wood,

Bernard Krigstein, and Joe Orlando. In this way its comics stand as a hallmark in the ongoing struggle for creative and economic control between comic book creators and publishers. This is a struggle that forms a continuing theme for Moore throughout his career, and it is one that—as I argue in the next chapter—shapes *Watchmen* in not immediately apparent but nonetheless crucial ways.

CHAPTER TWO

PROPERTY

Adrian Veidt / Ozymandias serves as the villain of *Watchmen* insofar as he engineers the byzantine plot, stumbled on first by the Comedian and then Rorschach, to purposely kill millions of people in New York City in order to trick the United States and the USSR into believing that they must cooperate to prevent a fictional alien invasion. As Moore has pointed out in interviews, Veidt's role raises "moral questions . . . which are problematical . . . because the perpetrator is a liberal and a humanitarian!"[1] The subject of a glowing tribute by the liberal journalist Doug Roth printed as the supplementary materials to the character's origin chapter—albeit a tribute that uneasily notes the trappings of Veidt's immense wealth, especially his three Vietnamese servants (whom he has killed in the preceding chapter in order to protect his secret)—Veidt has prior to the start of the graphic novel quit crime-fighting and amassed the fortune he needs for his plans.[2] Starting out with charging stations for electric cars, by the time the events of *Watchmen* take place he has diversified his product line with such items as a popular perfume named Nostalgia and toys based on his superhero career. In Veidt's first appearance in the series, when Rorschach goes to inform him about the Comedian's death, we see several Ozymandias action figures on Veidt's desk (figure 10). Rorschach, holding one, comments scathingly on the fact that Veidt has "set up a company selling posters and diet books and toy soldiers based on himself."[3]

The problem with Veidt's merchandising is not simply that he has decided to profit from his own heroic past, since as we learn in the sup-

FIGURE 10. The villain as cross-marketer
Source: Alan Moore and Dave Gibbons, *Watchmen*
I.18

plemental materials to a later chapter, his Marketing and Development department is urging him to expand his line of action figures to include ones of Rorschach, Nite Owl, and the villain Moloch. The employee who writes this memo notes that figures of Veidt's fellow superheroes seem "viable" despite "the trademark and copyright laws": "Our lawyers seem to think that since the costumed identities themselves are outlawed and illegal, there can be no legal claim to copyright upon their costumed images, leaving us free to register a copyright ourselves." Likewise Veidt can manufacture and sell a "Moloch figurine" since not only has the former supervillain recently died, but "once again there can be no legal claim on Jacobi's part concerning infringement of an identity which is illegal in the first place."[4] If, as I noted at the conclusion of chapter 1, Moore has repeatedly commented in interviews and other venues on the long struggle between comic book artists who created characters on a work-by-hire basis and the companies who then owned these trademarked characters, then the Veidt Corporation appears at this moment as an exaggerated figure for the latter, able to profit from the creations of others through a combination of Veidt's contingent relationship with the creators and a legal fiction. Rather than seeing the identities of Rorschach and Nite Owl as products of love and dedication (as superheroes and those who create them would), the Veidt Corporation understands them as sources of cross-media profit streams. The same memo suggests why Veidt should okay a figure of his pet Bubastis: because even though the genetically altered lynx "didn't play any part in your exploits while you were an adventurer, . . . the people doing the Saturday morning Ozymandias cartoon show . . . are keen that Bubastis should play a major role as a feline sidekick, making it therefore appropriate to play her up in our other merchandising."[5]

It is perhaps a (joking) sign of how seriously Moore takes this issue that Veidt—while enthusiastic about the Bubastis figure—demurs on the others for personal reasons: willing to kill millions of people, including ones he knows closely, to bring about his speculative plan to end the Cold War, Veidt is "ethically very uncertain" about profiting from the creations of others.[6] In what follows I read the conflict between Rorschach and Ozymandias as, among other things, an allegory of the conflict between the work-for-hire creative talent of the comics industry and the corporations which by and large controlled and profited from their creations, especially before changes in the 1980s led to greater creative control and profit sharing by at least some well-known writers and artists. This allegory predates the later hardening of Moore's attitudes about this situation as he fought with DC over control of his own creations, demonstrating that questions of creative control constituted an important element of his thought from early in his career. *Watchmen* is all the more interesting, however, to the extent that Moore and Gibbons's collaboration does not treat this allegory consistently but rather remains torn between Moore's idea of comics as literature, which as we have already begun to see allows him to relocate agency to creators, and a more medium-specific celebration of the aesthetics and modes of production of comics themselves.

That Rorschach stands in for the work-for-hire creator becomes clear when we note that Moore explicitly based him on the Question and other characters created by Steve Ditko after Ditko left Marvel due to a dispute over his enormously successful cocreation Spider-Man. According to Ditko's biographer Blake Bell, the artist continually fought with Spider-Man's other creator, Stan Lee, to keep the more realistic touches that had made the character successful. Bell contends that Lee, "prone" according to Ditko "to the formulaic trappings of the comics he had [previously] presided over" and "still smarting from the psychological scars caused by the Comics Code Authority in the mid-1950s," both sought to introduce "too many far-reaching elements of the 'fantastic' that would be incongruous in a strip about a plausible teenager" and self-censored ideas that he thought would run afoul of the Code.[7] Ditko, on the other hand, insisted "that the strip be grounded in the civilian life of Peter Parker"; rendered the book's supporting cast members, especially Peter's employer, J. Jonah Jameson, and his elderly Aunt May, unglamorously; and "push[ed] himself and Lee to introduce nuances to enhance the strip's believability."[8]

Bell probably overplays Ditko's (and underplays Lee's) contribution to Marvel's transformation of the superhero genre in the early 1960s: part of what set Marvel's heroes apart from those of their competitor DC was Lee's dialogue, which, as Bell claims, Lee sometimes "overd[id]"[9] but which lends an element of seeming realism to the superhero genre by adopting the soul-searching conventions of the romance comic and the soap opera. Still, Lee and Ditko did engage in a running battle over control—both creative and financial—of the title. Late in the first year of the series, Ditko took over plotting duties and eventually secured credit for doing so (something that Jack Kirby, who also plotted his books with Lee, never achieved).[10] But Ditko's desire for creative control and—increasingly as he came under the influence of Ayn Rand's ideas—his share of profits from the character brought him into conflict with both Lee, who was as much a manager as a creator at Marvel, and the company's owner, Martin Goodman, "a self-made man who didn't take any lip from the hired help."[11] Ditko eventually decided to leave Marvel over the profit-sharing issue, which crucially involved Marvel's growing income from exactly the sort of merchandise in which Ozymandias trades. In addition to arguing "with Lee and Goodman over promised royalties and monies from merchandising that were beginning to pour in near the end of Ditko's tenure," the artist also objected to Marvel's move into cartoon programming that used photocopied images of his and others' work to present minimally animated versions of previously published comic book stories.[12]

In leaving Marvel, Ditko chose creative control over profits. Angered by Marvel's failure to pay him what he thought was his due as Spider-Man's cocreator, he returned to Charlton, the small Connecticut comic book company for which he had created Captain Atom (Dr. Manhattan's precursor) in 1960 before devoting his time entirely to the

better-paying Marvel.[13] Charlton had, ironically, come into business
when its founders met in the New Haven County Jail, where one of
them, John Santangelo, was doing time for illegally selling copyrighted
song lyrics.[14] Upon their release Santangelo and his new partner, Edward Levy, went into the legitimate magazine business, in 1945 adding
comic books to their line mainly because it was more cost-effective to
keep their presses running at all times than to shut them down periodically.[15] This quantitative rather than qualitative approach to their
product led Charlton to cut as many corners as possible: "Charlton
produced material of the lowest artistic quality, on the lowest quality
paper, with the least enticing packaging exhibited in the industry."[16]
But it also ironically allowed the company to offer Ditko "the greatest artistic freedom in the industry."[17] In exchange for a low page rate
Charlton left Ditko more or less free to fill pages as he wished, giving
him the opportunity to dramatize the Randian ideas that he had tentatively begun to explore in *Spider-Man*.

Ditko's Randian turn achieved its fullest expression in the two main
influences on Rorschach, the Question and Mr. A—the latter an even
more extreme figure whom Ditko created for his fellow artist Wally
Wood's pioneering underground comic *witzend*. But it is also visible
in Ditko's Blue Beetle, a new version of a character that Charlton had
purchased from the comic book publisher Fox. The Blue Beetle, in his
Fox incarnation as well as his earliest appearances at Charlton, was an
archaeologist who received various ill-defined powers from an ancient
Egyptian scarab. When Ditko revamped the character for the backup
feature in *Captain Atom*, he introduced a new Beetle who had assumed
the identity out of guilt when his mad-scientist uncle was responsible
for the original's seeming death. Ditko's Blue Beetle was the precursor to Moore and Gibbons's Nite Owl in more ways than just being a
legacy hero: a scientist named Ted Kord, he fought crime using a range
of gadgets (including a flying Beetle similar to Nite Owl's Archie) and
an acrobatic, Spider-Man-like fighting style in lieu of actual powers. In
the character's early adventures Rand's influence is primarily visible in
the strip's villains: generally anonymous figures or members of gangs
rather than individuals, they include among their number a spy trying
to highjack a plane; a band of criminals led by an heir who has frit-
tered away his inheritance and now masquerades as a philanthropist;

and the bearded, pseudoanarchist Madmen. These stories—even after Ditko began writing as well as drawing them for the Beetle's own title, featuring the Question as its backup series—remain lighthearted and swashbuckling, with the hero prone to making Spider-Man-like quips while he fought.

By the final published issue of *Blue Beetle*, however (number 5, cover dated November 1968, almost a year after the issue that preceded it), Ted Kord not only fights a purely Randian villain—an artist who dresses up as his own creation, a grotesque statue called "Our Man," and attempts to smash works of heroic, figural art—but also sets aside his wisecracks in favor of set-piece speeches similar to those made by Rand's characters. At the end of the story Kord tells his admiring girlfriend why he sought to protect a statue called "The Unconquered":

> I was fighting for everything it stood for . . . to me! For the best in a man whatever it is, whatever it took to make that statue . . . whatever it takes to achieve anything worthwhile! It can only be done by struggling to succeed! "Our Man" could only have won if I gave up . . . on what that statue stands for, for what it means to me![18]

In that issue's backup story, meanwhile, the Question—whose alter-ego, Vic Sage, had aided the Blue Beetle in the preceding story—takes on the art critic who had championed "Our Man" and who himself seeks to destroy a heroic painting.[19]

Ditko pushes these Randian conceits even further in his Question and Mr. A stories, whose protagonists are so convinced of the righteousness of their crusades that they are willing to let criminals die. In the story published in Wood's *witzend* Mr. A—named after Rand's fascination with the law of identity (A is A) attributed to Aristotle[20]—allows a criminal named Angel to fall to his death while he delivers another set-piece speech to Angel's would-be victim: "I have no mercy or compassion for aggressors . . . only for their victims . . . for the innocent! To have any sympathy for a killer is an insult to their victims. Even if you weren't hurt . . . I wouldn't have saved Angel!"[21] In the Question story that appeared in *Blue Beetle* 4, where portraying such a denouement would have constituted a violation of the Comics Code, the scripter Steve Skeates has the hero note, "But they just might survive their trip to the river! I'd better call Captain Lash so he can pick 'em up . . . either way!"—still a fairly shocking denouement for a commercially published comic book in 1967.[22] The two characters, with their absolutist notions of morality, serve as clear influences on the violent, uncompromising vigilante Rorschach.

Moore's investment in the Question and Mr. A might initially seem puzzling, insofar as these characters—like Ditko's earlier efforts to move Spider-Man "away from Lee's initial paradigm of Peter Parker, the obsessive, neurotic teenager, and toward Rand's ideal of a young, romantic male hero"[23]—might seem to offer a retreat from *Watchmen*'s realist project. Rand's writing actively dismisses Freudian and other notions of psychological causation in favor of what she describes as reason: "guilt" is a common word in her fiction, but always in the service of a pseudo-Nietzschean argument that guilt is merely a weapon that lesser people use to exploit the capitalists who are society's true creators. In Rand's novels inner conflict is a sign of corruption or error that her heroes must move beyond. Her 1957 *Atlas Shrugged*, for instance, tells the story, among others, of steel-mill owner Henry Rearden, who must learn to eschew the guilt he feels for his success and to embrace the guilt-free existence already espoused by the novel's chief protagonist, John Galt. Rearden at his best appears with "no guilt in his face, no doubt, nothing but the calm of an inviolate self-confidence."[24]

This is to say that Rand's protagonists, whether the architect Howard Roark from *The Fountainhead* (1943) or the industrialists and artists of *Atlas Shrugged*, are already superheroes. They do not have superpowers as such, but Rearden and Galt are both brilliant inventors (the former has created the ultradurable Rearden metal, the latter a motor that generates unlimited energy), and their colleague Ragnar Danneskjöld is a former philosopher who has become a pirate (robbing the relief ships sent to the United States by the socialist government of Europe in order to one day repay the income taxes of those whom he considers creators). Indeed, one way to read the plot of *Atlas Shrugged* is as the origin story of a kind of superhero team, a capitalist Justice League or Avengers who watch the world from their secret headquarters in the Rockies and—this being Rand—refuse to help people.

Yet Ditko's Randian characters hold a fascination for Moore, and not simply as productive challenges to realist characterization. As I suggested in chapter 1, Moore did see the Question and Mr. A as such challenges, giving Rorschach their inability "to see any shades of grey in terms of morality"[25] while seeking to flesh out the psychological implications of such a worldview: "I used to ask," Moore told an interviewer in 1988, "'What does Mr. A think of when he masturbates?'"[26] But Rorschach is not only a realist revision of Ditko's Randian vigilantes, as suggested by the fact that he plays a larger role in *Watchmen* (and by many accounts holds a larger claim on readers' attention and sympathy) than the more ordinary Nite Owl.

Moore's fascination with Ditko's characters can also be understood, in this regard, as a function of Moore's respect for Ditko himself. If Moore sought to imagine a complicated psychology lying behind and shaping Rorschach's inflexible understanding of good and evil, Ditko earned Moore's admiration for his own, different brand of inflexibility. Moore told the magazine *Comic Book Artist* in a 2000 interview, "I at least felt that though Steve Ditko's political agenda was very different to mine, Steve Ditko *had* a political agenda, and that in some ways set him above most of his contemporaries. . . . There's something about his uncompromising attitude that I have a great deal of sympathy with. It's just that the things I wouldn't compromise about or that he wouldn't compromise about are probably very different."[27] Rorschach's unbending integrity as a violent crime-fighter takes on a different cast when transposed to Ditko's artistic integrity, and the latter shades Moore's depiction of the former. Moore makes the connection between Rorschach and Ditko explicit in an interview in the documentary *In Search of Steve Ditko*, noting, "[Rorschach] has this ferocious moral integrity that has made him one of the most popular characters in the book, and obviously that ferocious moral drive and integrity, that was kind of my take upon Steve Ditko."[28]

Rorschach can thus be read as a figure for the uncompromising artist and, more specifically, of the comic book artist for whom work-for-hire had historically meant a lack of ownership or control over his (usually) creations. As Eric Berlatsky notes in the introduction to his invaluable selection of interviews with Moore, one advantage of following Moore's comments over the course of his career is that

it demonstrates "his initial enthusiasm toward, and then disillusionment with, the comics industry."[29] Just as Ditko gave up his work for
Charlton and began working full-time for Marvel because it paid better, Moore left the British magazine *Warrior*, which featured creator-
owned strips, for the better-paying DC and even signed away his
rights to his series *V for Vendetta* (published in black-and-white in
Warrior between 1982 and 1985, then as a ten-issue color miniseries
by DC in 1988-1989).[30] But like Ditko returning to Charlton following
his dispute with Lee and Goodman, Moore in 1988–1989 left DC, and
for a time superhero comics entirely, out of what Berlatsky describes
as "a conscious choice to emphasize certain elements of his trajectory
over others, sacrificing a measure of economic security for creative
freedom when it seemed these two strands were no longer reconcil-
able."[31] Throughout the 1990s Moore worked on ambitious, nonsuperhero projects—the realistic *Big Numbers*, the historical/horror fiction
about Jack the Ripper *From Hell*, the pornographic *Lost Girls*—while
he also eventually returned to superhero work for Image Comics, a
creator-owned company that briefly rose to challenge the dominance
of DC and Marvel.[32] Moore agreed to do his own America's Best
Comics (ABC) line for Image's WildStorm imprint in 1998, just before DC purchased WildStorm. Having thus inadvertently returned
to DC, Moore found himself once again writing comics—the most
well known of which is *The League of Extraordinary Gentleman* with
artist Kevin O'Neill—for his old publisher.[33] After Moore argued with
DC over the film version of *V for Vendetta*, Moore and O'Neill took
League, which unlike Moore's other ABC series was creator owned, to
the independent publisher Top Shelf.

In 2009, following this dispute over the *V for Vendetta* movie,
Moore responded to an interviewer's question about which rights
to his works he owned by citing Gerard Jones's 2004 book *Men of
Tomorrow*—a brilliant, detailed account of Jerry Siegel and Joe Shuster's decades-long struggle with DC over credits for and profits from
their creation Superman. Alluding to Jones's discussion of early comics entrepreneurs' reputed involvement with bootleggers and other
questionable business associates, Moore told the interviewer, "The
industry . . . it's dark satanic mills. And in all my experience of them,
these people are gangsters by any other name."[34]

Most recently, Moore has taken issue with DC's decision to publish a number of prequels to *Watchmen* under the title *Before Watchmen*.[35] While Moore called *Before Watchmen* "completely shameless,"[36] Gibbons was more diplomatic, noting in a statement, "The original series of *Watchmen* is the complete story that Alan Moore and I wanted to tell. However, I appreciate DC's reasons for this initiative and the wish of the artists and writers involved to pay tribute to our work. May these new additions have the success they desire."[37]

This difference in tone aside, Gibbons's idea of *Watchmen* as a "complete story" gets at the heart of the tension between creators and companies here, to the extent that the very notion of a complete story runs counter to the business model, premised on an unending stream of new additions/editions, pursued by the mainstream comic book industry. There is no complete Superman story or Spider-Man story: Superman and Spider-Man are characters owned by DC and Marvel, respectively, the subjects of decades-long (since 1938 in the case of the former and 1962 in the case of the latter) series of stories told in multiple comic books by multiple creators, both over time and at any given time, and licensable for toys, films, Broadway shows, and whatever other projects the parent companies think will be profitable. As Dan DiDidio, one of the DC publishers responsible for *Before Watchmen*, quite accurately told *USA Today* in a story about the launch of the series, "The strength of what comics are is building on other people's legacies and enhancing them and making them even stronger properties in their own right."[38]

We need not understand this aspect of the medium strictly in mercenary terms: Moore was, after all, hired by DC to revamp the *Swamp Thing* series (created by Len Wein, now one of the writers on *Before Watchmen*) and initially conceived *Watchmen* as a story using the "properties" DC had acquired from Charlton. But DiDidio's use of the word "properties" rather than, say, "characters" points to the economic agenda of Marvel and DC, which already in the late seventies were rumored to be making "greater profits from licensing than publishing"[39] and which in their current status as subsidiaries of large media conglomerates (Time Warner and Disney) serve as cross-media marketing platforms for films and other much-more-lucrative enterprises.

We thus need to understand Moore's anachronistic model of literature as a response to the corporate world represented in *Watchmen* by Veidt, who makes money by marketing toys, cartoons, exercise programs—indeed, everything but comic books—based on his exploits as Ozymandias. As I discussed in the introduction, Moore criticized DC's plans for *Before Watchmen*, and implicitly described his and Gibbons's original graphic novel as a work of literature, by telling the *New York Times*, "As far as I know, . . . there weren't that many prequels or sequels to 'Moby-Dick.'"[40] While this assertion ignores the history of literary sequels (Is not James Joyce's 1922 *Ulysses*, for instance, among other things a sequel to his 1916 *A Portrait of the Artist as a Young Man*?),[41] it does make sense as a critique of what this tradition has become under the conditions of contemporary corporate publishing. Specifically, this practice has in recent years become less about authorial choice or literary homage than about the corporate branding of stories, characters, and even popular authors (whose names appear on books written by other people).

Mark Lawson, writing in the *Guardian*, describes this transformation as an extension of the logic of the film industry, although in ways that also clearly map onto what I have been saying about the comic book business:

> The movie business loves sequels for financial reasons—a studio accountant would always rather see *Tired Franchise 4* on the production slate than *Risky Concept 1*—but this enthusiasm also reflects an attitude to creativity. Among film producers, there is no sentimentality at all about sole creators or ownership of characters. The originating novelist is likely to have little or no involvement in the words delivered by the actors (even dramatists, a more complementary profession, are not guaranteed to script the picture made from their play) and so the link between author and story, integral to the experience of reading, is generally shattered before the camera turns.[42]

Moore's reference to *Moby-Dick*, then, is misplaced not only because it ignores the actual precedent of literary prequels and sequels but more importantly because it fails to acknowledge that the literary world has adopted qualities—a reliance on the financial profitability of sequels, what Caren Irr has described as a shift in focus from the authors who produce texts to the corporations that own them[43]—that make it more like the comics industry that Moore criticizes. In this respect we can understand the comic book industry not (as it is tempting to do) as an outmoded one dying a long death in the face of competetion from newer media but on the contrary as a pioneer (with roots in the branding operations of early newspaper comics syndicates) of the economic strategies through which big media conglomerates have more recently reshaped film, television, and publishing.[44]

The contradictions inherent in Moore's anachronistic model of literary production have become increasingly explicit as his disputes with the comics industry have intensified. His most recent graphic novel, for instance, the Top Shelf–published *2009* chapter of *League of Extraordinary Gentlemen* with O'Neill, features as villains unnamed versions of both Harry Potter and six different James Bonds—unnamed for legal reasons in a way that reinforces these characters' roles as avatars of corporate franchises. Moore has made clear in interviews that he sees *Century*, whose three volumes move from 1910 to 1969 to 2009, as among other things a commentary on the devolution of popular culture over the course of the past hundred years.[45] In this respect *2009* suggests a powerful contrast between the vibrant characters of late nineteenth-century fiction with which *League* began (Bram Stoker's Mina Murray, H. Rider Haggard's Allan Quatermain, H. G. Wells's Invisible Man, Robert Louis Stevenson's Mr. Hyde, and Jules Verne's Captain Nemo) and franchise figures such as Bond and Potter. The series in this way takes a legal necessity—unlike the public-domain characters of its first volume, subsequent volumes that move into the twentieth century cannot refer by name to copyrighted characters such as Bond and Potter—and makes it a part of its critique of contemporary mass culture. Yet *League* as a whole obviously celebrates the reimagination of existing characters in its very premise of making the protagonists of works of literature into comic book characters.

League thus seems, in a significant way, at odds with Moore's objections to both the film versions of his work and *Before Watchmen*. On one hand Moore opposes others' adaptions of his creations, especially *Watchmen*, which he sees as a sacrosanct work of art comparable to *Moby-Dick*; on the other hand he seeks to make other works of art grist for his own mill—Melville's Ishmael is, tellingly, a minor character in *League*—and rankles at characters such as Bond (owned by the Broccoli family and Metro-Goldwyn-Mayer) and Potter (owned by J. K. Rowling and Time Warner) whose legal status makes such reimagination difficult.

Yet *2009*'s sly critique of Time Warner via the figure of Potter suggests an important difference between these two seemingly similar processes, one grounded in the corporate understanding of stories as legal or economic entities rather than aesthetic ones. In the midst of a climactic battle with the surviving League members, after killing Quatermain and being attacked by a sword-wielding Orlando, the rampaging Harry-Potter-cum-Antichrist yells, "*Aoww!* That, like, really *hurt?* I could, like, sue you and shit?" (figure 11).[46] Both Bond and Potter have been the subjects of well-publicized legal disputes: in the former case over the rights to *Casino Royale* and *Thunderball*, both of which were adapted as films (the latter under the title *Never Say Never Again*) outside the official MGM franchise;[47] in the latter over the right of RDR Books to publish a print version of the school librarian Steven Vander Ark's website *The Harry Potter Lexicon*.[48] It is perhaps not too much of a stretch to imagine Moore's litigious Antichrist as a reference to the latter suit, especially insofar as it was brought by DC's parent company, Warner Bros. Entertainment.[49] In September 2009, moreover, Warner reorganized DC as DC Entertainment, placing Diane Nelson in charge of the new division. Prior to becoming president of DC Entertainment, Nelson, according to her official biography on the Warner Bros. website, served as "Executive Vice President, Global Brand Management for Warner Bros. Entertainment, a group she started in 2005 in order to continue the cross-company brand management work she began on the Harry Potter property in 2000, expanding efforts to include such iconic films as *Batman Begins*, *Superman Returns*, *Polar Express*, *Charlie and the Chocolate Factory* and *Happy Feet*."[50] Similarly, DC's press release announcing the reorganization claimed that its purpose was "to maximize the potential of the DC brand."[51] Behind Moore's rampaging Antichrist, we might say, is a vision of the media corporation seeking to maximize its brand potential; *2009* allegorizes, in this way, the conflict between corporations' desire to profit from characters and stories (what we might understand

FIGURE 11. The villain as litigator
Source: Alan Moore and Kevin O'Neill, *The League of Extraordinary Gentlemen Century: 2009*, n.p.

as the economics of the comics industry) and artists' desire to revise them creatively (which is central to the aesthetics of the comics medium).

The comics-specific revision of ongoing stories is, of course, at odds in fundamental ways with the notion of the autonomous, self-contained work of literary art, a tension that is in fact central to *Watchmen*. Crucially, Moore understood *Watchmen* as an autonomous work of art before his relationship with DC had soured—indeed, before he and Gibbons had even mapped out the "complete story" that the series would become. No doubt the main reason that Moore was unable to secure permission to use the Charlton characters for his planned story was that he wanted not only to use them but to render them unusable for future projects. As he wrote in his initial pitch,

We'll start from the outside of the concept and work inwards, beginning with the world that these characters inhabit. For a start, as I said over the phone, I think we should not even think for a moment which Earth this thing is set on, and make no attempt to tie it in with regular DC continuity. If you ever want to do a Captain Atom / Superman crossover then I suppose you could always do it as a special event in its own right like the X-Men / Titans crossover or something. Anyway, I don't think that the opportunity for casual crossovers is a good enough reason to include this in the DC Multiverse when weighed against the drawbacks of such a move and the limitations imposed.[52]

Elsewhere in the sketch Moore links his desire to take the Charlton characters out of "the regular DC continuity" to his plans to make the story "far more realistic in conception than any super-heroes' world has been before," arguing that he must have the ability to make drastic changes to the characters and their world in order to tell his story.[53]

It is small wonder that DC turned down Moore's request to use the Charlton characters, since he was essentially asking the company to eschew these characters' potential as renewable sources of profit for the sake of his story. Moore's reference to *The Uncanny X-Men and the New Teen Titans*, a comic book that DC and Marvel coproduced in 1982 with their then-most-popular titles, suggests a precedent in which DC participated in a project that it could not subsequently exploit, albeit because of the system of corporate ownership itself. While DC and Marvel have produced a number of such crossovers over the years, with each other and with other comic book companies, such projects undermine the idea of a continuously exploitable property through their status as coproductions: neither company can continue the story on its own, since it involves characters owned by someone else. Moore's attempt to analogize his planned project with the X-Men / Teen Titans crossover could not, ultimately, open up a space for his own control over the story as its creator, since this example in fact depended on and thereby reinforced the contrasting logic of corporate ownership. DC's eventual decision to turn *Watchmen* itself into a renewable revenue stream, via the prequels, eventually reasserted this logic even in the face of a story that, as Moore promised in his sketch, undermined generic conventions drastically enough to render sequels difficult. *Before Watchmen* circumvents this problem through the logic of the prequel, as the series's tagline—"It's not the end of the world. It's the beginning"—makes clear.[54]

If Moore's bid for the Charlton characters was thus a bit naive on his part, the model of the autonomous work of literary art nonetheless remains central to his engagement with DC's characters in the mideighties. This model shapes, for instance, the preface that Moore wrote in 1986 for the first collected edition of Frank Miller's *The Dark Knight Returns*. In this brief piece Moore praises Miller for taking "a character who, in the view of the wider public, . . . sums up more than any other the essential silliness of the comic book hero" (thanks to

Batman's association, in the pre–Tim Burton and Christopher Nolan era, with the 1960s television show starring Adam West) and treating him realistically: "Depicted over the years as, alternately, a concerned do-gooder and a revenge-driven psychopath, the character as presented here manages to bridge both of those interpretations quite easily while integrating them in a much larger and more persuasively realized personality."[55] Here we might note—recalling Moore's critique of the "grim and gritty" wave of comic books that he and Miller helped usher in[56]—that Moore does not locate the realism of Miller's story in its exposure of the dark underside of Batman's characters (something that he acknowledges, probably thinking of the famous-to-comics-fans stories by Dennis O'Neill and Neal Adams from the late sixties and early seventies, had already been done). Rather, in a way not unrelated to Moore's diffusion of various aspects of Batman among multiple characters in *Watchmen* (see chapter 1), Miller's Batman "integrat[es]" in one figure the radically different ways in which the character has been portrayed in order to produce something like the complexity of human psychology. Geoff Klock, as I noted in chapter 1, makes a similar claim around Miller's explanation of Batman's seemingly incongruous yellow chest symbol.

In the present context, however, Moore's account of *The Dark Knight*'s realism also functions as an imaginative transformation of the inconsistencies produced by multiple authors over long periods of time into a singular artistic vision. And indeed, immediately after praising Miller's realism, Moore then, seemingly contradictorily, celebrates the fact that Miller's "Batman has finally become what he should always have been: He is a legend."[57] These two statements are not in fact contradictory, however, insofar as Moore goes on to claim that "Miller has also managed to shape The Batman into a true legend by introducing that element without which all true legends are incomplete and yet which for some reason hardly seems to exist in the world depicted in the average comic book, and that element is time."[58] By "time" Moore means something very specific, the fact that "all of our best and oldest legends recognize that time passes and that people grow old and die." Here Moore cites Robin Hood's "final blind arrow shot to determine the site of his grave," the Norse Ragnarok, and Davy Crockett's last stand at the Alamo, then notes that comic books do not allow such stories "given *the commercial fact* that a given character will still have to sell to a given audience in ten years' time."[59]

Moore's dispute with DC over the Charlton characters is still clearly in play here, but in *The Dark Knight* Moore finds the example of artistic agency that the X-Men / Teen Titans crossover did not provide. In describing Batman as a "legend" Moore locates the inconsistencies in the character's portrayal not in his status as a commercial object but rather in his status as a subject of collective myth: as Moore is well aware, there are numerous inconsistencies in the stories of Robin Hood and the Norse gods. So far from undermining the role of the singular artist, this shift in fact affirms the artist's ability to shape such inconsistencies into something like a real, complex character. In Moore's preliminary sketch for what was to become *Watchmen* greater authorial control is the means to the end of the revisionist realist strategies that I described in chapter 1. Here, however, that relationship is reversed: realism provides the basis for asserting the authority of an artist giving shape to his version of a collective story. Moore casts Miller as a Shakespeare dramatizing earlier Italian works or a Wagner creating operas out of German folk tales or (to note a figure who is alluded to in *Watchmen*) a T. H. White retelling Arthurian legends.

Moore finally got the chance to write his own version of such a story the same year, when, following DC's decision to reboot Superman, he was invited to bring the character's previous incarnation to a conclusion with a two-part story that appeared under the title *Whatever Happened to the Man of Tomorrow?* Set in the then future of 1997, this story begins with a reporter interviewing Lois Lane about Superman's disappearance ten years earlier and has Lane relating the story of Superman's last battle against his greatest enemies. The opening of this story, set by letterer Todd Klein in another version of the faux-gothic font Moore and Gibbons used for the *Tale of the Black Freighter* excerpts in *Watchmen*, makes clear its continuity with Moore's description of *The Dark Knight Returns*:

This is an IMAGINARY STORY (Which may never happen, but then again may) about a perfect man who came from the sky and did only good. It tells of his twilight, when the great battles were over and the great miracles long since performed; of how his enemies conspired against him and of that final war in the snowblind wastes beneath the Northern Lights; of the women he loved and of the choice he made between them; of how he broke his most sacred oath, and how finally all the things he had were taken from him save for one. It ends with a wink. It begins in a quiet midwestern town, one summer afternoon in the quiet midwestern future. Away in the big city, people still sometimes glance up hopefully from the sidewalks, glimpsing a distant speck in the sky . . . but no: it's only a bird, only a plane. Superman died ten years ago. This is an IMAGINARY STORY. . .

Aren't they all?[60]

The image below this text, by penciler Curt Swan—arguably the consummate Superman artist—features a public statue of the hero labeled "IN MEMORIAM,"[61] as if to emphasize the character's transformation into a whole, finished work of art.

With this in mind we might read *Watchmen*, written around the same time as Moore's preface to *The Dark Knight Returns* and *Whatever Happened to the Man of Tomorrow?*, as an allegory of the struggle between the creative artist seeking to craft a finished work of art and the corporation which owns a profitable, because endlessly reproducible, set of intellectual properties. Within such an allegory Rorschach, Moore's "kind of . . . take on Steve Ditko," plays the uncompromising artist committed to his version of things, while Ozymandias, the head of a corporate empire based partly on licensing his own and other superheroes' images, plays the part of the big publisher like DC. As if to make the point even clearer, Rorschach dies not in a physical struggle of the sort we would expect with a costumed vigilante but because he insists on telling his version of the events engineered by Veidt: "People must be told," he insists to Dr. Manhattan, who then disintegrates Rorschach because he (Manhattan) is convinced that the best course of action is to preserve the fiction of an alien invasion that Ozymandias has created.[62]

What happens immediately after this scene, however, complicates any attempt to read the relationship between Rorschach and Ozymandias as a coherent allegory of the relationship between the comic book creator and the corporate publisher. For if Moore, in almost all of

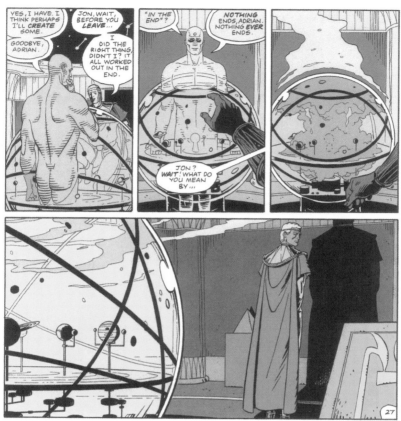

FIGURE 12. "Nothing ever ends" (including, at this point, the graphic novel)
Source: Alan Moore and Dave Gibbons, *Watchmen* XII.27

his work, essays, and interviews, locates the aesthetic potential of the comic book creator in his or her power to create the sort of autonomous artwork celebrated by modernism, the final pages of *Watchmen* undermine this connection by instead identifying Ozymandias—up until then fairly clearly the figure of the corporate owner—with aesthetic autonomy. Manhattan makes one final visit to Veidt, who clearly wants the godlike figure's approval for his actions. After Manhattan asserts noncommittally that he "understand[s], without condoning or condemning," and then announces his intention to depart "this galaxy for one less *complicated*," Veidt demands, "Jon, wait, before you *leave. . .* I did the right thing, didn't I? It all worked out in the end." Manhattan, crucially, interprets a question about ethics (Do the ends justify the means?) to be one about metaphysics (What is the nature of events?): "'In the end'?" he replies, "*Nothing* ends, Adrian. Nothing ever *ends*" (figure 12).[63] In the context of the current discussion we can take this as a statement about aesthetics as well: Veidt has constructed a fiction that he wishes to be finished and autonomous, the way Miller provided a conclusion to Batman's story or Moore to Superman's. Manhattan informs Veidt, however, that this is a false hope.

As if to confirm this, *Watchmen* does not end here, as I noted in chapter 1, but offers two epilogues. In the first a disguised Dan Dreiberg and Laurie Juspeczyk visit her mother (notably on Christmas, a recurring holiday) and speculate about reviving their superhero careers. And in the second Seymour, the "aptly as well as ironically named"[64] assistant at the right-wing tabloid the *New Frontiersman*, returns from lunch and is told by his editor to find a story to fill space in the next issue. In the final story panel of the series we see Seymour reaching for the crank file on which sits Rorschach's journal—which the vigilante mailed before leaving for Antarctica and whose final entry reveals Veidt's role in the conspiracy to kill or remove other superheroes.[65]

The second epilogue clearly extends the themes opened up by Manhattan's final conversation with Veidt. When Seymour returns from lunch, his editor sarcastically notes, "Three million New Yorkers died and you weren't one of them."[66] Seymour continues to exist—by chance rather than desert—after the conclusion of the fiction constructed by Veidt. And the column space that Seymour's editor orders him to fill is empty because of another official story related to Veidt's: the editor has had to kill his own column because in the new post–Cold War world brought about by Veidt's ruse "nobody's *allowed* to say bad things about our good ol' buddies the Russians anymore."[67] Most importantly, of course, *Watchmen* itself ends with Seymour's hand hovering over a counterfiction that could (if anyone believes it) unravel the whole conspiracy. Given Moore and Gibbons's understanding of *Watchmen* as what the latter calls "a complete work of art" and Moore's subsequent objections to the extension of the *Watchmen* story via the recent prequels, it is at least intriguing that the story itself all but ends with the caption, "To Be Continued?"

As I argued in chapter 1, Moore and Gibbons engage, in *Watchmen*, in strategies of self-conscious complexity and formal play that make the series the heir, within the comics medium, of earlier modernist movements. Bryan Dietrich, offering support for this point, contends that *Watchmen* undermines its characters' insistent "rage for order" both thematically—Silk Spectre discovers that that man she hates for attempting to rape her mother is her father; Rorschach, seeking absolute justice, "finds only darkness"—and formally, via the "near-infinite recursiveness of text, of metatext" that makes it endlessly available for close reading. "As with any significantly complex and recursive text," Dietrich argues, "the minute one sets out to reduce the infinite to the simple, sublimity to character and plot point, the sand beneath begins to shift; iconic connections, metatextual crosscurrents, all the subtleties of theme and symbol begin to tumble and lose footing."[68] This account of *Watchmen* as having, in Moore's own terms, "a kind of crystalline structure" whose "many levels and little background details and clever little connections and references . . . academics can pick over for years"[69] is, of course, completely compatible with the modernist notion of the autonomous artwork, whose elaborate structure renders it infinitely internally productive. It calls into question the rage for order, that is to say, thematically, but it ultimately affirms it on the level of form—as, in a meta-aesthetic moment, Dr. Manhattan describes the chaotic process that produces a specific individual from an infinitely complex alignment of factors as a "thermo-dynamic *miracle*" that, when seen in the proper light, "may still take the breath away."[70]

The epilogue with Seymour, however, suggests a different, more radical challenge to the finished work of art[71]—one in an aesthetic mode drawn not from literature or visual art but from the comics medium itself. In part we may begin to understand this mode through the still largely undertheorized modern (but not modernist) aesthetic category that Jared Gardner discusses under the rubric of "seriality." The "open-ended serial form" emerged, Gardner suggests, from the daily newspaper, which "was by definition one that never ended" but also "could guarantee no continuity, as stories were regularly dropped, threads lost in the cacophony of events and political upheavals."[72] In the nineteenth and early twentieth centuries various art forms emerged that "promised a way to bring to the newspaper the continuities and structures that the media intrinsically lacked,"[73] including the serialized novels of authors such as Charles Dickens[74] and the early serial film.[75] In both these cases seriality was far more than the delivery of a work in discrete sections: seriality was intrinsic to works' production, and it instilled in these forms a "messy pleasure" predicated on "the kinds of interactions made possible by the gaps between episodes, by the overlapping serialized stories, and by the range of paratexts and intertexts that made periodical fiction so ideally suited to the transforming urban landscape of the nineteenth [and early twentieth] centur[ies]."[76] In both these cases, moreover, seriality eventually gave way to the emergence of something like the coherent work of art: the modernist art novel in one case and the classical Hollywood narrative film in the other.[77] The different economics of the newspaper comic strip and later the comic book, however, made them preserves for the "open-ended serial form" that later also found homes in radio and television.[78]

The rise of the graphic novel in the eighties and nineties presented a similar challenge to the serial form of the comic book, and it is perhaps inevitable that *Watchmen* would bear the marks of this tension in its very shape. As Gardner suggests, the famous unadaptability of Moore and Gibbons's story to film reflects not its literary pretensions but, on the contrary, its embrace of forms of seriality no longer available to film (at least until the advent of the DVD technology, in which, Gardner claims, Snyder's adaptation achieved its "final text").[79] We might here say of *Watchmen* what Daniel Worden says about the work of Chris Ware, another comics artist who publishes serially but aspires to high cultural status, that it "thrives on the incomplete and yet continually strives toward some totality."[80] While the form of this sentence suggests a telos, with the totality that is striven for ultimately more important than the ground from which it emerges, *Watchmen*'s last minute undermining of the totality that is clearly central to Moore's artistic ambitions suggests that we should perhaps linger a bit longer on the incompleteness.

This point becomes clearer when we consider Dave Gibbons's somewhat different sense of *Watchmen*'s production and aesthetics. Gibbons, in his interview with Mark Salisbury, stresses the way the story was shaped by its initial appearance as a monthly series:

[Chapter V, "Fearful Symmetry," famous for the way its panels mirror each other front to back, is] more amazing when you realise it was written and drawn almost a page at a time, so that we could mess around with it a bit to make sure the mirror structure worked exactly. This is in the days before fax machines, so the script was physically sent down to me in a taxi, a couple of pages at a time. As it turned out, a lot of the later issues of *Watchmen* were also done a few pages at a time, mainly because the deadline pressure was such that it was the only way we could get it done on time.[81]

As this suggests, so far from seeing these conditions as debilitating, Gibbons understands them as making possible the forms of collaboration and contingency that underwrite the book's formal innovations. Elsewhere in the interview he describes the collaborative processes that led to the Comedian's famous smiley-face button and to the interpolated *Tales of the Black Freighter* story,[82] and he notes, "The first issue of *Watchmen* is actually quite straightforward, it's around issue #3 where the more experimental stuff started to fall in place," citing the same scene with "the news vendor and the kid"[83] that, as we have seen, Moore also identifies as a turning point between the "naturalistic" version of the superhero story he set out to write and the complicated, experimental narrative that *Watchmen* became.[84] *Watchmen*'s status as a multilayered work of formally experimental art did not come about, that is, through its projection as a finished, autonomous piece but rather emerged in the midst of (and in some instances because of) its production as a serial.

Gardner further argues that one of the key elements of "the open-ended serial narrative"[85] was the possibility for audience interaction, largely imagined but in some cases quite concrete, that it made possible: "This is the fantasy the serial encouraged: that by writing in you could be a collaborator in the production of the serial narratives, and by actively reading you could be a collaborator in the adventures themselves. And in the partnership between film studios and newspapers that was central to most of the serials produced in the silent era, numerous spaces were opened up for both the fantasy of collaboration and for a more meaningful role in the form of the numerous contests

inviting readers to contribute ideas for a conclusion or a sequel."[86] Gibbons, like many comics creators and aficionados, stresses the greater
degree of audience participation that comics, as opposed to other media, require, noting that "with a comic book," as opposed to a film, "the
reader can backtrack, you can reach page twenty and say, 'Hey, that's
what that was all about in that scene on page three,' and then nip back
and have a look."[87]

But Gibbons also suggests that the serial form realizes this "fantasy
of collaboration" for the creators themselves, both through their literal
collaboration in the case of a multiauthored book such as *Watchmen*
and through the possibility of reading and responding to earlier installments that the serial form opens up:

> If you look at issue #1, there is a news-stand and a kid reading a
> comic, but it isn't the kid we eventually ended up with, because
> at that time it didn't strike either of us as significant. I think we
> were both responsible for the accretion of detail in those scenes,
> but the majority of it happened originally as I was drawing it. I
> would often design a setting not realising we would come back
> to it later, and when we did, almost magically, we had elements
> that we could re-use. Without getting too mystical about it, we
> very much had the sense that rather [than] us doing *Watchmen*,
> it was being done through us. For instance, there are details that
> only became apparent afterwards. There's a thing I drew maybe
> twenty times; the little plug in the power hydrants in the street,
> and it wasn't until the very last issue that it was pointed out to me
> this thing with the two plug holes was also a smiley face.[88]

Gibbons, here referring to the third panel on page 4 of chapter I,
describes an initially unrecognized precursor to the scene in chapter
III that Moore discusses as emblematic of *Watchmen*'s formal sophistication (figure 1). What he in doing so characterizes as akin to magic
is, we might say, simply the unconscious creative intuition that the serial form allows him and Moore to foreground in the process of creating *Watchmen*. Of course one might argue that a novelist gets the same
advantage from multiple drafts, though the serial process does force a
certain public commitment to the installment (shared with the world

before the project as a whole) that drafting does not. In any case what I am trying to stress here is the way in which Gibbons describes *Watchmen*'s innovations not as a property of its final version but rather as a function of its serial production.

In *Watchmen*, all of this is to say, Moore's tendency to imagine the autonomous, modernist work of art as a site of authorial agency over against corporate control is balanced by a very different investment in the aesthetics of seriality characteristic of the comic book medium. Moore and Gibbons's graphic novel, as I have suggested, veers at the last minute from its investment in the finished work of art by associating this notion with Ozymandias's plan and his hopeful assertion—refuted by Dr. Manhattan—that this plan had the desired effect "in the end." This unexpected swerve gets at what I have described as the central tension in Moore's thoughts about the rights to his creations: between the idea that they are finished works that others (such as the directors of film adaptations and the writers and artists who have contributed to *Before Watchmen*) violate by reinterpreting and the idea that comics (like myth and legend before them) offer a common stock of stories that artists, including Moore and his collaborators, strive to reinterpret.

This tension is partly resolved by the fact that the reinterpretations to which Moore subsequently objected—both the films and the prequels—can be seen as the products of corporate decisions, made not on aesthetic but on economic grounds. But it would be a mistake to totally efface this tension, since already in *Watchmen* it opens up a (partially contradictory) adjunct to Moore's modernist aesthetics in the form of a commitment (equally shaped by Gibbons's thoughtful relation to the medium) to the aesthetic possibilities of the parallel, vernacular tradition of serial art—a tradition whose distinctly unmodernist investment in such things as collaboration rather than individual creation and reinterpretation rather than original invention bears its own creative payoffs.

Moore later found other models of opposition to the corporate control of intellectual property in magic and in collective political protest. The opposition between magic and corporate branding practices is limned briefly in an early scene from *2009*, in which Orlando and Mina Murray (who has just been released from years of involuntary confinement in a mental hospital) tour an unnamed, Hogwarts-like school that has been destroyed, and its inhabitants horribly killed, by the rampaging Antichrist. Orlando mentions the real-life school shootings that have occurred while Murray was committed, and Murray responds, "Then maybe this magical landscape mirrors the real world. Perhaps that's why it's so *awful.*" Orlando replies, "Yes. And it was meant to be so *marvellous. . .* Of course, it could be the other way *round*, couldn't it? If our magical landscape, our art and fairytales and fictions . . . if that goes bad, maybe the material world follows *suit.*"[89] Whatever the direction of causation here, Orlando's comments gesture toward Moore's longstanding dissatisfaction with the "grim, pessimistic, nasty, violent stories" that *Watchmen* helped engender.[90] And to a certain extent Orlando's indecision about what causes what points to a crucial (and, in the context of Moore's turn to magic, characteristic) inability to distinguish between the aesthetic and the "material" worlds. Moore's inclusion of fairy tales alongside art and fiction here is also telling. This scene, set amid *Century's* general narrative of the decline of popular culture, imagines a common stock of stories threatened by corporate control, but without the potentially redeeming agency (as in Moore's earlier heroic account of Miller's *Dark Knight*) of the individual artist.

In this context Moore's invocation of fairy tales resonates with Irr's account of the imaginative commons placed under siege by the contemporary regime of intellectual property. As Irr puts it, the "global expansion of capitalism since the 1970s" has been predicated not only on traditional commodities but also on "the sudden and immensely profitable treatment of a vast array of existing relations as property relations—a sort of virtual land grab, if you will." This move by "corporations . . . to claim monopolistic ownership in a range of potentially supervaluable intellectual commodities" has included not only efforts to patent traditional pharmaceuticals or to map the human genome but also Disney's "seiz[ure of] monopolistic hold over the folk and fairy tales of a Brothers Grimm–type European heritage" and—closer to Moore's own employment history—Time Warner's effort "to acquire exclusive access to recent history in the form of the Zapruder tapes."[91]

In recent years Moore's ideas have directly intersected with the anticapitalist movement against such developments through the transformation of the Guy Fawkes mask from *V for Vendetta* into a symbol of the Occupy movement and the hacktivist group Anonymous. Moore has expressed cautious approval of the way the mask "has lodged in the public imagination" and contends "that if the mask stands for anything, in the current context, that is what it stands for. *This* is the people. That mysterious entity that is evoked so often—this is the people"—even as the mask's ability to symbolize this commonality is ironically undercut by the fact that Time Warner owns and profits from the likeness.[92]

But Moore, always ambivalent about organized political movements, has been more likely to understand resistance to the corporate control of intellectual property via his turn to magic as both a subject of his comics and a form of performance art in its own right.[93] In this context we can see Moore's interest in magic not as an abandonment of real-world concerns but as an attempt to reactivate the creative commons in opposition to the corporate control of intellectual property. Moore describes magic as "giving you a different language of symbols to work with,"[94] one that offers access to a kind of common mental space—"The feeling that I have is more, 'Was everybody *everybody*?' which again ties back to, 'Everybody's sat here before me.' Is there some huge commonality? Are we all the same person? Is this all God talking to himself?"[95]—that is, crucially, not the one organized by corporations.

In a 2009 interview with Alex Musson and Andrew O'Neill in which Moore discusses his move into magic, he tells a story that we might read as a parable about the relationship of magic to the corporation. Following an incident in which his friend Steve Moore was offered the opportunity to do a novelization of the movie version of *Watchmen*, then had the option withdrawn, Moore tells the interviewers,

> I cursed the film and pretty much everything to do with it. And I use the word "curse" in a very professional sense.
>
> About a week later, I heard about the lawsuit between 20th Century Fox and Warner Brothers over the rights to make the film. On Christmas Eve, as a special present just to me, the judge awarded the case to Fox and now Warners will have to give them a chunk of the money. Apparently, it will now have to do as well as *The Dark Knight*. . . for Warners just to break even on it.[96]

In this literal instance of magical thinking Moore casts a curse that poetically subjects Warner Bros. to the same legal wrangling over property rights in which it itself engages ("I could, like, sue you and shit?") and blocks it from earning the profits that are its raison d'être.[97] During the same interview Moore remarks, "I think I've probably been more creative—my output's certainly been higher—since I formally took up magic."[98]

These options are not yet available in *Watchmen*, but they are anticipated to a certain degree by what we might understand as a romanticized vision of the comics industry running alongside (and indeed not entirely distinct from) its problematic history of work-for-hire and even sweated labor. This romanticized vision is implicit in the book that Moore cites in support of his view of publishers as "gangsters," Jones's *Men of Tomorrow*.[99] As Jones's subtitle—*Geeks, Gangsters, and the Birth of the Comic Book*—suggests, he addresses the purported links between the cheap publishing industry out of which comic books emerged and organized crime. Jones discusses, for instance, the ties between Harry Donenfeld, who published Superman's first appearance in *Action Comics* 1, and the mobster Frank Costello and raises the possibility that during the 1920s Donenfeld used his brother Irving's printing company, Martin Press, to smuggle liquor from Canada under cover of importing pulp paper.[100] To a large extent, however, Jones's book frames its account of the comics industry as the story of how these early days gave way, following the success of Superman, to a more standardized and bureaucratized corporate environment of organizational charts, legal dealings, and mergers. Discussing Donenfeld's partner Jack Liebowitz's midfifties acquisition of *Playboy*, for instance, Jones writes, "Independent News was in the pornography business again, but in such a different way and such a different world that it only illuminated the vast distance between the America of 1936 and the America of 1956. Jack Liebowitz had learned how to survive among the hustlers of the Depression. Now he was becoming a master of the efficient, corporate culture industry of the richest nation in the world."[101]

This narrative of increasing corporatization and bureaucracy, common in American writing since the post–World War II period during which DC's precursor National Comics became a large-scale, respectable business,[102] has the effect of retroactively casting a kind of nostalgic sheen on the period that came before it. It downplays forms of exploitation that existed in the comics industry from the start[103] and highlights the potential for upward mobility and creative agency for some of the players. Jones's invocation of gangsters in fact plays into this nostalgia insofar as it evokes a longstanding American romanticization of the criminal underworld as a zone of upward mobility for those who are specifically blocked from legitimate forms of success—whether because, like the Jews of numerous novels or Jones's real-life story, they are ethnic outsiders or because, in the case most recently of *Breaking Bad*, the system itself no longer works for those, like middle-class schoolteacher Walter White, for whom it is supposed to work. The underworld serves Jones as a sort of metonym, in this respect, for the fast, cheap, and loosely organized world of comics, a world that made it possible for at least some of its inhabitants to earn fortunes. The debut of Superman's own title sold nine hundred thousand copies in three printings, while Will Eisner and his partner, Jerry Iger, assembled a studio to provide content to multiple companies—employing fifteen artists and also buying work from freelancers, sometimes cutting up pages and adding new backgrounds so "one page could be resold as three"—and "cleared $100,000 in profit in the first year of the boom."[104] Much of the material produced during this land rush was dross, of course, though some of it, like Eisner's *Spirit*, was work of the highest order, and some—like Superman, whose rights Jerry Siegel and Joe Shuster sold to DC's precursor National Allied Publications for $130[105]—changed American culture forever.

Moore ignores this narrative of corporatization in the 2009 interview in which he mentions Jones's book, instead describing DC as still run by gangsters in the 1980s.[106] *Watchmen* offers a displaced version of this nostalgia in its depiction of the *New Frontiersman*, the right-wing newspaper to which Rorschach sends his journal and whose office provides the setting for the series's final scene. The magazine's political affiliation abets Moore's efforts, as he has said, "to avoid a sort of baby-bird school of moralizing"[107] by sympathetically depicting characters and organizations whose politics are far from his own left-of-center commitments. Thus, Ozymandias "can still be seen as liberal even though he's wiped out half of New York,"[108] while the right-wing Comedian and Rorschach come in for surprisingly sympathetic portrayals: "What I wanted to do was to give each of the characters, including the ones I politically disagree with—perhaps *especially* the ones I politically disagree with—a depth that would make it feasible that these were real, plausible individuals."[109] Yet despite Moore's invocation of "depth," it is not simply realistic characterization that is at stake here, as we can see if we add the *New Frontiersman*—not a character but an organization—to the mix.

The contrasts between Veidt's world and the *New Frontiersman* go far beyond their respective political affiliations and begin appearing long before the epilogue set in the paper's offices. The supplemental materials to chapter VIII, which features Nite Owl and Silk Spectre's rescue of Rorschach from prison, consist of layout pages from an issue of the *New Frontiersman* whose headline story—"Honor Is Like the Hawk: Sometimes It Must Go Hooded"—speaks out in defense of America's outlawed superheroes. The images are messy and include handwritten editorial notes and trompe l'oeil depictions of a razor blade, a paper clip, and a pencil. On one hand this story is full of right-wing rhetoric and is accompanied by a racist and anti-Semitic cartoon that shows a generic patriotic superhero, his hands chained behind his back, preparing to face off in a boxing ring against various caricatured foes. On the other hand it is followed by a story about the missing writer Max Shea and other "talented and prominent Americans [who] are being spirited away from under our noses," hinting at a dark conspiracy—the very conspiracy that the reader of *Watchmen* is in the process of discovering.[110] Like the preceding prison-break narrative, in which prisoners riot and commit horrible acts but Nite Owl and Silk Spectre also break the law to free Rorschach, these excerpts from the *New Frontiersman* ask the reader to differentiate between modes of opposition to official power—in this case between offensive articles such as one addressed "To the People of the Jewnited States of America"[111] and the story about Shea, whose paranoid account of events is in fact correct.

The *New Frontiersman*'s polemic in defense of superheroes refers, moreover, to a companion piece about Ozymandias that will appear as the supplemental material to chapter XI: "In the current edition of pseudo-intellectual Marxist-brat rock-star monthly *Nova Express*, cocaine-advocating editor DOUGLAS ROTH [shown chaining

and unmasking the superhero character in the accompanying car-
toon] makes a vitriolic and unfounded attack upon the tradition of
the masked lawman in our culture and attempts to stir up old prejudices and hatreds into a bloody wave of civil disorder."[112] This refers to
the fawning profile/interview "After the Masquerade: Superstyle and
the Art of Humanoid Watching," which appears following the series's
penultimate chapter (the one in which Veidt explains his plan to Nite
Owl and Rorschach and we see people die as his teleportation wave
hits New York).

Roth's piece on "one of America's best-respected and most consistently left-leaning superheroes" is presented at the end of chapter XI
not in its messy layout format but as a finished product. It is, in contrast to the material from the low-budget *New Frontiersman*, beauti-
fully designed and laid out, and the accompanying images, unlike the
messy cartoon from the *New Frontiersman*, are artfully composed.
The first image features Veidt and his cat, Bubastis, posed in front
of his symmetrically arranged exercise equipment; the second shows
him alone against the backdrop of his trademark bank of television
screens, their grid appearing like an even more regular version of the
comic book's pages themselves.[113] While the material from the *New
Frontiersman* mirrors the chaotic and morally ambivalent story from
the chapter that precedes it, the finished, image-conscious *Nova Express* article reflects the polished story that Veidt tells—a story that
not unrelatedly leaves out the deadly consequences of his actions.

Moore gives us a clue to the connotations of this formal contrast
between the two magazine excerpts by naming Roth's *Rolling Stone*-
like publication *Nova Express*. This is a reference to the 1964 novel by
William Burroughs, whom Moore cites in a 1988 interview with Christopher Sharrett as an influence for his "theoretical work" on "the relationship . . . between the word and the image."[114] Burroughs's theory of
the relationship between the word and the image is, however, not just
an aesthetic theory but also—in Moore's account and in fact—a theory
of power: "Burroughs," Moore says, "tends to see the word and the image as the basis for our inner, and thus outer, realities. He suggests that
the person who controls the word and the image controls reality."[115] The
novel *Nova Express* recounts the struggle of the Nova Police against
the Nova Mob and their "control lines of word and image."[116] Although

Moore in 1988 notes his reluctance to "duplicate" Burroughs's "style of writing"—"There have been various attempts to mimic his cut-up technique, most of which have been mannered imitations of Burroughs"[117]— we can understand Burroughs's cut-ups as anticipating Moore's own engagement with magic. This is the case because Burroughs's cut-ups, like Moore's magical performances, provide a means of arranging the materials of culture in terms different from those shaped by corporations and other powerful institutions. In this respect Veidt's plan to end the Cold War, as unquestioningly reproduced by *Nova Express*, clearly puts him in the position of the Nova Mob attempting to exert control over word and image. The *New Frontiersman*'s messiness, by contrast, takes on a positive cast to the extent that it demands readerly interpretation and thus active engagement.

The series's final scene in the *New Frontiersman* offices offers an analog to the Burroughsian aesthetics of resistance to ideological control. Prior to this scene the reader sees the paper's employee Seymour walking through the streets of New York after picking up lunch. When Seymour returns to the paper's offices, the editor tells him that he cannot eat because he has to fill two more pages to replace the editor's column, killed by government censors because it was critical of the United States' new ally the Soviet Union. Seymour suggests a piece about Robert Redford's plans to run for president in 1988, which sets up a Ronald Reagan joke ("Seymour, we do *not* dignify *absurdities* with *coverage*. . . Who wants a *cowboy actor* in the White House?"), then proposes something from the crank file. The editor agrees and tells Seymour to choose something. The final story panel shows Seymour reaching for the crank file (his smiley-face T-shirt splattered with ketchup to form an image identical to the Comedian's bloodstained smiley-face badge in the comic book's first panel), while a dialogue balloon theoretically emanating from the editor says, "I leave it entirely in your hands."[118]

In the 1988 interview in which Moore discusses both the politics of his characters and the influence of Burroughs, he places this scene in explicit contrast with Veidt's plan:

Perhaps what Veidt did was totally unnecessary. The real point is that power resides with everyone, that we are all responsible. The world is far more complex than our political systems sometimes would have us believe, although of course these powerful individual leaders have a prominent role, but that too must be seen as the responsibility of everyone. The last line of *Watchmen*, "I leave it entirely in your hands," was directed at the reader more than Seymour. The fate of the world is undecided: everyone has responsibility. What the reader does in the next ten minutes is as important as everything Ronald Reagan does.[119]

Moore here extracts a general political moral from the ending of *Watchmen*, one that I will consider at greater length in the next chapter. But for the remainder of this chapter I want to linger on the way that this dialectic of control and agency also plays a role in *Watchmen*'s engagement with the issue of corporate ownership of intellectual property in the comics industry. Just as Moore and Gibbons present the excerpts from the *New Frontiersman* at the end of chapter VIII as mock-ups—that is, as work in progress—in contrast to the finished version of *Nova Express* at the end of chapter XI, so the final scene of *Watchmen* shows us the *New Frontiersman* offices as a certain kind of workplace.

This workplace differs distinctly both from the offices of the Veidt Corporation and from the Antarctic headquarters where Rorschach and Nite Owl confront Veidt at the end of *Watchmen*. Veidt's work spaces, like the *Nova Express* story about him, function primarily as public displays that seek to impose an official narrative on (and for this reason misrepresent) the nature of Veidt's activities. Veidt's cavernous office, where Rorschach confronts him in chapter I, and the lobby of the Veidt corporation, where we see what appears to be an assassination attempt on Veidt in chapter V, are both designed primarily for display, with stylized marble and gold ornamentation modeled on the monumental Egyptian art that fascinates Veidt: in the very center of the double-page spread that lies at the very center of chapter V, the aforementioned "Fearful Symmetry," Veidt dispatches his would-be assassin in front of a giant golden letter "V."[120] Moreover, as the reader subsequently discovers, this assassination attempt is not even real but a bit of stagecraft managed by Veidt to make him seem like a victim of the conspiracy against his fellow heroes rather than its engineer.

Here we have returned, via Burroughs, to Veidt's investment in narrative closure not as the mark of the autonomous artwork but as a tool of those in power: not art but ideology. We can push this critique even further, moreover, and note how for Veidt the construction of narratives becomes a *literal* investment. So far from serving as a form of resistance to the corporate regime of intellectual property, that is, it actually provides the core of Veidt's ability to profit from such property. The centerpiece of Veidt's primary work space in his Antarctic retreat, a wall of televisions that he monitors in order to map out his corporation's investment plans, represents the ordered grid work that he seeks to impose over the chaos of world events (figure 13). This bears most obviously on the false story that Veidt will craft in his lethal effort to end the Cold War, but it also characterizes the unerring investment strategies that he extracts from the broadcast stream: turning "oiled muscleman with machine-gun, . . . pastel bears, [and] valentine hearts" into the more abstract "juxtaposition of wish fulfillment violence and infantile imagery, desire to regress be free of responsibility . . ." into a finally concrete plan to invest "into the major erotic video companies" in the "*short* term" and "selected *baby food* and *maternity goods* manufacturers" in the long term.[121] Veidt invests in pornography and baby food because, as he notes in this scene, he refuses on principle to support the arms industry. But he nonetheless demonstrates a consummate skill at transforming the raw materials of culture into a profit stream—much the same way that he raises "ethical[]" objections to action figures of others but nonetheless has turned his own superhero career into a merchandising opportunity. (The internal memo in which Veidt objects to selling action figures based on other superheroes suggests, moreover, that his ethical resistance to profiting from militarism is limited. Proposing instead of superheroes toy and cartoon versions of a "costumed army of terrorists," he writes, "More militaristic flavor will sell better. The American public has never really gone in for super-heroes in a big way.")[122]

Just as *Watchmen*'s visual and narrative representations of Veidt's work spaces ultimately reinforce his identification with the corporate comics industry circa 1986, so too do its depictions of the *New Frontiersman* identify the paper with the nostalgic version of the early comics industry that I mentioned earlier. And here as well this industrial

FIGURE 13. Adrian Veidt's rage for order
Source: Alan Moore and Dave Gibbons, *Watchmen* X.8

allegory works in and through a more general political allegory. The *New Frontiersman*'s office contrasts visually with Veidt's work spaces in that it is cramped and messy, a messiness emphasized by the disordered pile of papers that Gibbons places in the foreground of the panels in the final scene (figure 14).[123] Insofar as it is this crank file toward which Seymour reaches in the final story panel, this messiness literally makes possible the contingent popular agency that Moore associates with the line, "I leave it entirely in your hands." But insofar as the messiness extends to office procedure as well, the scene also offers an allegory of work that resonates with the romanticized vision of the early comics industry. In this vision creative control is made possible by a sort of benign neglect. If the editor's words upon Seymour's return with their sandwiches invokes the world of cheap mass culture occupied by comics—"What, did you go to *Dimension X* for 'em?"[124]—the remainder of this scene invokes such neglect. The editor lets Seymour choose the article to replace his censored anti-Russian piece not because he respects Seymour's judgment but because he wants to eat his lunch. If it seems like a stretch to see a connection to the comics industry here, we might recall that Steve Ditko left, and Alan Moore was subsequently to leave, mainstream publishers for independent ones whose marginal operations gave creators more room to do as they pleased.

FIGURE 14. The messiness of political possibility
Source: Alan Moore and Dave Gibbons, *Watchmen* XII.32

So far from merely anecdotal, Ditko and Moore's experiences point to a general dynamic of the comics industry. As Gardner notes, comic books arose as a way of squeezing a bit of extra profit from newspaper comic strips, bound and cheaply printed in tabloid format first as promotional giveaways and then later for sale,[125] but in the midthirties "publishers began to realize that it was cheaper to hire amateurs to produce original material than to pay the syndicates for reprint rights."[126] Even after the success of Superman made clear that there were significant profits to be made from comic books, they were often produced by writers and artists free to exercise a great deal of creative control simply because those who were running (and, of course, extracting the most profit from) the business did not particularly care about the content. The final scene of *Watchmen*, I would argue, is thus not simply a political allegory of the power of the common man as opposed to the exceptional leader. It is also an allegory of the early comic book industry as a place where the imperative to produce a great amount of material and the frequent lack of editorial oversight produced both much ephemera and the work of masters such as Eisner, Jack Cole, Jack Kirby, and Joe Kubert.

The very contingency of the final story panel—"Who knows," Moore suggests in an interview, "maybe Seymour didn't reach for Rorschach's diary but took another piece of crank mail instead. Perhaps the whole thing didn't work"[127]—drives this point home. Just as the early comic book industry made possible the work of a few creative geniuses amid a great deal of dross, Seymour may not make the choice that ultimately reveals Veidt's conspiracy. But this contingency distinguishes his choice from the kind of top-down imposition of control imagined by Veidt in his "dream of utopia."[128] As the contrast with the *Nova Express* makes even clearer, Moore makes the *New Frontiersman* a right-wing paper not simply for the frisson of offering a three-dimensional version of politics with which he disagrees but because this sort of right-wing tabloid represents—at least in the days before Fox News and the corporatization of right-wing opinion—a fringe operation similar to the early comic book business.

Watchmen's final scene thus contradicts Moore and Gibbons's sometimes notion of the series as a finished work of literary art and instead strikes a hopeful note about the ongoing aesthetic potential of the comics medium amid the creeping corporatization represented by Veidt and his lawyers. We can partly free this celebration of the medium from its problematic nostalgia if we note that as a matter of fact such corporatization characterized the comics industry from its earliest moments: Harry Donenfeld and Jack Liebowitz were already reaping the profits of the *Superman* radio show and merchandising, while continuing to pay Jerry Siegel and Joe Shuster by the story, in 1940.[129] So far from undermining a redemptive account of the medium, this fact opens up the possibility of understanding the industry's history not as a fall from an early creative heyday to an era of corporate control but as an ongoing struggle between corporate and more marginal elements.

In any case *Watchmen*'s metaengagement with the history of comics necessarily complicates the question of the series's literary status with which this book began. *Watchmen* was part of a wave of comics in the mideighties that made a bid for such status on a number of levels: by appearing (after initial serialization) in book form, by treating their narratives more realistically, by engaging in formal innovation rather than simply adhering to the orthodoxies of form and genre. These strategies lend themselves—both in the abstract and concretely in the case of some of Moore's comments—to a latter-day modernist celebration of the individual artist who transcends convention to wrestle great works of art into being. But as Gibbons's contrasting account of *Watchmen*'s genesis suggests, the story of the series's formal innovations is much more complicated than that narrative allows. This point is driven home by one of the artist's most frequently cited claims about *Watchmen*'s form, the series's reliance on a traditional nine-panel grid layout:

> The nine-panel grid layout comes largely from the EC Comics of the forties and fifties, and from those early *Amazing Spider-Man* issues that Steve Ditko drew. Both had a kind of hypnotic power, mainly because they were done on that very structured nine-panel grid. There was also a strip called *Bogie*, by a Spanish artist, Leopoldo Sanchez, that was reprinted in [the British comic] *Warrior*. It was black and white, and while it was quite a complex and densely illustrated story, the straight-forward grid system he'd used really seemed to simplify it. I think I just liked the feeling of authority that the nine-panel grid gave you as an artist. It's like watching something on television or at the movies, this idea of a proscenium arch, where you have a single, fixed viewpoint in front of which things move.[130]

Here Gibbons celebrates not the overthrow of convention but, by contrast, the power that comes from convention, as a poet might celebrate the sonnet, or a film director continuity editing. Such aesthetic conventions are present, we might say, even in the breach—indeed, they make the breach possible.[131]

Even more challengingly, many of *Watchmen*'s formal innovations came into being through a process of collaboration that has long distinguished comics from forms of high art—literary, visual, and otherwise—which still privilege the individual creator. As Douglas Wolk's comments on the power of auteurism in determining the contemporary graphic canon suggest, this ethos of individuality has crept into the comics field itself and is one of the reason why creators such as Art Spiegelman, Chris Ware, and Alison Bechdel are more consistently celebrated than are figures such as Moore and Gibbons and those who work in the superhero genre more generally. *Watchmen*'s self-conscious account of its creation within a very different cultural field, one that might be celebrated because of its marginality, makes a case not only for the graphic novel's inclusion in the body of works to which we give serious attention but also for the rethinking of our aesthetic standards that would necessarily ensue from such inclusion.

Ultimately, *Watchmen* turns both to the modernist notion of the autonomous literary work and to a vision of comics as a collaborative, serial medium for countermodels to the corporate world of the mainstream comics industry circa 1986—in particular this industry's approach to intellectual property as a source of profit rather than as a site of aesthetic and social engagement. Both these countermodels are fantasies: one the fantasy of the heroic artist who stands apart from the world of institutions to create works of genius, the other the fantasy of collaborators who pursue their work on the margins of such institutions. In both cases it is the institution that is the enemy. It is thus possible to argue that this critique, which has a long and powerful genealogy in postwar Anglo-American thought, makes a category mistake, vilifying institutions in general instead of a particular kind of corporate capitalism organized around intellectual property. In the specific case of *Watchmen* this critique links the writings of William Burroughs, the sixties counterculture in which Moore formed his politics and began his career, and—more surprisingly—the Thatcherite politics against which the series at least nominally sets itself. This irony forms the complicated center of *Watchmen*'s explicit political stance, which I discuss in the next chapter.

CHAPTER THREE

POLITICS

Watchmen self-evidently engages with the politics of the Cold War, which the Reagan administration's bellicose rhetoric and policy of military buildup had restored to the center of US public consciousness,[1] and the increased fear of nuclear war that this rhetorical and practical escalation brought about. Concern about a possible nuclear war was arguably greater in Reagan's first term than at any time since the Cuban missile crisis in the early 1960s and was registered in numerous works of mass culture besides *Watchmen*—most directly in the 1983 ABC television movie *The Day After*, about the aftermath of an all-out nuclear engagement on the residents of Lawrence, Kansas, and Kansas City, Missouri. If *The Day After* presents a world in which nuclear warfare has broken out, *Watchmen*'s own science-fiction conceit of the alternate world functions differently, presenting a world that has already been changed long before by the presence of superheroes and in which these changes bring about the possible end of the Cold War.

On the surface *Watchmen* would thus seem to be the more optimistic of the two works. Yet in what follows I argue the opposite point. *The Day After* offered its story as a cautionary tale meant to sway public opinion by depicting the horrific aftermath of a war—a warning effective, according to some accounts, not only with ordinary Americans but with the president himself, whose second term was marked by a greater emphasis on arms-reduction talks.[2] *Watchmen*, on the other hand, presents a world that in the mideighties finds itself, despite other enormous differences—the US monopoly on superheroes, the fact that the United States won the Vietnam War—in much the same danger of nuclear conflict. In this way Moore and Gibbons's series suggests that the Cold War, if not exactly fated, is the product of structural politics that are all but impossible to change.

The series thus presents the success of Ozymandias's scheme to end the Cold War as in some ways less of a change than a continuity; indeed, Peter Paik has argued that it brings about an even worse situation, insofar as Veidt institutes a kind of totalitarian order in which "world peace is won not only through deception and genocide, but also extorted by means of myths concocted by the very perpetrators of the slaughter, imposing new illusions that effectively blackmail the world into abstaining from its violence."[3] Insofar as totalitarianism was the ideological conceit through which the United States in general— and the Reagan administration in particular[4]—vilified its communist opponents, this suggests a certain ironic complicity on *Watchmen*'s part with the very order it seems to be critiquing.

In order to fully explore this irony we must consider *Watchmen*'s 1980s, in which Richard Nixon is a fifth-term president, as a displacement not only of Ronald Reagan's United States but, at an additional remove, of Moore and Gibbons's England: Moore was born in 1953 in Northampton and has remained a lifelong resident of the small East Midlands city;[5] Gibbons was born in London in 1949 and was living fifty miles away from Moore when they were working on the series.[6] Moore's other major production of this period, the series *V for Vendetta* with David Lloyd (begun before *Watchmen* in 1982 and finished in 1988–1989 after DC purchased the rights), depicts a totalitarian near-future England as an obvious projection of England under Margaret Thatcher. I argue that *Watchmen*, by contrast, surreptitiously reproduces a key tenet of Thatcher's own rhetoric, in the process demonstrating the link between the postwar countercultures, literary and social, in which Moore cut his teeth and the emergent neoliberalism of the mid-1980s. While this link does not simply invalidate the left-wing anarchist populism that Moore associates with the image of Seymour reaching for the pile containing Rorschach's journal, it does complicate it in significant ways. Attending to these complications gives us a fuller picture of the politics of both *Watchmen* and the Cold War intellectual framework from which it emerges.

Paik's account of *Watchmen* stresses the graphic novel's intense cynicism about the brand of utopian thought it associates with Ozymandias. Paik reads *Watchmen*, like the other works of popular science fiction he discusses in his book *From Utopia to Apocalypse*, in relation to what he describes as "an ongoing repression of foundational violence amid the praise lavished upon the wisdom of Utopian institutions and their achievement of socioeconomic equality."[7] This theme obviously resonates with Cold War critiques of totalitarianism, as Paik recognizes, although he makes clear that "neoliberal capitalism" shares this potential "to inflict bloodshed on a massive scale in the name of peace and liberty."[8] Speculative fiction such as science fiction and the superhero narrative, Paik writes, provides a special insight into this residuum of violence and oppression through its perhaps surprising realism, understood not "in the sense of the nineteenth-century novel and its representational conventions" but rather as "a discourse which analyzes in an impartial and dispassionate manner the workings of power."[9] Moore's works, like the other speculative fictions that Paik considers, take a realistic approach to "the values contained in political theology, whether of revolutionary socialism or neoliberal capitalism," seeking not "to create new myths or to reinforce existing theologies but rather to display, with unblinking candor and rigorous equanimity, the violence committed in the name of founding new modes and orders as well as for the sake of destroying unjust regimes."[10]

This form of political realism, Paik argues, shapes *Watchmen*'s unsparing portrait of the violence subtending utopian schemes such as Veidt's. Veidt's efforts to found a new and lasting peace on a repressed foundation of genocide result "not in a peace that is equated with justice but in a peaceableness that is enforced by the terrors of a most outrageous form of injustice."[11] The central problem with Veidt's plan, that is to say, is that it breaks the Gordian knot of mutually assured destruction only by installing another equally intractable problem in its place: at the series's conclusion the heroes are faced with the nonchoice of endorsing genocide or exposing it or, in the words of Manhattan, "destroy[ing] any chance of peace, dooming earth to *worse* destruction."[12]

Paik suggests, moreover, that *Watchmen*'s cultivation of fatalism extends to the reader's affect, in a way that resonates with what I described in the previous chapter as the graphic novel's ambivalence about the modernist notion of the finished, autonomous artwork. In chapter 2 I argued that Veidt's question to Dr. Manhattan—"I did the right thing, didn't I? It all worked out in the end"[13]—links this modernist account of the artwork to Veidt's scheme, while Manhattan's response—"*Nothing* ends, Adrian. Nothing *ever* ends"[14]—implicitly reasserts the serial and participatory aesthetics of the comic book. Paik goes further than this, however, suggesting that even Manhattan's response registers a kind of formal closure parallel to the ideological closure of the world that *Watchmen* describes:

> The cumulative effect of the astonishing level of attention with which Moore and Gibbons bring their world into being is a palpable sense of suffocation, in that the world of *Watchmen* ultimately takes shape in the form of a totality that has become wholly closed in upon itself. Its profusion of discourses and plural registers of meaning serve only to reinforce and bind ever more tightly the fabric of an unassailable and immutable reality, in which is ruled out any form of change other than an abrupt and global transformation of the very conditions of existence, such as would take place with the extinction of *Homo sapiens*. Accordingly, the remark by Dr. Manhattan that "nothing ever ends" may not so much be taken as words of consolation and fellow feeling than as a neutral observation of nonhuman fact, attesting, perhaps, to the vitality and dynamism of subatomic particles.[15]

Yet Paik too asserts that *Watchmen* does not "finally endorse[] . . . the methods by which Ozymandias coerces the nations of the world to embrace the path of peace or the decision of the other heroes to refrain from pursuing justice or revenge,"[16] a demurral that he locates, somewhat surprisingly, in Moore and Gibbons's depiction of Rorschach.

Noting Rorschach's subtle softening after Nite Owl and Silk Spectre rescue him from prison—his gesture of mercy toward his landlady in the presence of her young son and his efforts "to speak in longer sentences, rather than his usual clipped style of speaking"[17]—Paik contends that "these manifestations of compassion and courtesy, however

small, indicate that [Rorschach's] rejection of compromise and his acceptance of obliteration might have to do with something other than
a fanatic's inflexibility."[18] Rather than an act of stubbornness, that is,
Rorschach's acceptance of death at the hands of Dr. Manhattan is an
act of radical sympathy, an expression of "an extreme form of solidarity with the victims of the fake alien attack."[19] In what is perhaps Paik's
most compellingly counterintuitive claim about the graphic novel, he
argues that "Rorschach is in fact the character who undergoes a far
more fundamental change in the final chapters of the narrative than
Laurie Juspeczyk and Dan Dreiberg, who, being the most reasonable
and reassuringly human personalities in the group, take a brief moment to express their moral outrage and thereupon proceed to make
their peace with Veidt's horrifying deed."[20]

Paik argues, that is, that Rorschach embodies a form of character
development that goes beyond the political realism of Veidt/Ozyman-
dias's character (What would a superhero do with his or her abilities
in the real world?) or the quotidian realism of Juspeczyk and Dreiberg
(What would a real human being who dressed up and fought crime act
like?), one that can be expressed only implicitly via his decision not to
survive in the brave new world brought about by Veidt's mass murder.
In this way Rorschach is the character who comes closest to embody-
ing the graphic novel's own formal commentary on Veidt's action,
which takes the shape of a rejection of the closure it elsewhere seeks
to enact—perhaps most strikingly in the scenes of the fake alien's fa-
tal materialization[21] and its corpse-strewn aftermath,[22] through which
"Moore and Gibbons confront us directly with the lives that are extinguished for the sake of achieving this perfected and unsurpassable order, whose power to haunt the survivors, it seems, has become defused
by the blackmail of universal well-being."[23]

Paik's deeply immanent account of *Watchmen*'s aesthetics allows
us to see the graphic novel's simultaneous fascination with and with-
drawal from the modernist artwork in a different light than the histo-
ries of modernist art and comics that I discussed in chapter 2. In this
other, more explicitly political light, *Watchmen* courts formal closure
as an analog for the ideological closure of totalitarianism, intensify-
ing this closure in order to register the difficulty of thinking outside
accepted paths. Ultimately, however, the graphic novel surreptitiously

invests not in such closure but in the evanescent remainders that flicker on its edges, in things such as Rorschach's minimal development of empathy and the images of the dead victims of Ozymandias's scheme. This is a compelling reading, one that squares not only with Moore's claims to have learned from an author like Burroughs but also with Moore's own account of the final story panel with Seymour as a vision of potential—but only potential—agency.

Paik's account does not, however, acknowledge the extent to which this political framework is itself symptomatic of the ideology that emerged in such places as the United States and the United Kingdom during the Cold War and that to a certain extent remains central to post–Cold War thinking. This ideology was organized, I have suggested, around the construction of the concept of totalitarianism. During the Cold War totalitarianism was frequently defined, in Hannah Arendt's influential formulation, as a form of government distinguished even from other forms of authoritarian rule by its colonization of private life: "Totalitarian government, like all tyrannies, certainly could not exist without destroying the public realm of life, that is, without destroying, by isolating men, their political capacities. But totalitarian domination as a form of government is new in that it is not content with this isolation and destroys private life as well. It bases itself on loneliness, on the experience of not belonging to the world at all, which is among the most radical and desperate experiences of man."[24] Closer to Moore's acknowledged influences, Burroughs asserts the same colonization of interiority via the metaphor of language as a virus: "In the West," the critic Ann Douglas notes in the aptly titled Burroughs reader *Word Virus*, "language had become the 'word virus,' the dead heart of the control machine."[25] Language, that is, functions like a virus, penetrating and colonizing the organism for its own purposes, and "Burroughs' avant-garde experiments in montage, the cut-up, and disjunctive narrative were attempts to liberate Western consciousness from its own form of self-expression, from the language that we think we use but which, in truth, uses us."[26] In Moore's own formulation Burroughs "suggests that the person who controls the word and the image controls reality" insofar as he "tends to see the word and the image as the basis for our inner, and thus outer, realities."[27]

Burroughs's account of power clearly jibes with Paik's reading of

Watchmen, insofar as Burroughs considers language itself as the site of ideological programming yet still seeks the possibility of some saving resistance. But Burroughs's understanding of language as virus is also broadly complicit with the Cold War critique of totalitarianism, insofar as it posits an all-encompassing and invasive system against which the individual struggles to defend him- or herself. Timothy Melley has demonstrated in detail how Burroughs's discourse of addiction, seemingly committed to the radical dismantling of all distinctions between the individual and his environment, in fact depends on "an exceptionally romantic ideal of selfhood" that is threatened by congress with the outside world: "Only by assuming that individuals should owe *nothing* to the 'outside' for their actions and identity," Melley writes, "can Burroughs sustain a panic-stricken vision of the individual as a total addict and the world as a hostile place full of controlling agents."[28] The ideological nature of this agon between virtuous individual and malevolent system becomes more apparent when we note that it has survived the end of the Cold War to become a central tenet of neoliberal capitalism, which continually challenges the welfare state, regulations, and institutions in general (except of course the corporation) in the name of unimpeded growth and profit. Anti-institutionalism is central to the neoliberal program that arose, according to David Harvey, from experiments with privatization in Chile and New York City in the 1970s and then became the centerpiece of the policies of Reagan and Thatcher, the latter of whom was even more uncompromising in her assertion that "all forms of social solidarity were to be dissolved in favour of individualism, private property, personal responsibility and family values."[29]

Harvey includes, among the social currents that prepared the way for the rise of neoliberalism, the shift from an old class-based left to a new left and counterculture more committed to individual expression and suspicious about institutions per se:

> The earlier rise of a significant youth movement (given to political satire) and the arrival of a freewheeling pop culture in the "swinging London" of the 1960s both mocked and challenged the traditional structure of networked class relations. Individualism and freedom of expression became an issue and a left-leaning

student movement, influenced in many ways by the complexities of coming to terms with Britain's entrenched class system as well as with its colonial heritage, became an active element within British politics, much as it did elsewhere in the movement of '68. Its disrespectful attitude towards class privileges (whether of aristocrats, politicians, or union bureaucrats) was to ground the later radicalism of the postmodern turn.[30]

To note this is not to blame the left counterculture for the rise of neoliberalism, but it is to assert that that the sixties left propagated a number of ideas that were subsequently appropriated by the apostles of a neoliberal individualism focused on lifestyle, consumer choice, and market competition.

From this perspective Moore and Gibbons's decision to make their main villain a liberal may be seen not just as an effort to defy political expectations but also as a canny insight into this phenomenon. Veidt has given up his do-gooding career as Ozymandias and now makes enormous amounts of money by selling, among other things, the Veidt Method, a mental and physical regimen based on his training techniques. With its incorporation of "powerful spiritual disciplines" including "lateral thinking, Zen meditation, and the power of dreaming and the subconscious,"[31] the Veidt Method is a fairly clear metaphor for the transformation of the sixties counterculture into a series of New Age lifestyle choices. Similarly, Doug Roth's 1975 piece on Veidt for *Nova Express* (which, with its resemblance to *Rolling Stone*, is itself an emblem for the transformation of an alternative publication into a profitable mainstream one) presents Veidt as criticizing Richard Nixon but also making cocaine jokes, living in a luxurious Antarctic retreat, and employing servants (whose presence generates a combination of ambivalence and preemptive justification on Roth's part).[32]

Perhaps even more tellingly, Moore's post facto account of why he and Gibbons set the story on an alternate earth where Nixon is president subtly but powerfully links Veidt to Reagan. According to Moore, he and Gibbons set *Watchmen* in an alternate time line in order to avoid the implications of Reagan's popularity: "Rather than, say, mention Ronald Reagan, who for some reason many people seem to like, we used Richard Nixon. Mentioning Reagan within the confines of this story would probably cause a lot of people simply to switch off and not get to the more important ideas we wanted to transmit."[33] If the *Nova Express* article on Veidt specifically likens the ex-superhero to John F. Kennedy,[34] Moore's comments here suggest a triangulation with Reagan: like the liberal Veidt in 1975 (and the liberal JFK in the previous decade) the conservative Reagan in the mideighties represents a triumph of style over substance that transcends the political divide. This is also the point of the joke in the second epilogue, which has Seymour walking past a newspaper machine displaying the headline "RR to Run in 88?" and then suggesting a piece on the Robert Redford candidacy to his skeptical editor, who replies, "Who wants a *cowboy actor* in the White House?"[35]

Watchmen links Veidt and Reagan not only through their shared resemblance to Kennedy, moreover, but also through their shared distance from Kennedy's foil in the postwar US political imaginary, Nixon. Moore and Gibbons replace the popular Reagan with Nixon, who while self-evidently well liked enough to be repeatedly reelected within the world of the graphic novel would still be associated by real-world readers with the taint of Watergate. Veidt explicitly invokes this taint with his comments, in the *Nova Express* piece, about C.R.E.E.P. and his habit of "referring to Nixon's close subordinates as humanoids."[36]

Finally, Moore offers a displaced version of the Veidt-Reagan connection in his account of the final panel as stressing that "what the reader does in the next ten minutes is as important as everything Ronald Reagan does."[37] This equation directly links the reader to Seymour, who is the figure in the narrative poised to do something; in the process it connects Reagan to Veidt as the powerful and famous figure whose control of the fictional world Seymour may undo.

Seymour and the reader, in this formulation, have an agency unavailable to Veidt or Reagan. But what kind of agency is this, exactly? In order to answer this question we must first consider the forms of agency that are available—or, better, unavailable—to the characters in the series. The first thing we might note in this regard is the series's somewhat surprising commitment to the lack of agency on the part of the seemingly powerful. Veidt initially seems to be a figure of complete agency, the man who models himself on Alexander the Great and imposes his will on the world to end the Cold War (as Reagan would, of course, be given credit for doing, although Moore had no way of knowing that when he and Gibbons wrote *Watchmen*). As Paik's reading suggests, however, Veidt's semblance of agency is false because "nothing *ever* ends," in particular the power politics that Veidt merely reinstates at a different level by founding his new order on genocide. This suggests that we might better understand what Veidt possesses not as authentic agency but as will, the chief characteristic of the totalitarian dictator central to the Cold War imaginary. It is thus fitting that Veidt's belief that he has ushered in utopia is deflated by Dr. Manhattan, whose own chief characteristic is the fatalism paradoxically produced by his omniscience. Manhattan can see the future, so while he acts—killing Rorschach, for instance, to preserve Veidt's plan or (in perhaps the most profound assertion of will imaginable) responding to Veidt's "But you'd regained interest in *human life. . .*" with "Yes, I have. I think perhaps I'll *create* some"[38]—he is merely fulfilling a script that has already been written.

This assertion of the actual powerlessness of the seemingly powerful in fact works to reinforce the agon between the individual and the system, insofar as it suggests that all power lies with the latter, even in the case of those who seem to wield more than their fair share. *Watch-*

FIGURE 15. The powerlessness of the powerful
Source: Alan Moore and Dave Gibbons, *Watchmen* X.3

men's depiction of Nixon makes this dynamic clear. In his final (and most extended) appearance in the series Nixon is definitively associated with the interminability of the Cold War, traveling in the opening pages of chapter X to an underground military complex where, in the final panel, we see him sitting chained to the case containing his nuclear launch codes while he concludes his response to the question "what do we do *next*?" with the words "And we sit . . . and we *wait*" (figure 15).[39] If Nixon here resembles Manhattan, his seeming abundance of power in fact revealed as imprisonment in a larger system, the point is to remind us to look through Veidt's own semblance of agency (burnished by his Reagan-like mastery of his image) for a corresponding inability to actually shape events.

What distinguishes the powerful from the powerless in *Watchmen* is not agency but—in keeping with the critique of totalitarianism—a willingness to treat human life as a mass rather than an individual phenomenon. Veidt's plan is an assertion of dominance designed to surpass his hero, Alexander—"He'd not united *all* the world," Veidt soliloquizes before the Vietnamese servants he has just poisoned, "nor built a unity that would *survive* him"[40]—but it is also a calculation, the murder of millions to save humanity itself. Veidt treats human beings as a mass rather than as irreducible individuals, that is, a perspective he believes Manhattan to share, as he suggests in his interview with Doug Roth for *Nova Express*:

> VEIDT: *Jon*? Right-wing? (*Laughs*) If there's one thing in this cosmos that that man *isn't* capable of doing it's having a political bias. Believe me . . . you have to meet him to understand. I mean, which do you prefer, red ants or black ants?
> NOVA: Uh . . . ? Well, I don't have any particular preference . . .
> VEIDT: Exactly. Well, imagine how Jon feels.[41]

Of course we might understand this as a moment of projection that tells us more about Veidt than about Manhattan: Veidt thinks, "Manhattan is a godlike being, so he shares my view of human life, which is justified because it is an attribute of godlike beings," and so forth. But an earlier scene in fact shows Manhattan making a parallel calculation. Referring to an incident in which he used his powers to disperse a group of rioters by teleporting them back to their homes, he notes, "The next day, I am reading in the paper of two people who suffered heart attacks upon suddenly finding themselves indoors. More would have suffered during a riot, I'm certain."[42] Although Moore and Gibbons give Manhattan a seemingly redemptive moment on Mars when he claims to have learned from Laurie Juspeczyk that each human life is so improbable as to constitute a "thermodynamic *miracle*,"[43] when he confronts Veidt, he tells him, echoing Veidt's own earlier words to Doug Roth, "You are a *man*. . . and this world's *smartest* man means no more to me than does its smartest *termite*."[44] By the end of the story Manhattan is stating his intention to go off into space and "*create some*" human life[45]—the "some" reinforcing the massifying implications of the collective noun.

In fact *Watchmen* suggests that Manhattan misunderstands his encounter with Juspeczyk on Mars, in ways that make clear that the series is less concerned with the opposition between power and its lack than with the opposition between systems and individuals. Even at the conclusion of that earlier chapter Manhattan is impressed not so much with Juspeczyk's individuality as the mass phenomenon it exemplifies. "But . . . if me, my birth, if *that's* a thermodynamic miracle . . . I mean, you could say that about anybody in the *world!*" she cannily notes, and he replies that she is correct: "Yes. Anybody in the world . . . but the world is so *full* of people, so *crowded* with these miracles that they become *commonplace* and we *forget*. . ."[46] What draws Manhattan even in this moment is the mass phenomenon of individuality, which he compares to physical phenomena—"Dry your eyes," he tells Juspeczyk, again using the collective noun, "for you are *life*, rarer than a *quark* and unpredictable beyond the dreams of *Heisenberg*."[47] For Juspeczyk, however, the result of their encounter is a deeply personal revelation, the realization—as I noted in chapter 1—that the Comedian is her father.

It is this connection with personal life and the uniqueness of individual narratives that distinguishes Nite Owl, Silk Spectre, and even Rorschach from Manhattan and Ozymandias. The former characters all demonstrate even less agency than the latter ones at the level of world events. Nite Owl and Silk Spectre, as Paik contends, disagree with Veidt's actions but accept them. Rorschach refuses to give up in the face of his own powerlessness, walking out of Veidt's headquarters declaring his trademark "Never compromise," but in the end all he wills—telling Manhattan "*Do it!*"—is his own death, which fails to change anything.[48]

These three characters do, however, act out of different but equally profound commitments to individual human lives. The first epilogue, with Dreiberg and Juspeczyk, takes place in a world in which, as Paik argues, nothing fundamental has changed despite the end of the Cold War. Hence, the couple's plan to resume their superhero careers flirts with the reversal of all the revisionist energy that the preceding story brings to the superhero genre. But in fact this epilogue remains committed, in other ways, to the psychological realism that has been central to this revision. For one thing it refuses to show a particular outcome, depicting—in anticipation of the panel with Seymour's hand hovering over Rorschach's journal that will follow—only Dan and Laurie (now living under assumed names) "talking about *adventuring.*"[49] And it ends not with Dan and Laurie but with four panels featuring Laurie's mother, Sally Jupiter, the original Silk Spectre. In this sequence Jupiter looks at a photograph, kissing it while tears run down her cheek and then, in the final panel of the sequence, sitting on the edge of her bed turned away from the reader. In the foreground of this image lipstick marks enclose the head of the Comedian in the photograph taken just prior to his rape attempt.[50] This brilliant panel at once puts the past in the past and—given the relationship between the photograph and the comics panel that I discuss in chapter 1—Jupiter's superheroics back into their medium of origin. But it also intimates the possibility of change, at least the private—but resolutely novelistic—change of a character's relationship to her past.

This suggests that Dreiberg and Juspeczyk's return to private life following the events in Antarctica, while not necessarily political per se, is perhaps something more than a simple disavowal of what the pair know about Veidt's plan. And while the ascetic Rorschach would be the last character to embrace personal life in this manner, there is nonetheless a parallel between the first epilogue's return to psychological realism and Paik's argument that Rorschach grows as a character through his tentative acknowledgment of others' individuality. With this in mind we can return to the two moments of Rorschach's split origin and note that they both involve his response to violations of others' individuality. The Kitty Genovese murder that causes Rorschach to put on a mask and begin fighting crime provides a (literal) textbook example of the abdication of individual responsibility. In a panel from the sequence in which Rorschach recounts this story to his prison therapist, Malcolm Long, we see someone (presumably Rorschach) looking at a newspaper headline reading, "Woman Killed While Neighbors Look On." In the captions Rorschach calls her Kitty Genovese and then notes, "I'm sure that was the woman's name," thereby emphasizing the importance of recalling her in her particularity.[51] The botched kidnapping and child murder that Rorschach cites as his true origin, meanwhile, hinges on a case of mistaken identity: "Blaire Roche. Six years old. Kidnappers believed she was connected to Roche chemical fortune. Stupid mistake. Father was bus driver. No money at all."[52] Rorschach takes the case, as he tells Long, for "personal reasons"; as in the later scene in which he spares his landlady, he empathizes with an "abused" and "frightened" child.[53] The senselessness of the girl's murder, in turn, underlies the revelation of life's randomness that, as I discussed in chapter 1, makes him fully Rorschach.[54]

The problem with Rorschach's commitment to individuality is that he can understand it only in terms of avenging and/or punishing individuals, and it is this commitment that is stymied by both the scale and the moral ambiguity of Veidt's plan. The first epilogue with Dreiberg and Juspeczyk, meanwhile, hinges on the latter's reconciliation with her mother after she reveals that she knows the Comedian is her father, an act that requires accepting Sally Jupiter in her flawed individuality: "People's *lives* take them strange *places*. They do strange *things*, and . . . well, sometimes they can't *talk* about them. I know how that is."[55] Here, as with Rorschach's reactions to abused children, empathy begins with an act of recognition, although *Watchmen* does not see this as a problem so much as a basis for beginning to embrace others' individuality. If in Rorschach's case the problem is that this embrace only extends as far as setting himself up as a judge—thereby reducing people's complexity to an abstract choice between the innocent and the guilty—in Nite Owl and Silk Spectre's case the problem is that this embrace remains resolutely private, unable to extend beyond the realm of the family. Paik notes that even the Comedian experiences "a twinge of pained sympathy" when his daughter presses him on the rape without yet knowing that he is her father;[56] in this regard Juspeczyk proves herself her father's daughter when she too limits her expressions of sympathy to the family circle.

If these characters' figurations of individuality emerge from a Cold War framework that pits them against Veidt and Manhattan's pseudo-totalitarian disregard for human life, however, they also illuminate the continuities between this Cold War template and the emergent neoliberalism of the seventies and eighties. Insofar as *Watchmen* associates these characters with law and order (Rorschach) and the family (Nite Owl / Silk Spectre), the series links them to the conservative domestic policies that accompanied the rise of neoliberal market reforms in the United States and—especially—Great Britain during these years. Harvey, noting that the "drive towards market freedoms and the commodification of everything can all too easily run amok and produce social incoherence," argues that under such conditions "the inevitable response is to reconstruct social solidarities, albeit along different lines—hence the revival of interest in religion and morality, in new forms of associationism (around questions of rights and citizenship, for example) and even the revival of older political forms (fascism, nationalism, localism, and the like)."[57]

Thatcher combined both elements of this dialectic with her support for market deregulation on one hand and her neoconservative championing of the family and law and order on the other. A year after *Watchmen* appeared, in a 1987 interview for *Woman's Own* magazine following Thatcher's election to a third term as prime minister, she uttered her infamous motto of conservative individualism: "There is no such thing as society." As the unedited transcript of this interview with journalist Douglas Keay makes clear, this statement summed up a range of conservative policy and rhetoric from Thatcher's first two terms: "I think we have gone through a period when too many children and people have been given to understand 'I have a problem, it is the Government's job to cope with it!' or 'I have a problem, I will go and get a grant to cope with it!' 'I am homeless, the Government must house me!' and so they are casting their problems on society and who is society? There is no such thing! There are individual men and women and there are families and no government can do anything except through people and people look to themselves first."[58] As both supporters and detractors of Thatcher's sentiment forget, she immediately goes on to note that people have "obligations" to others as well as "entitlements."[59] But this quote nonetheless encapsulates the steps taken under Thatcher's Conservative Party governments to eliminate or weaken institutional structures that might promote such responsibility outside the confines of (a narrowly defined version of) the family: the "stripping of functions in social policy from the state, such as care of the elderly, and returning them to the family."[60]

Even as British conservatives, like their colleagues in the United States, sought to make the family ideologically and practically responsible for a host of functions previously performed by the welfare state, they also built up the state's policing functions. As the historian of the Thatcher era Andrew Gamble notes, her administrations actually expanded the powers of "central government."[61] This meant on one hand disempowering the local authorities who had been largely responsible for regulating the economy and redistributing resources and on the other ramping up the state's policing powers in the name of "internal security": "Substantial increases were made in police pay, manpower and equipment. Several acts were passed to give the police greater powers and enforce tougher sentences. The Criminal Justice Act of 1982 introduced a new framework of custodial sentences for offenders under 21. The Police and Criminal Evidence Act, 1984, gave the police new powers in respect of stop and search, entry, search and seizure, arrest and detention and the interrogation and identification of suspects. The Public Order Act, 1986, gave the police new powers to control demonstrations and crowds."[62] While the Conservative government stopped short of "formally organis[ing] the police as a national force," it established the National Reporting Centre to coordinate police activity around such events as the miners' strike of 1984–1985, and during the early eighties "policing took on a more repressive character as those opposed to the Thatcher government came to be stigmatized as the 'enemies within' and likened to Argentineans [with whom the United Kingdom fought the Falklands/Malvinas War in 1982] and [Irish Republican] terrorists."[63]

Watchmen thus appeared during a period in British history when the state was simultaneously shrinking programs designed to improve

FIGURE 16. *Watchmen*'s British 1980s
Source: Alan Moore and Dave Gibbons, *Watchmen* II.16

citizens' lives, as in the United States, and expanding its repressive powers (a situation somewhat different from that in the United States, where police repression was still largely understood as a local problem of specific cities such as Philadelphia, where the MOVE bombing took place in the summer of 1985). With the exception of the scenes in which punks attack Dreiberg and Juspeczyk[64] and kill the original Nite Owl, Hollis Mason[65]—which replace the racial elements common to US depictions of violent urban crime with the punk iconography that Americans by and large associated with a lifestyle choice rather than class antagonisms—*Watchmen* nowhere betrays its British origins more than in the scenes of the Comedian, armed with riot gas and rubber bullets, putting down an urban riot in New York City (figure 16).[66]

This riot might initially seem to depart significantly from the British milieu, insofar as it is led by supporters of the police, who are on strike to protest the activities of the superheroes: a woman yells at the Comedian and his companion Nite Owl, "My *son* is a *police officer*, you *faggots*."[67] The riot serves, however, as a prelude in the graphic novel to the passage of the 1977 Keene Act, a piece of legislation that outlaws those superheroes not working for the government, as Manhattan and the Comedian do. The Keene Act, that is to say, either forces superheroes into private life or makes them into agents of the state's repressive powers. These two options in turn mirror the ideological limits within which Rorschach on the one hand and Nite Owl and Silk Spectre on the other find their commitments to individual lives constrained: they can either commit themselves to law and order wholeheartedly, eschewing private life altogether as the ascetic Rorschach does, or commit themselves wholeheartedly to private life, giving up their erstwhile careers as public heroes. When Dreiberg and Juspeczyk decide to return to superheroics, crucially, they rescue victims of a fire rather than capture criminals. In this respect their final discussion about resuming their crime-fighting careers is not (wholly) a retreat into the unexamined assumptions of the superhero genre, although it does remain bound to the realm of private citizens rather than of state activity.

This dilemma of a desire for agency that can find no means for institutional expression provides, we might say, the ideological limits of *Watchmen* as a work composed under the Thatcherite rollback of the British state's "functions in social policy." With this in mind we can finally return to the question of the agency that Moore ascribes to the reader in the 1988 interview in which he discusses the final story panel. Here it is helpful to recall that discussion:

> Perhaps what Veidt did was totally unnecessary. The real point is that power resides with everyone, that we are all responsible. The world is far more complex than our political systems sometimes

would have us believe, although of course these powerful individual leaders have a prominent role, but that too must be seen
as the responsibility of everyone. The last line of *Watchmen*, "I
leave it entirely in your hands," was directed at the reader more
than Seymour. The fate of the world is undecided: everyone has
responsibility. What the reader does in the next ten minutes is as
important as everything Ronald Reagan does.[68]

As I argued in the last chapter, the final scene with Seymour and his
editor works, within the series's metaimagination of comics history,
as an evocation of the industry's recurrent smaller-scale, less rigidly
organized modes of production in contrast with the corporate model
represented by DC.

As a directly political gesture, however, this scene is problematic.
How is what the reader does as important as what the president does?
Does saying so simply efface the massive disparity in institutional
power between the two? How, exactly, is the reader's power, or potential power, related to the possibility that Seymour might expose the
story of Veidt's conspiracy? What are the chances that this story will
reach someone beyond the *New Frontiersman*'s regular readers? And
that that audience might take this story, written by an escaped convict
and published in a fringe tabloid, seriously? And that, having taken
it seriously, they would or could do something—what is not entirely
clear—about it? Paik writes that "the cruelty that freezes Seymour's
hand in mid-gesture over Rorschach's journal in the very last panel of
the narrative stems largely from the likelihood that, were the public
to be informed that the alien attack was indeed a hoax, they would
be as little inclined as the masked heroes in acting on the truth and
pursuing the claims of justice."[69] Given this, on what basis does Moore
retrospectively claim that he and Gibbons intended the final panel as
a gesture not of cruelty but of possibility?

One way to begin thinking through these questions is to ask if
we can imagine a more directly political analog to the institutional qualities of the *New Frontiersman* in its role as a stand-in for the
early comics industry. As I noted in chapter 2, these qualities include
the paper's small size; its social marginality; its association with process rather than finished product; and, perhaps most importantly, its

openness to nonconventional creativity. When we phrase the issue in this way, we find that there is in fact a very close analog in Moore's accounts of his time during the early seventies with the Northampton Arts Lab,[70] an offshoot of the original (and by then defunct) London Arts Lab founded by the American expatriate and underground newspaper editor Jim Haynes in 1967. Maggie Gray's account of Moore's time with the Arts Lab and the regional underground press of early seventies England constitutes an important effort to provide an institutional framework for the development of Moore's political and aesthetic ideas. Gray notes that "while most historical chronologies [of the sixties counterculture] focus on major centres of activity such as London and San Francisco, they neglect to account for the more disjointed provincial and regional scenes, where many key countercultural practices persisted long after their apparent departure from the national and international stage."[71] These regional scenes found embodiment not only in the various Arts Labs that carried on after Haynes's original folded in 1969 but also in regional alternative newspapers that took up where the first-wave underground press of the late sixties left off and generally balanced national and international stories with more local ones about "city council corruption, strikes, squats and police raids," as well as "reviews and listings of local arts events."[72]

Moore's earliest cartooning work (which he drew as well as wrote) includes strips for two such papers: "Anon E. Mouse" for *anon.* (*Alternative Newspaper of Northampton*) and "St. Pancras Panda" for Oxford's *Backstreet Bugle*. Gray argues that Moore's experiences with such institutions played a significant role in shaping his political and aesthetic views, citing for instance the Northampton Arts Lab's "insistence on unfettered collaboration between artists themselves, and between artists and audience," and its "emphasis on complete autonomy and the realization of creativity through ongoing experimentation rather than production for the market."[73] Similarly, she describes the underground press as "an alternative space to commercial media, less constrained by rigid deadlines, hierarchical editorial structures and hypocritical claims to journalistic objectivity," a setting in which "cartoonists felt they could produce work with complete self-determination, authenticity and freedom from censorship," insofar as they were working in "a raw, democratic and accessible medium open to all practitioners regardless of technical accomplishment."[74] Gray locates in Moore's early underground strips the first stirrings of "a Brechtian formal self-reflexivity" that is tuned, she argues, not to the production of "a self-contained narrative whole" (of the sort that, as we have seen, characterizes some of Moore's more modernist pronouncements for comics' status as art) but on the contrary to a "refusal of objective authorial detachment, and activation of a critical awareness of the strip's constructedness on the part of the reader."[75] In her conclusion Gray argues that Moore's work since these early strips "has been marked by a struggle to realize in more mainstream commercial contexts (with varying success), the formal innovation, direct political relevance, autonomous and non-coercive creative conditions, and dialogic, participatory reception that characterized his underground work, formed in the crucible of the hippie counter-culture."[76] These are, of course, many of the same qualities that, I argue in chapter 2, *Watchmen* and its creators associate with the comics medium and the comics industry outside the two major companies, here taken to an even more self-conscious (and self-consciously political) level.

While Moore frequently describes his time with the Arts Lab as formative, his most extended discussion of this period occurs in his 1998 conversation with Matthew De Abaitua. There, following a glowing account of his collaboration with Gibbons on *Watchmen*—which he describes as "the result of an almost sexual union"—Moore declares,

The only organisation I have ever enjoyed being a part of was the Northampton Arts Lab, when I was seventeen. Arts Labs are a phenomenon that no longer exist. They only existed for the late sixties, early seventies. I can't even begin to describe the effect that had upon me, and I suspect that it would be difficult to measure the effect they had on British culture. It was basically the idea that in any town, anywhere, there was nothing to stop like-minded people who were interested in any form of art, getting together and forming completely anarchic experimental arts workshops—magazines, live events, whatever they could imagine doing. And it was completely nonhierarchical, it worked fine. There would be other artists you respect, and you could talk about possible collaborations. . . . To me, that is the only organisation that works. To me, any other organisation has got a whiff of fascism.[77]

Moore goes on to specify that he means this not in the political sense but in a structural one: "It's 'facia', the roman word for a bunch of bound twigs. . . . The twigs will be tied together in a neater and stronger bundle if they are all the same size and length. That's fascism."[78] Against this "linear, meccano-like"—and obviously anti-individualistic—"organization" Moore contrasts "anarchy," which he describes as "a more fractal, more natural, more human organisational system."[79]

The fact that Moore recalls this period immediately after issuing a paean to his collaboration with Gibbons reinforces Gray's stress on counterculture institutions as sites of "unfettered collaboration," and in general Moore's account of his time with the Arts Lab supports Gray's characterization of this period. With reference to *Watchmen* itself, however, perhaps the most important thing to note about Moore's reminiscence is that it begins by explicitly placing the Arts Lab and what it represents in the past: "Arts Labs are a phenomenon that no longer exist." With this preliminary declaration, we might say, Moore enacts the antinostalgic sentiment that he and Gibbons thread through *Watchmen* via running references to Veidt's popular Nostalgia perfume line. As an interoffice memo from Veidt that is included with the supplementary materials at the end of chapter X makes clear, Nostalgia represents another success of Veidt's skill at assessing consumer psychology: "In the soft focus imagery and romantic atmosphere, the advertisements conjure an idyllic picture of times past. It seems to me that the success of the campaign is directly linked to the state of global uncertainty that has endured for the past forty years or more. In an era of stress and anxiety, when the present seems unstable and the future unlikely, the natural response is to retreat and withdraw from reality, taking recourse either in fantasies of the future or in modified visions of a half-imagined past."[80] Both the Thatcher and Reagan eras were, of course, replete with "modified visions"—differently coded for their respective national frameworks—"of a half-imagined past," and here

Moore seems to comment on the nostalgia of eighties conservatism, describing it as a shield against Cold War anxiety.

Moore and Gibbons use Nostalgia perfume as a running motif in the series, and by the time the reader reads this memo, he or she has already seen numerous references to the perfume serving as commentary on characters' subjective states: Juspeczyk walks under a billboard advertising the perfume after she leaves Dr. Manhattan, a television commercial for it plays following Juspeczyk and Dreiberg's first (abortive) attempt at sex, a bottle sits on Sally Jupiter's nightstand when she takes a phone call from the soon-to-be-dead Hollis Mason, and—most tellingly—Juspeczyk uses a bottle to smash Dr. Manhattan's clockwork construction on Mars after she realizes that the Comedian was her father.[81] In this last scene three panels follow an image of the spinning bottle thrown by Juspeczyk under captions in which she recounts a childhood encounter with a broken snow globe: "I figured inside the ball was some different sort of time. *Slow* time . . . and inside there was only water."[82] In the context of Juspeczyk's discovery about her father these captions indict nostalgia as a form of repression, here linking the psychological to the political. We might thus take Moore's 1998 statement that "Arts Labs are a phenomenon that no longer exist" as a refusal to indulge in similar nostalgia about his own countercultural origin.

But another aspect of Moore's retrospective account of the Arts Lab—his insistence that any organization beyond the most impromptu is "fascistic"—should remind us of Harvey's assertion of the relationship between certain strains of left countercultural thought and the neoliberalism that emerged in the seventies and eighties.[83] And in fact another of Moore's accounts of his Arts Lab experiences offers an even more concrete anticipation of Thatcher's rhetoric. Moore tells a story of that earlier time: "Against my advice, the rest of the group decided to ask the arts council for a grant because we had been putting out magazines, doing performances, we'd been doing performances at mental hospitals, things like that"; in exchange for "a detailed account of all of [the group's] activities for the last two or three years in a phone book-sized report," they received an offer of five pounds. Summing up this story, Moore declares, "These things convinced me that if you want to do anything it was probably best to do it yourself. Don't look to the authorities or anybody to necessarily support you. Do the show right here. Just put it out in some half-fisted amateurish way. If it's any good then the energy will convey what it was you were trying to communicate."[84]

Moore here refers to the Arts Council of Great Britain, a nondepartmental public body (an organization which functions independently of government departments but which receives its remit and funding from the government) tasked with promoting the arts. He seeks to distinguish the nonhierarchical collaborative work he did with the other members of the Arts Lab from the bureaucratic procedures of the Arts Council, in the process revealing the strain of libertarian individualism informing his left anarchist politics and not infrequently on display in his comments. This strain is even more apparent in a 2011 interview in which he discusses his decision to forge ahead with his career as a cartoonist:

> Once that little light bulb had gone on in my head I realized that I should just do something that I thought would be appropriate, send it in to somewhere, and if it got rejected, do something else. I did a fairly half baked comic strip for possible inclusion in one of the music papers that was over here at the time, Sounds. I got a telegram, we didn't have telephones at the time, asking me to get in touch and saying that they'd like to run the strip. This was the start of my career, and all it really took was me making the decision I was responsible for my own life, for my failures and for my successes, should there be any. Taking responsibility for something, I have found, tends to give you power over it. Taking responsibility for yourself, certainly gives you power over yourself, and that is the only power I'm politically comfortable with. Power over others is tyranny, in whatever context it occurs, whether it is in a nation or in a family. Whereas power of one's self is a necessity for being a complete human being.[85]

A different version of Moore's origin from the one grounded in his time with the Northampton Arts Lab, this one casts him as a successful entrepreneur. It also partly effaces a crucial component of Moore's story, which is that he was able to make the leap to his first commercial strip thanks to government benefits.[86] Moore made the decision to support himself and his family on social security "for a few months, or a year"—until, he says, "I established myself as an artist."[87]

More generally, the language of "power" and "tyranny" in this quote casts individualism ("power over yourself") as the only viable form of opposition to a social field that is itself only conceivable in terms of power relations. Later in this same interview Moore once again discusses the etymology of fascism and notes that he is a proponent of magic because whereas "fascism and religion have a certain parallel," he sees magic "as a spiritual equivalent to anarchy, in that magic is purely the relationship of an individual with the universe."[88] The difference here is institutional organization, which is a problem for Moore no less than it was for Thatcher.

This does, of course, ignore a crucial distinction between Moore and Thatcher, which is that Moore takes his position absolutely seriously while Thatcher observes it mostly in the breach, excoriating all institutions while demonstrating a willingness to support and even strengthen those (the police, the military, corporations) that are central to neoliberal capitalism. But this difference only reinforces the problematic fact that Moore's dislike of institutions leaves him with no space from which to build any sort of lasting opposition to the Thatcherite England that he dislikes. Regional Arts Labs such as the one in Northampton, and the underground press, might have provided one such space, but instead they disappeared. In the case of the latter Gray notes that by the end of Moore's time with the *Backstreet Bugle*,

the UK underground had faded, with many of its more established writers migrating to the music papers like *NME*, while the energy, oppositionality and design innovations found fresh articulation in punkzines. The regional press fell victim to the practical pressures of diminishing financial viability, and the ideological problems of sustaining egalitarian working practices in the absence of independent printers. Standalone comix publications faced similar problems exacerbated by detachment from a wider radical media, which left them vulnerable to deterioration into merely a form of grassroots capitalism that ultimately reproduced alienating hierarchies between artists, editors, producers and readers.[89]

Faced with these conditions, comics producers either joined an alternative comics industry whose "more expensive" products, "while aimed at an adult audience and distinct from mainstream titles, . . . lacked the confrontational politics of the underground" or, like Moore, made the transition to the mainstream.[90] As I have suggested, *Watchmen* alludes to the mainstreaming of the underground press in its depiction of *Nova Express*, while relocating the underground's erstwhile oppositional energies in the right-wing *New Frontiersman*—a move that reinforces the idea that the marginality of institutions is more important than their explicit political stances.[91]

Similarly, Moore's critique of the bureaucratic procedure required to secure Arts Council funding for the Northampton Arts Lab ignores the role that the state played in maintaining "an authentic cultural space outside of capitalist social and economic relations."[92] This role was, to be sure, always less than it might have been. In 1942 no less a figure than John Maynard Keynes—the originator of the macroeconomic theory of state regulation behind the postwar welfare state in Britain, the United States, and elsewhere—became the first chairman of the Arts Council. As Chin-tao Wu notes in her book *Privatising Culture*, the Arts Council's precursor had been a wartime body, funded partly privately and partly by the government, dedicated to bringing art to the masses and, in a manner similar to the WPA, making work for artists; under Keynes (who was not only an economist but an associate of the Bloomsbury group which included Virginia Woolf and others) the Arts Council instead emphasized the promotion and support of the elite arts.[93] From at least the midfifties on, moreover, the history of the Arts Council was marked by tension between those who were focused on London and proponents of a regional strategy "concentrating on crafts and local activities."[94] Moore's anecdote of preparing "a phone book-sized report" for the sake of five pounds suggests that support for initiatives such as the Arts Labs was never strong.

Acknowledging these failures, however, is not quite the same thing as suggesting, as Moore does, that organizations such as the Arts Labs can only be ephemeral—are, indeed, admirable because of their ephemerality. Such an argument was especially problematic in the eighties, given that the Arts Council was a prime target of the Thatcherite agenda "of reducing public spending and expanding the private sector."⁹⁵ In Britain as in the United States this meant not only direct cuts but also a program of shifting arts funding onto the private sector in a way "designed to put the arts as far as possible at the mercy of the marketplace."⁹⁶

My point here is to note that Moore participates in and is shaped by a left-wing intellectual tradition that has significant affinities with the Thatcherite motto "There is no such thing as society." Both the Thatcher and Reagan governments promoted themselves as enemies of bureaucracy, and even the fact that they identified government with bureaucracy did not so much distinguish them from but establish their continuity with the thought of the sixties counterculture. Moore's belief in self-responsibility and his assertion that it is "probably best to do [things] yourself" rather than apply for Arts Council grants are sentiments that Conservative ideologues might well have endorsed. Indeed, if one wanted to, it would be easy enough to produce a Thatcherite reading of *Watchmen*. Sara Van Ness rightly identifies as crucial to the series a moment in chapter XI when Malcolm Long's wife, Gloria, tries to get him to come home after their split, but only on the condition that he takes a less demanding position. She tells him, "I'm not going to share you with a world full of *screw-ups* and *manic depressives*. I'm not going to share *my* life with them." Even as she does so, however, Long insists on intervening in a fight between two other characters. Van Ness reads Long's reply to his wife—"I mean, it's all we *can* do, try to *help* each other. It's all that *means* anything . . ."; "Gloria . . . I'm *sorry*. It's the *world*. . . I can't *run* from it"—as a crucial moment of growth and empathy on Long's part, one in which he rejects the extreme form of private self-interest espoused by his wife.⁹⁷ Yet Long's rejection of such self-interest replaces it with individual acts of kindness and empathy that are, after all, the sorts of things that Thatcher herself promoted in her famous 1987 interview, declaring, "It is our duty to look after ourselves and then also to help look after our neighbour and life is a reciprocal business and people have got the entitlements too much in mind without the obligations."⁹⁸ In this regard the only moments of connection that seem unambiguously positive in *Watchmen* are private ones, such as when Dr. Manhattan looks on approvingly as Dreiberg and Juspeczyk hold each other in their sleep.⁹⁹ By contrast the one moment of mass action in the series's present, a mob's angry reaction to Nite Owl and Silk Spectre's rescue of Rorschach from prison, leads to Hollis Mason's death in a riot of the sort used to justify increasing police repression during the Thatcher era.[100]

To read *Watchmen* as a dramatization, however inadvertent, of Thatcherite ideology is, of course, inaccurate, especially given Moore's explicit disdain for Thatcher's England. Yet the very terms in which Moore expresses this disdain suggest the problematic limits of his understanding of Thatcher's regime. In his 1988 introduction to the first DC issue of his series *V for Vendetta*, Moore writes,

> It's 1988 now. Margaret Thatcher is entering her third term of office and talking confidently of an unbroken Conservative leadership well into the next century. My youngest daughter is seven and the tabloid press are circulating the idea of concentration camps for persons with AIDS. The new riot police wear black visors, as do their horses, and their vans have rotating video cameras mounted on top. The government has expressed a desire to eradicate homosexuality, even as an abstract concept, and one can only speculate as to which minority will be the next legislated against. I'm thinking of taking my family and getting out of this country soon, sometime over the next couple of years. It's cold and it's mean-spirited and I don't like it here anymore.[101]

Here Moore depicts England under Thatcher (as he does in the sustained allegory that is *V* itself) not as a realm of freedom but as the type of the bureaucratic police state: epitomized by the concentration camp, opposed to difference, engaged in the totalitarian attempt to control even "abstract concept[s]." He emphasizes, that is to say, the Thatcher state's expansions of state power while disregarding its (in the long run arguably more harmful) reductions of such power.[102]

Watchmen's dystopic projection of the Reagan/Thatcher eighties, while somewhat more complex, functions in a similar way. In the graphic novel the US government seems to exist primarily (if not exclusively) in the guise of its military and police functions, managing the march to nuclear apocalypse and employing its state-sanctioned agents in paramilitary operations. Meanwhile, the forms of powerful mass protest that characterized Thatcher's Britain, like the 1984–1985 miner's strike, are nowhere in sight, the last protest having taken place in 1977 with the riots preceding the Keene Act. Similarly, the government's censorship, on the series's final page, of the *New Frontiersman's* criticism of the Soviet Union seems like a residual nod to Cold War critiques of totalitarianism. But while Thatcher's government made fairly extensive use of the Official Secrets Act "to prevent information about the operations of the British secret service and British government itself from reaching the public,"[103] she also had a particularly close relationship during the eighties with Rupert Murdoch's tabloid the *Sun*, which backed her war with Argentina and attacks on trade unions.[104]

It is the top-down institutional power exemplified by this act of censorship—behind which lies, of course, Veidt's act of deception—against which Seymour's final gesture appears as a model for the reader's potential agency. The contingency that Moore has argued is central to the final story panel—"Who knows, maybe Seymour didn't reach for Rorschach's diary but took another piece of crank mail instead. Perhaps the whole thing didn't work"[105]—functions much as Burroughs's famous cut-up method of randomly rearranging pieces of text does in Melley's account: "The point of using cut-ups is to reintroduce the accidental into what appears determined and determining, thereby short-circuiting the power of social messages."[106] Here, crucially, *Watchmen* escapes the airless closure with which Paik associates it, albeit only by gesturing outside the narrative itself and to the reader. As Moore notes, "I think some people were disappointed with the ending because they wanted something rock-solid and conclusive. We wanted the reader to make the decisions."[107]

The problem with this formulation is that while such open-endedness is good at disentangling the individual from top-down ideological messages, it does so only by sacrificing the social altogether. As Melley notes about the cut-up, "If we follow the idea to its logical conclusion and keep in mind that all messages are suspect, it is clear that a successful program of cut-ups would effectively isolate the individual from communication and thus from social relations in general. The cut-up promotes a form of hyper-individualism—a defense of atomistic selfhood against a 'penetrating' and controlling social order."[108] As Melley incisively notes about Burroughs's distrust of "communications," "Social relations would be impossible if communications did *not* influence human behavior."[109]

Perhaps, however, there is another way to think of *Watchmen*'s relationship to the conservative Britain and United States of the 1980s, using Michael Clune's very different account of Burroughs's project. For Clune the true potential of the aesthetic is its ability to "open a space outside the social world,"[110] a task which in the post–World War II era has paralleled accounts of the market as an imagined "nonsocial way of ordering human action, perception, and desire."[111] Burroughs is one of a number of writers of what Clune calls "economic fiction," which is Clune's name for "that genre of aesthetic works in which the market organizes experience."[112] With this in mind Clune insists that the seeming "randomness" of the cut-up method is in fact "virtual," insofar as "it stands in for something else: a kind of order Burroughs thematizes in his choice of the elements submitted to chance operations, in the non-randomized passages, and in the [Nova] trilogy's supporting theoretical texts."[113]

As in Melley's reading Clune's Burroughs sets himself against the social world, which he understands not as "the necessary horizon of meaning and action" but rather as "a space of the sadistic torture and brutal repression of human bodies and capabilities."[114] But in Clune's account Burroughs does not proceed in the interest of individualism. Rather, he seeks to limn a realm beyond the individual and the social altogether in which "there is no trace of the split between human decision and impersonal process, between coordination and cooperation."[115] And this realm works, Clune argues, strikingly like F. A. Hayek's contemporaneous account of the price system. In particular Clune finds a striking resonance between a section of *The Soft Machine* (1961) organized by the arbitrary coordination of vowels and colors[116] and the way in which the price system, contrary to classic economic theories that see the market as a way for expressing individual agency, in fact projects "a world where market prices are left to organize things without the interference of other kinds of order"[117]— in which they make possible a kind of collective intention that is neither simply the aggregate of individual intentions (since price shapes individual desires) nor a reflection of social norms (since "price does not represent information, it 'places' things: less than, or more than, closer to or farther from, easier or harder to get, ready to hand or not ready to hand").[118] For both Burroughs and Hayek, that is, "self-interest and an interest in the collective cannot be separated"; rather, "*The spontaneous coordinating action of these quasi-symbols is the ontological basis of intention itself.*"[119]

I suggest in chapter 2 that Moore finds such a nonsocial coordinating principle in magic. While in contrasting magic with religion Moore insists that the former "is purely a thing of the individual,"[120] he elsewhere suggests that magic might provide access to "some huge commonality" coordinated by systems such as the Kabbalah which "giv[e] you a different language of symbols to work with. And having a different language is the same as having different consciousness. It's a linguistic phenomenon."[121] While *Watchmen* predates Moore's turn to magic, we might retrospectively reconfigure the stress on contingency in Seymour's final gesture as a similar longing for such a collective principle; as Moore notes in his account of this scene, "The fate of the world is undecided: everyone has responsibility."[122]

Yet if Clune's theory of economic fictions thus suggests the possibility of reading *Watchmen*'s final image as intimating some collective realm, this account still hinges on an act of negation that testifies to the power of revolutionary change only through the very difficulty of imagining it:

> What art can do is make things disappear. The vast body of critical work on utopia is linked by the common argument that utopia is hard to see. Most writers understand this negatively, and read this feature as a sign of the difficulty or impossibility of seeing a world unlike our own. In the economic fiction, invisibility is not a sign of the impossibility of another world, but its guarantee. Here invisibility is a practice. The theory of fictional economics revolves around the claim that art disembeds economic form from the social. Its practical aesthetics are concerned with disappearance.[123]

In this light the lack of closure in the final story panel is the only way in which Moore and Gibbons can intimate a utopian alternative to the existing world. The impossibility of representing collective agency, we might argue, ultimately indicates the series's peculiar engagement with what Fredric Jameson calls "the inner limits of a given ideological formation"[124]—in this case, the Reagan/Thatcher eighties.

More concretely, if the system is so all encompassing that change can only ever come about through the contingent actions of individuals, then what hope exists of systemic transformation? *Watchmen's* "realistic" critique of utopian thinking depends, as Paik's reading asserts, on locating the only efforts to change the system in its nominal villain and on linking these efforts not to a desire for something new but to the repetition of an ancient pattern. Moore and Gibbons make this clear by means of what otherwise might seem like a plot mistake. Why does Veidt cover up a string of killings, from the Comedian to the assassin he has had hired to make an attempt on his own life to the artists who participated in his project to his own servants to millions of New Yorkers, and then (after having confessed his plot to Nite Owl and Rorschach) do nothing to stop Rorschach when he threatens to reveal the conspiracy?

It is true that Veidt questions Rorschach's status as a *"reliable witness,"*[125] although Dr. Manhattan (his ability to see the future temporarily stymied by Veidt) takes the threat seriously enough to pursue Rorschach and kill him. Veidt, moreover, also lets Nite Owl and Silk Spectre leave Antarctica and return to their private lives, although they too know his secret. The answer to this seeming inconsistency lies in Veidt's backhanded confession to Nite Owl and Rorschach: "No one will know. Those involved are all dead, killed by killers who killed each *other*, a lethal *pyramid. . .* my *servants'* death from exposure, after drunkenly opening my *vivarium*, provides its silent *capstone.*"[126] Veidt's reference to a pyramid here points to the name of one of his shell companies, Pyramid Deliveries, the entity that not only hires his would-be assassin but whose ship explodes while transporting the artists he has hired to work on his conspiracy. Pyramid's name perhaps suggests an implicit critique of corporate capitalism as a kind of pyramid scheme. But it also alludes to Veidt's Egyptophilia, which comes to the fore when Nite Owl accesses his computer records by correctly guessing that his password is "Rameses II, the Egyptian name for *Ozymandias*," and then deduces that he is at his Antarctic retreat by deciphering a reference to Karnak, where "Rameses built a gigantic *hall. . .* ; a *monu-*

ment."[127] During this scene Rorschach muses on the Egyptian artifacts lining the walls of Veidt's office, noting, "Funny . . . ancient pharaohs looked forward to end of world: believed cadavers would rise, reclaim hearts from golden jars. Must be currently holding breath with anticipation. Understand now why always mistrusted fascination with relics and dead kings . . . in final analysis, it's us or them."[128]

Rorschach here suggests a connection between Veidt's desire to bring about a new world and his seemingly opposed "fascination with relics and dead kings." And indeed over the course of the remaining chapters Veidt's desire to monumentalize himself emerges and to some degree overtakes the future-oriented impulse he associates with Alexander's severing of the Gordian knot. If Alexander's actions represented "lateral thinking . . . centuries ahead of his time," Veidt declares to his now-dead servants, it was also "under rule from Alexandria [that] the classic culture of the great pharaohs was restored." Describing a hashish-induced vision he experienced in Alexandria at the conclusion of his pilgrimage to retrace Alexander's steps, Veidt declares, "Alexander had merely resurrected an age of *pharaohs. Their* wisdom, *truly* immortal, now inspired *me."*[129] Veidt here goes from apostle of the future to vessel of the past, and indeed the following page makes clear that he has killed his servants not to preserve his conspiracy but out of symbolic kinship with the Egyptians, whose "*greatest* secrets . . . were entrusted to their *servants,* buried *alive* with them in sand-flooded *chambers."*[130]

On this basis we might surmise that Veidt disregards Rorschach's threat and lets Nite Owl and Silk Spectre leave because—contrary to what he tells Rorschach and Nite Owl—he needs someone to know what has happened and more importantly that he has engineered it. In doing so he chooses monumentality over life, as suggested by a series of images in which he unfolds his conspiracy to Nite Owl and Rorschach. The three characters appear as tiny background figures in these images, while in the foreground of the most prominent one a museum case holds, among other artifacts, a Greek breastplate and helmet and an Egyptian cat's head. "My plan," Veidt tells the others in this image, "required preparation for the day when I'd assume the aspect of kingly *Rameses,* leaving Alexander the *adventurer* and his trappings to gather *dust."*[131] This is, of course, an ironic reference to the ironic fact that Veidt's superhero name is most famously the title of a Percy Bysshe Shelley poem in which "a traveller from an antique land" relates the story of a broken statue in the desert whose pedestal invites the viewer, "Look on my works . . . and despair!"[132] But the fact that Veidt's desire to monumentalize himself is—if we take this hint—as doomed to failure as his desire to break definitively from history does not diminish the role that this desire plays in his actions.

As Joshua Lukin has suggested, Moore's suspicion of radical change goes so far as to implicate his own professed anarchist politics via the title character of *V for Vendetta*, a figure who appears in Lukin's reading as something of a trial run for Veidt/Ozymandias. V's "actions," Lukin argues, "are not those of a revolutionary idealist but of a bitter control freak whose ethos has a built-in paradox: if suffering is so important to building character, why strive to improve society at all? Wouldn't the greatest of souls then be created in the most oppressive of milieux?"[133] Noting that comics written in the wake of the revisionist masterpieces of Moore and others did not "go further in an anarchist agenda, supplementing their rejection of authority with a plan for a reorganised, nonauthoritarian society," Lukin speculates that "perhaps the superhero genre, with its Romantic inclinations, would have difficultly supporting a story in which society had at least as much prominence as an individual hero."[134] In Lukin's reading *Watchmen* and *V for Vendetta* go as far as the genre can by inverting its tropes to "present[] the superhuman as incompatible with humanitarian ideals."[135] Crucially, this "cautionary tale"[136] involves not only the will to power but also the fixation on the past that Veidt shares with V (who, like Veidt, has a secret headquarters filled with art treasures).

There is, however, a difference between V and Veidt's collections: whereas the former's Shadow Gallery is filled with books, records, and movie posters that have been banned by the neofascist British government—that is to say items of popular culture that might well bear preserving in the gray Orwellian world that V inhabits—Veidt collects the trappings of power themselves, trappings that Rorschach explicitly associates with death rather than life. While this difference might seem to work in *V for Vendetta*'s favor, I would in fact argue that it speaks to the more complicated nature of *Watchmen*'s politics. V mounts a relatively straightforward dystopian tale in the British tradition, updating the genre's tropes for the Thatcher era and providing, as Lukin notes, a cautionary tale about the potential of corruption by the totalitarianism against which one contends. *Watchmen* certainly evinces elements of such a cautionary tale, among other places in the *Tales of the Black Freighter* story and the Nietzsche quote that provides the title ("The Abyss Gazes Also") and concluding epigraph of Rorschach's origin chapter. But while these elements of the book clearly reflect on the crime-fighter-cum-world-savior Veidt, Veidt unlike V leaves behind superheroics and becomes a successful capitalist prior to putting his scheme in place.

Whereas V has had a (perhaps undertheorized) afterlife as an icon of Anonymous and the Occupy movement, Veidt the liberal capitalist seems in retrospect like a prophetic figuration of what Francis Fukuyama called, in a controversial 1989 essay, "The End of History." Veidt in effect desires to bring about what Fukuyama, writing several years after the Cold War's actual end, called the "unabashed victory of economic and political liberalism" ushered in by the West's triumph over communism.[137] The triumph ends history itself insofar as communism was the last major historical idea, in Fukuyama's Hegelian view of history, to challenge liberalism's claim to universalism:

> For human history and the conflict that characterized it was based on the existence of "contradictions": primitive man's quest for mutual recognition, the dialectic of the master and slave, the transformation and mastery of nature, the struggle for the universal recognition of rights, and the dichotomy between proletarian and capitalist. But in the universal homogenous state, all prior contradictions are resolved and all human needs are satisfied. There is no struggle or conflict over "large" issues, and consequently no need for generals or statesmen; what remains is primarily economic activity.[138]

Of course the USSR remains in place in Veidt's new order, but we do not in fact see it. Instead we only glimpse a United States in which the key marker of change appears to be the appearance of a new fast-food chain named Borscht 'n' Burgers;[139] as Fukuyama notes, the end of history "can be seen also in the ineluctable spread of consumerist

Western culture"; "we might summarize the content of the universal homogenous state," he writes, "as liberal democracy in the political sphere combined with easy access to VCRs and stereos in the economic."[140]

The resonances between Veidt's plan and Fukuyama's account of the end of history, which subsequent critics have characterized as an apologia for neoliberalism, suggests the possibility of a more critical edge to *Watchmen*, or at least a sense that it is not quite as stuck in a Cold War mind-set as it in many ways seems. From this perspective Veidt's flaw, which I have elsewhere characterized as his desire for narrative closure, lies in his Fukuyama-like insistence that the end of the Cold War portends a new, ideology-free "posthistorical global neoliberal dispensation" rather than the novel forms of ideological struggle— whether the revived left internationalism stretching from Seattle and Genoa to Occupy or the neoconservative mobilization of the War on Terror—in which Fukuyama's ideas themselves participated.[141] More generally, the very nature of Veidt's plan belies the notion of an end to history. Contrary to Fukuyama's assertion that "the universal homogenous state" emerges when the final historical contradiction has been overcome, Veidt can only "save[] Earth from *hell*" and "help her towards *utopia*"[142] by establishing a new, fictional contradiction imagined to exist outside Earth itself. Here the persistence of Cold War thought appears as a problem not of *Watchmen* but of the character Veidt: Veidt only imagines he breaks the Gordian knot, when in fact he simply re-creates it at a further remove, much as American neoconservatives would mobilize the War on Terror as the impetus behind a US-guided version of neoliberal expansion.

The problem remains, however, that *Watchmen* can imagine nothing more substantial than Seymour's gesture to give flesh to Moore's contention that "what the reader does in the next ten minutes is as important as everything Ronald Reagan does." As I argued at the end of chapter 2, the second of the series's two epilogues offers a vision of the noncorporate comics shop as an alternative to the corporate world of DC and Marvel. In the context of Moore's ongoing concerns about the artist's right to his intellectual property, this form of workplace— embodied by the early comics industry, small comics producers such as Charlton, and British magazines such as *Warrior*—does indeed offer an alternative to the big companies' pursuit and exploitation of profitable brands, opening up a space where creativity can fly under the radar and where the amateur and the genius alike can have their day. But in addition to the fact that *Watchmen*'s depictions of the *New Frontiersman* office seem—given the gruff editor, the hapless assistant Seymour, and the publication's explicit politics—like an ambivalent tribute at best, the *New Frontiersman* also does not promise a sustainable version of the "authentic cultural space outside of capitalist social and economic relations" that Moore experimented with in his earliest work for the British underground press.[143] As the actual history of the comics industry suggests, such shops either become big concerns, as National Comics did on the strength of Superman, or go out of business—often making their properties available to the majors, as Charlton did with its heroes and *Warrior* did with *V for Vendetta*.

As a product of the Cold War 1980s, then, *Watchmen* is perhaps most accurately understood as expressing a concern about political events beyond ordinary people's control, due to both the "atomic deadlock" whose seemingly inexorable effects extend beyond the possibility of mutual destruction[144] and, particularly in Britain, the Thatcherite erasure or absorption of local authority into an increasingly centralized state. Veidt attempts to overcome the nuclear stalemate, but his own top-down efforts, which extend to sacrificing both specific individuals and faceless millions for what he believes is the greater good, provide safety at the risk of ideological lockstep—an extreme version of what Thatcher and Reagan themselves promised their citizens. Yet in critiquing eighties conservatism as a form of totalitarianism, Moore misses the way in which this conservatism itself mobilized the critique of totalitarianism in the interest of neoliberal capitalism.

Moore has arguably found a way out of this impasse through his founding of the magazine *Dodgem Logic*, whose first issue appeared in 2009. An explicit return to the values of his underground press days, *Dodgem Logic* employs Northampton contributors and remains committed to local material, and the magazine donated the proceeds of its first issue back to the town in the form of Christmas food packages and uniforms for the local basketball team. Yet Moore also intends the magazine to appeal beyond the local context. As he told *Wired* magazine, "We're hooked up in a way we were not hooked up previ-

ously. The world has changed. Now, we all have an individual neighborhood and locale, but we are also bombarded by information from
every other neighborhood and locale in the world." Featuring pieces
on topics such as urban guerrilla gardening as well as more purely
entertainment-oriented material, *Dodgem Logic* both espouses and
embodies the DIY logic of Moore's Arts Lab days: "I would like to
think that in our present time, not just in comics but in almost every
form of the arts, I think that creative expression is within the reach of
more people that it ever has been. Now, that is not to say that there
are more people with something to say than there ever have been before. But I would like to see a situation where people finally got fed
up with celebrity culture. Where people started this great democratic
process in the arts where more and more people were just producing
individually according to their own wants or needs." Again invoking
the final story panel of *Watchmen*, Moore contends that "this might
be the time in which big, centralized authorities prove that they are
no longer capable of running the show, or even pretending to run the
show. Increasingly, it is going to be up to us if our culture gets through
these next couple of decades in any shape at all. It is going to be down
to us."[145]

 Dodgem Logic thus seeks to give some institutional shape to Moore's
anarchist politics, although it retains a suspicion of organization that
continues to limit its political prescriptions primarily to negative ones.
Arguing that the DIY ethos might apply not only to the arts, as a countermodel for the corporate control of culture, but to politics as well,
Moore contends that "in the 21st century, if you see some situation you
are not happy with, it's probably not the best idea to vote for somebody
who tells you that they are going to do something about that situation
if elected, because frankly they're not. Historically, they never do. If
there is something that genuinely upsets you, don't vote for somebody who tells you that they are going to fix it. Try and fix it yourself;
that's the only way it is going to get fixed." The specific problems with
electoral democracy as a political strategy aside, Moore here critiques
the established system while providing only an optimistic hope that
the individual him- or herself can fix what ails it. As he goes on to
stress, "It is down to the individual. If individuals do not like the world
that we happen to be living in—and who could blame them?—then

I suggest it is up to them to change it."[146] Moore's unaltered devotion to individualism arguably undercuts *Dodgem Logic*'s own efforts to imagine a set of circumstances that might disperse power to ordinary people rather than maintaining it as the preserve of a privileged elite of political leaders, capitalists, and (the genre-fiction avatars of these real-world figures) superheroes.

But there remains another problem here, one still keyed to the specific historical shape that capitalism has taken in the past thirty years. In a recent essay arguing that films such as *Django Unchained* and *The Help* seem progressive while in fact reinforcing the neoliberal ideology of individual uplift, Adolph Reed attributes neoliberal capitalism's success in part to the compatibility of some of its guiding assumptions with the beliefs of its opponents. These include anarchists, who in Reed's account "fetishize direct action and voluntarism and oppose large-scale public institutions on principle" and thereby prove "indistinguishable from the nominally libertarian right in their disdain for government and institutionally based political action."[147] *Watchmen* provides evidence for Reed's claim from nearer the beginning of the neoliberal era: Moore and Gibbons criticize top-down power but are unable to imagine any means of confronting it that would not itself be tainted by the corrupting nature of institutional power. For this reason *Watchmen* is able to critique the neoconservative aspects of the Reagan/Thatcher eighties but not the neoliberal ones that were themselves premised on a distrust of institutions.

In the end this element of the series finds its most unintentionally elegiac expression in the generic in-joke of its title. To name a superhero narrative *Watchmen* is to court the expectation, as Moore and Gibbons were well aware, that this title refers to the name of a superhero group such as the Justice League, the Avengers, or the Fantastic Four. But as everyone who has read the series knows, this is not the case. The World War II–era superheroes who appear in flashback belong to a group called the Minutemen, and the former Minuteman Captain Metropolis attempts (unsuccessfully) to found a successor group named the Crimebusters in the 1960s. The flashbacks to this abortive meeting are the only scenes in which the Comedian, Dr. Manhattan, Nite Owl, Ozymandias, Rorschach, and Silk Spectre all appear together.[148]

The series's title is in fact a reference to the quote from Juvenal,

"Who watches the watchmen?" that a protestor—according to the Co-median, one of many—spray paints on a wall during the riots pre-ceding the 1977 Keene Act.[149] It thus points to another of *Watchmen*'s intentional violations of generic convention, like making the villain a nominal hero or allowing the presence of superheroes to change his-tory. As a kind of unofficial epigraph for the series as a whole, the quote—originally a line from the satire "Roman Wives," about the dif-ficulty of keeping disobedient matrons under lock and key[150]—clearly functions as a critique of state and police oppression. Yet insofar as it also refers back to the unlikelihood of its superhero protagonists banding together to fight evil, as in other comic books, the violation of conventions for the sake of realism here merges into a brand of political realism that is dangerously close to cynicism: the notion that collaboration is only possible or desirable in its most minimal and contingent forms and that any institutionalization of these forms in-herently risks corruption.

AFTER *WATCHMEN*

As I noted in chapter 1, Moore's fellow comics writer Grant Morrison and others have suggested that Moore drew ideas for *Watchmen* from Robert Mayer's 1977 novel *Superfolks*, about a Superman-like hero drawn out of retirement on Long Island to fight one last threat. In a three-part series for the comics website *The Beat*, Pádraig Ó Méalóid exhaustively details the resemblances between Mayer's novel and Moore's work, showing that while it is incorrect to argue that Moore simply pirates his ideas from Mayer, he may well have been influenced by *Superfolks*.[1]

These claims mostly concern specific plot devices, however; Moore's work seems less indebted to Mayer's at the level of style. *Superfolks* is primarily a postmodern burlesque of seventies culture that combines references to the Golden Age of superhero comics with cameos from both real-life celebrities and fictional characters. In addition to the protagonist (whose superhero name is never given, although several other characters refer to him by his codename "Indigo"), Superman, Batman, and other heroes are mentioned by name, while other characters clearly resemble Lois Lane, Captain Marvel, and Plastic Man. The protagonist's secret identity is David Brinkley, after the NBC nightly news anchorman, and because he is from the planet Cronk, his sole weakness is Cronkite. He lives next door to a recently retired policeman named Kojak and encounters characters named Bella Abzug (driving a cab) and Fred Astaire (serving as the fictional president's valet). Mayer's novel is descended from Donald Barthelme's campy 1964 story "The Joker's Greatest Triumph," in which Batman pursues the Joker with his friend Fredric, while the novel's blend of real and fictional characters resembles Robert Coover's surreal retelling of the Rosenberg spy case *The Public Burning*, which also appeared in 1977. While *Superfolks* does, albeit in the spirit of parody, offer a number of twists on comic book conventions that anticipate what Geoff Klock calls "the revisionary superhero narrative"[2]—Brinkley's hometown girlfriend, Lorna Doone (Lana Lang), has become a stripper; he uncovers a far-reaching corporate/government conspiracy to eliminate him—its tone and language are far from the more realistic ones of *Watchmen*. Mayer's recounting of Brinkley's origin, for instance, describes "The Lord God Nietzsche" deciding to destroy Cronk for its inhabitants' wickedness and telling Archie and Edith, the real parents of the child who will become Indigo, "Make thee a rocket of sturdy steel" with "a window . . . of durable plastic" in order to send "thy newborn son, Rodney," to Earth.[3]

As Ó Méalóid notes, though, Mayer's novel "cannot make up its mind, from page to page and sometimes from sentence to sentence, whether it's attempting to be serious, humorous, cynical, flippant, or something else."[4] As a result *Superfolks* does, in a few places, achieve something like the elegiac tone and psychologically realistic strategy of *Watchmen*, for instance in an early scene of Brinkley reminiscing about his life since he retired his alter ego:

> To find the fears, the conflicts, the frustrations, you had to look inside. He was worried about how they would pay all their bills, with inflation eating away his salary, and the baby coming. He was bored with his job; he did not like going to an office every day; he wanted to be his own boss, but did not know what else he could do. He was beginning to feel his years in his bones, and wondered what earthly diseases he was now susceptible to. His family was an island of calm; but an island in a sea of boredom. There was no excitement in his life anymore, no challenge, no commitment to anything beyond himself. It left a void somewhere deep inside him.[5]

This passage's explicit language of interiority and, especially, its exploration of middle-aged male malaise are not unique within *Super-*

folks. But it and other passages like it are, as Ó Méalóid suggests, at odds with the more cartoony approach of much of the novel—brief snippets of what seems like the minimalist prose of Raymond Carver and others (a body of work notoriously concerned with topics such as aging and failure) amid Mayer's more typically postmodernist style.

Moore may well have been influenced by such passages, but he also talks explicitly about another source for his own style, the Liverpool poet Brian Patten's 1967 "Where Are You Now, Batman?" A meditation on the loss of childhood, Patten's poem presents a series of lyrical images featuring the denouements of superheroes and characters from legend such as Superman, Sir Galahad, and Flash Gordon. Moore contends that poetry taught him "how to use words really effectively," specifically invoking "Where Are You": "There's a poem by Brian Patten called, 'Where Are You Now, Batman?' It has a haunting line about, 'Blackhawk has gone off to commit suicide in the hangers of innocence.' It made you think, 'Ah! If only they'd look at those characters with a bit of poetry in the comics themselves!' I think that's where my attitude came from."[6]

Unspoken here is the fact that poetry was able to serve as this influence because it operated in a different tonal register from the more parodic appropriations of mass culture central to the work of fiction writers such as Kurt Vonnegut, Thomas Pynchon, and Barthelme—a register similar, in Patten's case, to the lyric appreciations of mass culture that appear in the works of Frank O'Hara and the other New York School poets. Of course Moore's style is no doubt overdetermined. Another possible source for his interest in psychological realism—one to which he directly alludes in *Watchmen*—is T. H. White's 1958 retelling of Arthurian legend, *The Once and Future King*. White's book does for the characters of fantasy fiction what Moore does for superheroes, giving them, as in the following passage about Sir Lancelot, interior lives and complicated motives: "But the curious thing was that under the king-post of keeping faith with himself and with others, he had a contradictory nature which was far from holy. His Word was valuable to him not only because he was good, but also because he was bad. It is the bad people who need to have principles to restrain them. For one thing, he liked to hurt people. It was for the strange reason that he was cruel, that the poor fellow never killed a man who asked for mercy, or committed a cruel action which he could have prevented."[7] *Superfolks* may well have taught Moore some lessons about approaching popular genres with literary seriousness, all this is to say, but he learned more direct lessons from lyrical poetry about mass culture and from earlier works of mass culture themselves. Whatever *Watchmen*'s borrowings from Mayer's book, it brings to bear a host of other influences, and the series's revisionist approach to genre conventions is more concerned with challenging such conventions in the interests of realism than with parodying them.

While Moore and Gibbons's series looks in many ways very little like Mayer's typically postmodern superhero novel, however, it looks quite a bit like a series of novels published in the early twenty-first century. These novels embrace the superhero story and other popular genres while still aspiring toward literary seriousness. One such book—perhaps the groundbreaking one—is Michael Chabon's 2000 novel (and 2001 Pulitzer Prize winner) *The Amazing Adventures of Kavalier & Clay*, about a pair of Jewish cousins who invent a superhero called the Escapist in the period just before the United States enters World War II.

While *Kavalier & Clay* is primarily concerned with the Golden Age comics of the period in which it is set, Chabon is clearly familiar with *Watchmen*. He mentions it at a number of points in his 2008 essay collection *Maps and Legends*, for instance in his piece "Kids' Stuff," an expanded version of his keynote speech at the 2004 Eisner Awards.[8] "Kids' Stuff" is an account of comics' rise to artistic respectability—the success of the "battle . . . to elevate the medium, to expand the scope of its subject matter and the range of its artistic styles, to sharpen and increase the sophistication of its language and visual grammar, to probe and explode the limits of the sequential panel, to give free reign to irony, tragedy, autobiography, and other grown-up-type modes of expression"[9]—at the cost of a mass audience of children.

Chabon's wistfulness about the loss of this audience, and his assertion of the aesthetic possibilities of stories aimed at children, suggests nostalgia for the comics published before groundbreaking revisionist work such as *Watchmen*. At the same time, however, these qualities mark "Kids' Stuff" as a projection of Chabon's by-then-explicit dissatisfaction with realism in print fiction—the boredom with his "own short stories, plotless and sparkling with epiphanic dew," that he confesses in the essay "Trickster in a Suit of Lights: Thoughts on the Modern Short Story," with which he opens *Maps and Legends*.[10] The solution for Chabon, as his celebration in "Trickster" of writers who work in the "borderlands" between literary fiction and "the 'nonliterary' genres" highlights,[11] has been the incorporation of genre fiction into his writing.

Kavalier & Clay is in this respect a transitional book between the more conventional realism of *The Mysteries of Pittsburgh* (1988) and *Wonder Boys* (1995) and the full-blown genre exercises of Chabon's Sherlock Holmes novella *The Final Solution* (2004), his alternate-Earth hardboiled detective novel *The Yiddish Policemen's Union* (2007), and his pulp sword-and-sorcery story *Gentlemen of the Road* (2007). (He has more recently returned to what he now understands as "the genre of mainstream quote-unquote realistic fiction" with his 2012 *Telegraph Avenue*.)[12] *Kavalier & Clay* mostly concerns itself with the realistic story of its title characters, the artist Josef Kavalier and the writer Sam Clay (né Klayman): Kavalier's escape from occupied Czechoslovakia to the home of his cousin Clay; Clay's relationship with his absentee father, a vaudeville strongman with the stage name the Mighty Molecule; the cousins' creation of the Escapist and subsequent exploitation by their publishers; Kavalier's love affair with the artist Rosa Saks; Clay's tentative exploration of his homosexuality; the events of one tragic night in which Kavalier's brother is lost at sea while trying to escape Europe and the police break up a party of homosexuals Clay is attending on Long Island; Kavalier's experiences as a serviceman stationed in Antarctica and Clay's closeted marriage with Saks; and the pair's eventual reunion in New York City and the Long Island suburb where Clay has been raising Rosa's son with Kavalier as his own.

The novel's thematic interest in mass culture, however, allows Chabon to include a number of expository digressions about (real or lightly fictionalized) comic book history. For instance when Kavalier, fresh off the boat and being recruited for his fast-talking cousin's scheme to produce a comic book, asks, "What is a comic book?" Sam Clay produces one, and the narrator launches into a three-and-a-half-page mini-essay beginning, "In 1939 the American comic book, like the beavers and cockroaches of prehistory, was larger and, in its cumbersome way, more splendid than its modern descendant." This essay addresses, among other topics, comic book covers, the medium's early history repackaging newspaper strips, the lack of artistic or anatomical knowledge on the part of the first generation of comic book artists, and the birth of Superman.[13] Similarly, at the height of their fame the two cousins attend the opening night of Orson Welles's 1941 film *Citizen Kane*, which allows Chabon to offer a fictionalized version of the frequently cited story of *Kane*'s influence on Will Eisner's strip *The Spirit*.[14]

It would be a mistake to see these expository passages as merely providing content, though, since in their very form they violate one of the major rules of the specific kind of realism in which Chabon was trained and found his early success. The short story, "plotless and sparkling with epiphanic dew," was the chief genre of the minimalist writers such as Carver and Ann Beattie who had captured the mainstream of American fiction—and, as Mark McGurl points out, the American creative writing program[15]—from the postmodernists by the time that Chabon attended the MFA program at the University of California–Irvine in the late eighties.[16] But even more than plot, exposition was a violation of the rules of minimalist fiction, which proceeded under the Hemingwayesque banner of "Show, don't tell."[17] Chabon, by presenting his research so baldly in the novel, intentionally thumbs his nose at the rules of proper minimalist form.

This is worth noting because it nicely demonstrates *Watchmen*'s relationship to the early twenty-first-century fiction influenced by the superhero comic book: not direct formal influence per se (although the influence is real in the case of Junot Díaz, as I will discuss momentarily) but a kind of mutual interest in blurring the high-low divide from opposing sides. If Moore seeks to bring to comic book superheroes the psychological realism and formal experimentation of literature, writers such as Chabon turn to superhero narratives to escape the now stifling formal limitations (Show, don't tell) of literary realism in its late twentieth-century minimalist mode. Whether it is Moore and Gibbons trying to infuse realism into genre aesthetics, however, or Chabon and his successors trying to infuse genre aesthetics into realism, what gets produced is a self-conscious, at times tense combination of the two. And it is this tonal and formal hybrid, perhaps more than any other feature, which characterizes the American literary fiction of the early twenty-first century, serving as the successor to both postmodernism and the minimalist realism which itself succeeded postmodernism shortly before *Watchmen* appeared.

For Chabon, for instance, the superhero narrative provides a running counterpoint to the problem with realism that *Kavalier & Clay* identifies early on in its discussion of young Sammy Klayman's relationship to literature:

> In that narrow bed, in that bedroom hardly wider than the bed itself, at the back of an apartment in a solidly lower-middle-class building on Ocean Avenue, . . . Sammy dreamed the usual Brooklyn dreams of flight and transformation and escape. He dreamed with fierce contrivance, transmuting himself into a major American novelist, or a famous smart person, like Clifton Fadiman, or perhaps into a heroic doctor; or developing, through practice and sheer force of will, the mental powers that would give him a preternatural control over the hearts and minds of men. In his desk drawer lay—and had lain for some time—the first eleven pages of a massive autobiographical novel to be entitled either (in the Perelmanian mode) *Through Abe Glass, Darkly* or (in the Dreiserian) *American Disillusionment* (a subject of which he was still by and large ignorant). He had devoted an amazing number of hours to mute concentration, . . . to the development of his brain's latent powers of telepathy and mind control. . . . But like most natives of Brooklyn, Sammy considered himself a realist, and in general his escape plans centered around the attainment of fabulous sums of money.[18]

Here the young Sammy imagines three modes of escape from his (literally) narrow surroundings: being a writer, being a doctor, and having actual superpowers. This series suggests a continuum running from purely imaginative work; to a form of work in and on the real world, associated with practical achievements but still heroic; to a fantasy of direct impact on people. If we read "preternatural control over the hearts and minds of men" figuratively, however, this may be less of a continuum than a circle: both writers and telepaths use their mental abilities to influence others. As the next sentence suggests, however, the middlebrow modernist literary field with which Sammy is familiar accepts formal constraints on its imaginative power, limiting itself (like the minimalism in which Chabon will be trained fifty years later) to narratives of darkness and disillusionment. It promotes, that is, a form of realism as inherently limiting as Sammy's association of escape—in contradiction with everything that comes before it in this passage—solely with money. This early passage sets the tone for the entire novel: the main problem faced by both Sammy and his cousin throughout their lives will be distinguishing between necessary forms of realism (Sam's homosexuality is stigmatized; Josef cannot save his family from the Nazis) and unnecessary ones (Sam can choose not to live in the closet; Josef need not flee guiltily from happiness with the woman he loves).

While *The Amazing Adventures of Kavalier & Clay* is by and large a realist novel, moreover, Chabon departs formally from this realism via chapters that translate scenes from the cousins' comic books into print narrative. These chapters reinforce the novel's critique of certain kinds of realism thematically, insofar as the pair's characters embody the desire for escape from restraints in various ways: the Escapist, their breakthrough creation, is a super-escape-artist who, when his mentor is killed, receives a magic key that heals his lame legs and gives him superpowers to use in liberating others;[19] Luna Moth is a shy librarian who interrupts an attempt to steal the Book of Lo, "the sacred book of the ancient and mysterious Cimmerians," and is granted the power to shape reality with her imagination.[20]

Chabon both does and does not integrate these passages into the novel's primary realist narrative. On one hand the cousins' characters clearly offer displaced representations of their actual experiences and subjectivities: Sam, like the Escapist's alter ego Tom Mayflower, has weak legs; Luna Moth is based on Joe's lover Rosa Saks; Sam's testimony, late in the novel, before the Kefauver commission investigating comic books is dominated by gay-baiting mentions of his penchant for writing about sidekicks—a penchant which, the narrator notes, "stand in" not for Sam's sexual desires but "for his *father*, and by extension for the absent, indifferent, vanishing fathers of the comic-book-reading boys of America."[21] In this way, Chabon's descriptions of the cousins' characters can be seen as devices for exploring their inner lives.

On the other hand, however, the passages devoted to the Escapist and Luna Moth allow Chabon to exploit the formal possibilities of a medium and a genre whose standards differ markedly from those of realist fiction circa the late twentieth century. These standards include not only an abundance of plot and baroque dialogue far removed from Hemingway or Carver ("Know that before my homeland, great Cimmeria, was plunged into eternal darkness," the goddess explains, "it was ruled by women")[22] but also an inherent resistance to interiority and correspondingly elaborate surface description: "Now, imagine that somewhere, says Uncle Max, in one of the secret places of the world (Tom envisions a vague cross between a bodega and a mosque), a copy of the Empire City *Eagle* bearing this outrageous headline was crushed by an angry hand emerging from a well-tailored white linen sleeve. The owner of the hand and the linen suit would have been difficult to make out in the shadows. But his thoughts would be clear, his anger righteous, and from the lapel of his white suit there would have been dangling a little golden key."[23] In this passage Tom Mayflower's uncle and predecessor as the Escapist is relating how he himself received the gold key from the man in the white linen suit, who died while attempting to free him—until then a wealthy "playboy, spoiled and fast"[24]—from kidnappers seeking "to gain control over all the crime and criminals in the United States of America"[25] Here we might note not only that the imprecision of the story's setting (the bodega-mosque, the faux–New York Empire City) is the opposite of the skinny bedroom "at the back of an apartment in a solidly lower-middle-class building on Ocean Avenue" in which Sammy grows up but also that the lack of interiority does not necessarily imply a lack of thought or feeling: "his thoughts would be clear, his anger righteous."

Chabon expresses this notion that interior description has become a kind of trap to which the formal inventory of the comic book offers a key most directly and movingly in one scene from Joe's life on the road between his time in the navy and his reunion with Sam and Rosa in the 1950s:

The escape from reality was, he felt—especially right after the war—a worthy challenge. He would remember for the rest of his life a peaceful half hour spent reading a copy of *Betty and Veronica* that he had found in a service-station rest room, . . . wholly absorbed into that primary-colored world of bad gags, heavy ink lines, Shakespearean farce, and the deep, almost Oriental mystery of the two big-toothed, wasp-waisted goddess-girls, light and dark, entangled forever in the enmity of their friendship. The pain of his loss . . . was always with him in those days [but for] that half hour . . . the icy ball had melted away without him even noticing. . . . It was a mark of how fucked-up and broken was the world—the reality—that had swallowed his home and his family that such a feat of escape, by no means easy to pull off, should remain so universally despised.[26]

Here Chabon expresses through Joe a faith in naive escapism that *Watchmen*—with, as I described in chapter 3, its realist skepticism about political change—withholds (although Moore indulges such faith in subsequent projects such as *Supreme* and some of his ABC titles, written after his own disillusionment with the "grim and gritty" trend that *Watchmen* had helped foster). Toward the end of *Kavalier & Clay* Chabon has Joe preparing to purchase the Escapist's old comic book company in the hopes of returning to his partnership with Sam and bringing about the revolution in comic book aesthetics that would wait until the 1980s in the real world. Considering the formal sophistication that EC has brought to other genres, Joe thinks—in a kind of gloss, inadvertent or not, on the place of *Tales of the Black Freighter* in *Watchmen*—"What if . . . the same kind of transformation were attempted on the superhero? If they tried to do stories about costumed heroes who were more complicated, less childish, as fallible as angels."[27]

Chabon's novel, concerned thematically with the history of comic books, is concerned at a different level altogether with the history of realist fiction: a history it disrupts among other ways by its willingness to indulge in a happy ending. Whereas the epiphany, from Henry James to Carver, tends to focus on a retrospective revelation of past failures,[28] Chabon ends his novel with Sam (having turned down Joe's offer to work together again) headed to California to begin a new life presumably more open to his sexuality and Joe and Rosa reunited both romantically and professionally under her married name as—in the novel's capitalized last words—a new "KAVALIER & CLAY."[29]

Yet if Chabon's novel seems more optimistic about the possibility of change than *Watchmen* does, the resemblance of the former's ending to only the first of *Watchmen*'s two epilogues—a pair of lovers, contemplating their possible romantic and professional partnership—should remind us that *The Amazing Adventures of Kavalier & Clay* remains resolutely bound within the orbit of personal life. Its invocations of historical events function primarily to illuminate our understanding of Sam, Joe, and to a lesser extent Rosa, and for this reason the novel does not ultimately move beyond realism as far as it might or as far as Chabon's next three books do.

Indeed, with its melancholy tone *Kavalier & Clay* does not entirely escape conventional realism's attraction to failure, and at its most minimalist the novel is ironically most like *Watchmen*. A third scene of superheroics describes not one of Kavalier and Clay's creations but rather the thought processes of Carl Ebling, an American anti-Semite and Nazi sympathizer whom Joe has antagonized and who now plots to sabotage a bar mitzvah at which his enemy is performing as a magician. This chapter, which begins with Ebling's fantasy of himself as the Saboteur, one of the Escapist's enemies, and ends with him working as a waiter at the event he hopes to disrupt, reads like an absorption of the comic book's energies into one of the "plotless" short stories Chabon will subsequently critique.

The chapter opens, "The Steel Gauntlet, Kapitan Evil, the Panzer, Siegfried, Swastika Man, the Four Horsemen, and Wotan the Wicked all confine their nefarious operations, by and large, to the battlefields of Europe and North Africa, but the Saboteur, King of Infiltration, Vandal Supreme, lives right in Empire City—in a secret redoubt, disguised as a crumbling tenement, in Hell's Kitchen."[30] While the reader does not yet know that this is *not* a scene from the cousins' work, it already seems less imaginatively free than the other comic book scenes in the novel, for reasons that have to do with more than just the focus on a villain: the sentence emphasizes a sort of putatively chosen isolation from a group of others elsewhere, and it inverts the logic of young Sammy Klayman dreaming in his narrow Brooklyn apartment to end with a "crumbling tenement" wishfully posed as a disguise for something much more grand. The passage keeps chipping at the fantasy in this manner—"Next he goes into his laboratory and picks up the disassembled parts of the Exploding Trident, cleverly concealed inside of a pink cake box from a Ninth Avenue bakery"[31]—until the Saboteur exits his headquarters and the narration shifts into full-on banal realism: "He hops a bus across town to Fifth Avenue, then another to ride the twenty blocks uptown. Ordinarily he dislikes taking the bus, but he is late already, and if you are late, they take it out of your pay."[32] These scenes featuring the mostly hapless Ebling—Joe will, in the next chapter, thwart his plans, and Ebling will be the only one seriously injured—offer an almost sadistic rebuke to the escapism the book elsewhere promotes.

This rebuke is associated with Ebling's isolation and loneliness, which are driven home in the minimalist epiphany of the chapter's final sentences: "The Saboteur pushes the cart back toward the ballroom doors. At the last moment, as he is passing the magician, he cannot prevent himself from raising his head and looking his adversary in the eye. If there is a flicker of recognition there, it is extinguished in an instant as the doors to the ballroom fly open and, laughing and shouting and crying out in their loud barnyard voices, the first of the guests arrive."[33] This passage not only psychologizes Ebling's anti-Semitism in ways consistent with the novel's overall focus on personal life; it also treats his fantasy of being a powerful agent in the same way that Moore and Gibbons treat characters' decisions to dress up in costumes and fight (or commit) crime. Ebling is an avatar not of the attempt to reimagine realism using the tools of genre but of the realistic treatment of the superhero as perverse and slightly sad.

This same melancholy tinge dominates Jonathan Lethem's 2003 *The Fortress of Solitude*. Lethem's novel goes beyond Chabon's in its appropriation of genre forms, becoming what we might call a work of comic book magic realism: the protagonist, Dylan Ebdus, receives a ring from an injured homeless man that gives Dylan and his friend Mingus Rude the powers of flight and, later, invisibility. But given that premise, the ring plays a strikingly minor role in the novel as a whole. And as the marginality of the figure who bequeaths the ring makes clear, it is a symbol not of power but of powerlessness. Dylan imagines that "he'd sew a costume and take to the rooftops, begin *bounding down on crime.*"[34] But in fact he uses the ring's power to fly only once, when, during a summer away from Brooklyn with a host family in Vermont, he soars alone around a pond. Dylan shares the ring with his admired but troubled friend Mingus and, when he retrieves it, discovers that it now confers invisibility rather than flight. After using it in an ill-fated adventure in Oakland that gets him branded as a West Coast version of the vigilante Bernhard Goetz, he then gives it to a former childhood bully, now in prison, who, unaware of the change in its properties, leaps to his death.

Florence Dore, in an essay on *Fortress of Solitude* as a contemporary rock novel, notes that Lethem's titular reference to Superman's Arctic headquarters, which the book more specifically links to Dylan's father, Abraham—an avant-garde artist toiling in isolation on a hand-painted film—invokes the "hyperbolic potency" of the superhero as an ironic register of "the experience of human diminishment."[35] Abraham's film, especially in contrast to the science-fiction paperback covers he paints for money, clearly represents a high-modernist disdain for mass success: "By expelling onto the jacket designs his corruptest impulses—the need to entertain or distract with his paints, the urge to do anything with his paints apart from *seeing through them* to the absolute truth—he'd further purify his film. . . . Meanwhile, thriving in seclusion, like a *Portrait of Dorian Gray* in reverse, would be the austere perfection of the unpublished, unseen film."[36] The narrator's slip here—films are not published—suggests that Lethem, who began his career as a science-fiction writer in the vein of Philip K. Dick, is thinking about a problem of cultural hierarchies across media. And while acknowledging the beauty of Abraham's film (during an awkward showing at a science-fiction festival), the novel also insists on the aesthetic achievements of soul singers and graffiti artists.

Yet the novel by no means simply attempts to invert the hierarchy between high and popular art: Dylan's superheroics, associated with the Marvel comics to which Mingus introduces him, make nothing so clear as his similarities to his father. When Dylan appears to Heather, the daughter of his Vermont host family with whom he has been conducting a precocious romance, wearing his homemade costume, she tells him that "it looks weird" and leaves before he can demonstrate his flying ability—though not before she suggests, "If you stayed here you wouldn't have to go to private school," and he "perhaps cruelly" rebuffs her.[37] Heather does not get him, but he is an elitist snob: as he flies, he thinks, "Heather might be watching from high in the grass at the field's edge; it was possible. Or not, didn't matter now. He didn't need to be known in Vermont, this null area that was only measured in its distance from the city, its use as a restorative, a place to get your act together before returning to the real world."[38] The scene ends, moreover, with a deflationary quotidianness similar to the one that Moore and Gibbons employ in *Watchmen*: "When he landed running on the dock he took a splinter in his heel: never fly without proper footgear. And the corner tips of the cape had dangled and were soaked. . . . So: 1. Wear sneakers. 2. Hem cape. One way or another, you were always learning something."[39] Dylan's later adult exploits in Oakland and at an upstate New York prison, meanwhile, simply get people hurt. In contrast to Chabon's tentative faith that escapism can lead to actual change, Lethem uses superheroics primarily as a metaphor for human awkwardness and isolation.

At first glance this also seems to be what Díaz does in *The Brief Wondrous Life of Oscar Wao*, his 2007 novel about a Dominican American "ghetto nerd"[40] whose love of comic books, science fiction, and fantasy plays a major role in his monumental social isolation. *Oscar Wao*, as I have mentioned before, does not simply engage with the superhero genre but directly mentions Alan Moore and *Watchmen* at a number of points. Oscar de León (who acquires his titular nickname when he dresses like Dr. Who for Halloween and the narrator, Yunior, then his Rutgers roommate, tells him "how much he look[s] like that fat homo Oscar Wilde"; 180) has a pair of high school friends with whom he discusses "Los Brothers Hernández, Frank Miller, and Alan Moore."[41] After a high school romance ends unhappily, Oscar "even lose[s] interest in the final issues of *Watchmen*, which were unfolding in the illest way."[42] And, in the most extended reference, the penultimate chapter of *Oscar Wao* ends with the narrator describing a specific scene from the dead Oscar's copy of Moore and Gibbons's graphic novel:

And yet there are other days, when I'm downtrodden or morose, when I find myself at my desk late at night, unable to sleep, flipping through (of all things) Oscar's dog-eared copy of *Watch-*

*men. . . . * The original trade. I flip through the book, one of his top three, without question, to the last horrifying chapter: "A Stronger Loving World." To the only panel he's circled. Oscar—who never defaced a book in his life—circled one panel three times in the same emphatic pen he used to write his last letters home. The panel where Adrian Veidt and Dr. Manhattan are having their last convo. After the mutant brain has destroyed New York City; after Dr. Manhattan has murdered Rorschach; after Veidt's plan has succeeded in "saving the world."

Veidt says: "I did the right thing, didn't I? It all worked out in the end."

And Manhattan, before fading from our Universe, replies: "In the End? Nothing ends, Adrian. Nothing ever ends."[43]

This extended ekphrastic citation alerts the reader to an even more thoroughgoing resonance between *Watchmen* and *Oscar Wao*. Just as *Watchmen* ends with two epilogues, *Oscar Wao* follows Yunior's description of this scene from the graphic novel with a last, unnumbered chapter ("The Final Letter") in which Yunior describes two packages sent by Oscar from the Dominican Republic before his death at the hands of policemen whose captain's girlfriend he was seeing. The first package includes chapters of a science-fiction book Oscar is writing and a letter to his sister Lola which reveals that he did in fact lose his virginity before he died. The second package, Oscar promises in this letter, will contain "everything I've written on this journey. Everything I think you will need." But, as Yunior declares, "the fucking thing never arrived!"[44] Like *Watchmen*, that is, *Oscar Wao* ends with the deferred promise of a narrative that might explain the mysterious logic underlying events.

The first thing to note in beginning to unpack Díaz's thoroughgoing intertextual engagement with Moore and Gibbons's graphic novel is Díaz's participation in the by then well-established minitradition of novelists using the tropes of superhero narratives to transcend the formal repertoire of realist fiction. *Oscar Wao* appears eleven years after Díaz's 1996 short-story collection *Drown*, which was produced in the MFA program at Cornell and quickly became a writing-workshop staple, and the long-in-coming novel indulges in some of the same intentional improprieties as Chabon's *Kavalier & Clay* (including upping the expository game via lengthy digressive footnotes). Daniel Bautista relates what he calls *Oscar Wao*'s "comic book realism" to the Latin American tradition of magical realism (a comparison Díaz invites), suggesting that Díaz eschews magical realism's commitment to cultural authenticity for a more hybrid array of popular genres in which he finds "many useful metaphors for the immigrant experience in general."[45] This is true as far as it goes, although Díaz does not invent comic book realism so much as pick up a nascent tradition and adapt it to the transnational New Jersey–Dominican Republic setting of his fiction.

And indeed to the extent that *Oscar Wao* narrates the personal lives of Oscar, Yunior, Lola, and Oscar and Lola's mother Belicia, its superhero references operate in part, as they do in the work of Chabon and Lethem, as metaphors for or ironic counterpoints to characters' subjectivities. For Oscar and Yunior, himself a covert nerd, this link to superhero comics and other popular genres is direct, although Yunior as narrator also applies it to other characters for whom it has no biographical referent: describing the adolescent Belicia's discovery, in the Dominican Republic, of her burgeoning sexual attractiveness, for instance, Yunior writes that "the undeniable concreteness of her desirability . . . was, in its own way, Power. Like the accidental discovery of the One Ring. Like stumbling into the wizard Shazam's cave or finding the crashed ship of the Green Lantern!"[46] Through the device of Yunior's narration—*Kavalier & Clay* and *Fortress of Solitude* are both narrated in the third person—Díaz frees up comic book tropes and language (consider the exclamation point) to apply to characters and situations with no link to the medium as creators or fans. But in the case of Belicia we see a familiar pattern, insofar as her newfound powers prove as much curse as blessing, leading her to romance with a gangster married to the dictator Rafael Trujillo's sister, a savage beating in a cane field, and flight from her homeland to the United States. Bautista intuits this aspect of the novel when he notes, using the sort of deflationary language with which we should now be familiar, that "Díaz does not draw on the sense of wonder or redemption that Tolkien sometimes offers, as much as on the more cynical sense of evil and failure that his texts also provide."[47]

Bautista is referring to what we might describe as *Oscar Wao*'s preference for supervillains over superheroes: Díaz likens Trujillo to Tolkien's Sauron as well as to Jack Kirby's Darkseid and others,[48] but Bautista notes that "we find no characters who might compare to Gandalf, the Elves, or Tom Bombadil, and the few positive characters who are mentioned are alluded to in a uniformly negative fashion."[49] In part this corresponds to the revisionist approach to the superhero narrative that Díaz inherits from Chabon and Lethem and (more explicitly than either of them) from *Watchmen*. But it also points to a key difference between Díaz's novel and those of his predecessors: Díaz *is not* revisionist about supervillains, largely because they provide a sadly apt metaphor for the kind of local and global abuses of power that also concern him.

Oscar Wao has a directly political dimension, that is to say, that *Kavalier & Clay* and *Fortress of Solitude* lack. Anne Garland Mahler relates this political dimension to the superhero genre, and in particular Moore's brand of revisionist superheroes, in her essay "The Writer as Superhero: Fighting the Colonial Curse in Junot Díaz's *The Brief Wondrous Life of Oscar Wao*." Chabon and Lethem, I have argued, employ mainstream superheroes as hopeful or ironic counterpoints to their protagonists' foibles, much as Moore and Gibbons employ Nite Owl's admiration for an earlier generation of superheroes or the heroes of Arthurian legend. Díaz provides similar counterpoints to Oscar de Léon's lonely, isolated life, raising them to the level of tragedy in Oscar's final speech to the Dominican policemen, nicknamed after DC comics villains, who are about to kill him in a cane field: "They walked him into the cane and then turned him around. He tried to stand bravely. . . . He told them . . . they would sense him waiting for them on the other side and over there he wouldn't be no fatboy or dork or kid no girl had ever loved; over there he'd be a hero, an avenger. Because anything you can dream (he put his hand up) you can be."[50]

But Díaz also, as Mahler argues, takes a page from Moore and Gibbons's book and "creates a superhero novel that is self-aware, revealing the line separating the hero and the villain to be ambiguous."[51] This more direct appropriation from *Watchmen* enables Díaz to address not simply his characters' personal lives but also the global political situation that shapes them, providing a commentary on "the United

States as an imperial power that veils its true intentions under the guise of spreading democracy"[52]—that claims to fight on behalf of the Dominican people but in fact installs the tyrannical Trujillo in power.

Díaz thus takes very seriously *Watchmen*'s depiction of Veidt as a cautionary figure for the abuses of power, seeing in this depiction a parallel with the hemispheric policies that have played a central role in the history of the Dominican Republic and the Dominican diaspora. But Díaz also avoids, as Mahler helps us see, the critique of power in general that undermines *Watchmen*'s political allegory and renders it problematically complicit with the emergent neoliberal ideologies of the late Cold War. Díaz escapes this bind by also applying Moore and Gibbons's revisionist account of the superhero to his own and his narrator's vocations as writers. In a footnote that Mahler cites, Yunior writes,

> What is it with Dictators and Writers anyway? Since before the infamous Caesar-Ovid war they've had beef. Like the Fantastic Four and Galactus, like the X-Men and the Brotherhood of Evil Mutants, like the Teen Titans and Deathstroke, Foreman and Ali, Morrison and Crouch, Sammy and Sergio, they seemed destined to be eternally linked in the Halls of Battle. Rushdie claims that tyrants and scribblers are natural antagonists, but I think that's too simple; it lets writers off pretty easy. Dictators, in my opinion, just know competition when they see it. Same with writers. *Like, after all, recognizes like.*[53]

The list of similes at the heart of this passage opens with several that seem to cast the writer in the role of the superhero (the Fantastic Four, the X-Men, the Teen Titans) versus the dictator as supervillain (Galactus, the Brotherhood of Evil Mutants, Deathstroke)—or so we presume, although this actually reverses the order of the opening question and the invocation of Caesar and Ovid, and as the sequence progresses, at least some of the pairings become less clear-cut: why Foreman and Ali, and why is Ali in the second (villainous) position? By the time we get to Rushdie's assertion, the passage has already deeply confused the issue, and we are prepared for Díaz's Moore-and-Gibbons-influenced revision: that writers and dictators are in fact difficult to distinguish, just like heroism and villainy in *Watchmen*.[54] "Díaz," Mahler writes in her summation of the dynamic this passage sets up, "gives his critique of hierarchical power a sharp double edge by exposing the forces of domination present within his own writing, applying his criticism even to himself and thus exposing the limits of his own anti-colonial project, which threatens to slide back into the mold of the colonial tyranny that it seeks to unseat."[55]

The solution the novel proposes is not, however, to stop writing but rather to continue with "an unflaggingly self-critical posture."[56] This is not incompatible with *Watchmen*'s closing suggestion that power lies with readers, but Díaz does not suggest that the other sort of power wielded by the writer is inherently fascist. Rather, he makes the writer responsible for carrying on with an awareness of his or her power and a good-faith effort to expose rather than compound abuses of it. It is worth noting that this "unflaggingly self-critical posture," an extrapolation from the revisionist superhero subgenre, is central to Díaz's writing in ways that are not strictly linked to his interests in geopolitics: his most recent short-story collection, *This Is How You Lose Her* (2012), for instance, takes up another element of *Oscar Wao*—Yunior's problematic gender politics—in the interests of a relentless, and in intention feminist, exposure of bad masculine behavior.[57]

At least some readers remain skeptical of Díaz's claims to write as a feminist,[58] in ways that should remind us not only of his work's similarities to that of another New Jersey writer, Philip Roth, but also to the subgenre of serious fiction concerned with comic books that we have been discussing. If this subgenre is a generational phenomenon—Chabon, Lethem, and Díaz range in age from forty-four to fifty and thus were all in their late teens or early twenties precisely when the direct-market boom targeted this demographic—it is also a gendered one: "Comic book culture during the direct market boom," Paul Lopes notes, "was a decidedly teen and adult male culture of fanboys."[59]

As all three novels demonstrate to varying degrees, however, the literary engagement with the superhero genre produces formal innovations distinct from its realistic representation of the masculine comics subculture. Díaz depicts the world of the direct-market boom most directly, setting his novel in the mideighties and having his title character read *Watchmen* in its serialized form. But he also, as I have noted, uses the device of his crypto-nerd narrator, Yunior, to apply the tropes and language of comic books (and other popular genres) to settings far removed from this one.

More recently, Aimee Bender—who, at six months younger than Díaz, is on the young end of the generational cohort I have been discussing—has put these devices to great effect in a literary genre even further removed from their origins. Bender's 2010 *The Particular Sadness of Lemon Cake* is a lyrical coming-of-age novel about a girl's relationship with her mother and others, a book concerned not only with personal relationships but with literally domestic ones: as the title indicates, much of the story centers around food and eating. The first chapter begins with the intimation of an unspecified event—"It happened for the first time on a Tuesday afternoon, a warm spring day in the flatlands near Hollywood, a light breeze moving east from the ocean and stirring the black-eyed pansy petals newly planted in our flower boxes"[60]—and concerns nothing more out of the ordinary than the narrator's mother baking a cake for her daughter's upcoming ninth birthday. The chapter relates this process in a series of primarily descriptive paragraphs that are nostalgic and intimate in tone, concluding, "The room filled with the smell of warming butter and sugar and lemon and eggs, and at five, the timer buzzed and I pulled out the cake and placed it on the stovetop. The house was quiet. The bowl of icing was right there on the counter, ready to go, and cakes are best when just out of the oven, and I really couldn't possibly wait, so I reached to the side of the cake pan, to the least obvious part, and pulled off a small warm spongy chunk of deep gold. Iced it all over with chocolate. Popped the whole thing in my mouth."[61] What happens next, however—after a brief and seemingly unrelated flashback—is that the narrator experiences the first instance of her ability to read the emotions of whoever prepares her food.

As with *Fortress of Solitude* this discovery of actual superpowers does not shift *Lemon Cake* into a full-blown genre narrative: the narrator carries on with her life, at book's end training as a cook and perhaps finding a way to put her powers to use at a school for "at-risk kids."[62] But Bender ultimately mounts a much greater formal challenge to the literary genre with which she begins than does Lethem. We can see how if we compare the narrator's first experience of her powers to the passage from the first chapter that I just quoted. Both passages consist primarily of description, but whereas the passage from the first chapter glides smoothly over the things it describes, with an unquestioned sense that everything is as it seems, in the later passage description becomes a task, an effort to delineate in halting, impressionistic terms something that is grasped only imperfectly:

> I could absolutely taste the chocolate, but in drifts and traces, in an unfurling, or an opening, it seemed that my mouth was also filling with the taste of smallness, the sensation of shrinking, of upset, tasting a distance I somehow knew was connected to my mother, tasting a crowded sense of her thinking, a spiral, like I could almost even taste the grit in her jaw that had created the headache, that meant she had to take as many aspirins as were necessary, a white dotted line of them in a row on the nightstand like an ellipsis to her comment: I'm just going to lie down. . . . None of it was a bad taste, so much, but there was a kind of lack of wholeness to the flavors that made it taste hollow, like the lemon and chocolate were just surrounding a hollowness.[63]

Compared with this passage, the lyrical descriptions from the opening chapter seem both to depict a lost childhood world of wholeness and also, retrospectively, to be not really doing their job, to be taking things for granted rather than truly trying to grasp them.

Bender uses the device of superpowers, that is, as more than just a (by now familiar) metaphor for characters' subjectivities. She does this, to be sure: superpowers run in the narrator's father's family, it turns out, and her painfully shy brother has the ability to disappear into furniture. But Bender also employs the narrator's particular superpower as a kind of formal metaphor for the difficulty of writing about such subjectivities. The difficulty of knowing another's, or even one's own, subjectivity is a running theme in the novel: the narrator's grandmother on her mother's side lives alone and periodically sends the family strange, used or broken objects for reasons no one can understand; in a late scene the narrator sees a picture—"a brown-haired girl with a pony-tail in a red T-shirt that reminded me of one of my T-shirts"[64]—and must be told by her mother that the girl is her. The narrator's power figures this difficulty but extends it outward to the formal question of what language can convey in general: with time she learns to taste beyond the emotions of the food's preparer to the factories or farms from which ingredients originate and even becomes adept at identifying ingredients' geographic origins: "See, there are two different milks, I said, leaning in, on my stool. One is cream, from Nevada, I think, due to the slightly minty flavor, but then there's regular milk too, from Fresno."[65]

Here, perhaps, we return to where we began chapter 1, with Alan Moore's efforts to imagine what it would be like to possess superspeed like the Flash, to see other people as "an endless gallery of statues." *Watchmen* emerges from an effort to cast a superhero story in realistic terms: to imagine superheroes on one hand as ordinary people (here Gibbons's renderings of the short, ugly Walter Kovacs and the overweight, gone-to-seed Dan Dreiberg are as important as Moore's script) and on the other as figures whose outsized powers and abilities (Manhattan's near omnipotence, Veidt's superhuman intellect) necessarily bring about great changes in the world.

In crafting a more realistic superhero story, and one that might be taken in however circumscribed a way as a work of true ambition, Moore and Gibbons also laid the groundwork for subsequent writers to challenge the distinction between comic books and literature from the other side—to import the themes and forms of superhero comic books into the realist fiction that had, by the end of the twentieth century, exhausted the innovative energy that it had acquired from the modernist revolution at century's beginning. Moore and Gibbons, working within a medium characterized both by its own largely unformulated aesthetic standards and by a comparatively industrial mode of production, but aware of other aesthetic traditions, were among the artists in the mid-1980s who helped push the comic book to new levels of artistic achievement. Knowledge of their innovative contribution, however, remained for a long time largely confined to practitioners and fans of their still-disreputable medium and genre.

Yet it was precisely this hint of disreputability, perhaps, that ultimately attracted fiction writers who had taken comic books seriously prior to their formal aesthetic educations and were now casting about for examples of *bad* form to contrast with the minimalist good form they saw as confining rather than freeing their abilities. Rainbow Rowell's young-adult novel *Eleanor & Park*, which is set during the 1986–1987 school year, returns the reader to a time and a context (comic book reading) in which Moore and Gibbons's innovations, not yet digested into the body of mainstream superhero comics, constitute—like all avant-garde experiments initially do—just such a moment of disruptive bad form.

Rowell, who is slightly younger than the members of the generational cohort I have been discussing (she was born in the seventies rather than the sixties), nonetheless joins Lethem and Díaz in treating the discovery of comic books as a central element in a generational coming-of-age story. Her title characters are two high school misfits—a violently redheaded girl from a poor household headed by an abusive stepfather, and a boy whose Korean mother is still an anomaly in the Omaha of the time—who bond during their sophomore year in high school. Initially intent on ignoring each other when Eleanor is forced to share Park's seat on the bus to school, the breakthrough comes when she begins reading his comic books over his shoulder. These include *Watchmen*, of which Eleanor is initially skeptical because "it looked so ugly": "She liked it best," the narrator notes, "when he read the *X-Men*."[66] She becomes hooked, however, when Park gives her the issue to take home, and she also devours the back issues of *Swamp Thing* that he gives her the next day.

Rowell is well aware of the gender dynamics presented by this picture of a boy and a girl, rather than two or more boys, bonding over comic books. Eleanor and Park debate the gender politics of *X-Men*, with Eleanor pointing out that "the girls are all so stereotypically girly and passive. Half of them just think really hard. Like *that's* their superpower, *thinking*. And Shadowcat's power is even worse—she disappears."[67] Rowell does not explicitly say why Eleanor comes to like *Watchmen*, but the implication, given the series's opening association with ugliness, is that it is continuous with the punk elements of both the music that Eleanor and Park also share (though she does not like pure punk)[68] and their strategies of self-presentation (he infuriates his father by wearing eyeliner; she wears men's ties and torn jeans).[69] The novel also suggests that Eleanor has an affinity—even though she claims to find the pirate sections of *Watchmen* boring and gently mocks Park when he tries to explain how the series "completely de-constructs the last fifty years of the genre"[70]—for *Watchmen*'s realist inversion of superhero tropes: she dislikes it when Park's beautician mother gives her a makeover, saying, "I look like I'm in costume. Like I'm trying to be something that I'm not."[71]

Yet this commitment to realism aside, *Eleanor & Park* ends with an assertion, albeit in purely personal terms, of precisely the commit-ment to contingency with which *Watchmen* ends. Park and Eleanor's brief romance comes to a halt when she discovers that her stepfather is the author of the obscene, sexual notes that have been appearing on her schoolbooks, and Park drives her to the home of her aunt and uncle in Minneapolis. Park writes Eleanor long letters, but she refuses to reply, until finally—the day after he attends prom with someone else—he receives a postcard bearing "her scratchy handwriting" and carrying a message "just three words long."[72] These are the last words of the novel, and Rowell thus leaves the reader to wonder what these words are: "I love you"? "Wait for me"? Careful readers, though, may well suspect that the words are a quotation from another work that Park recalls just three pages earlier: "The final issue of *Watchmen* came out a few months after Eleanor left. He wondered if she'd read it, and whether she thought Ozymandias was a villain, and what she thought Dr. Manhattan meant when he said, 'Nothing ever ends,' at the end."[73] If so, these words signal a refusal both of falsely happy endings and of despair in the face of present circumstances. *Eleanor & Park* does not simply invoke Moore and Gibbons's work for period authenticity, that is, but offers a strong reading of its aesthetic lessons for realist fiction.

In this way Rowell inserts *Watchmen* into a larger story of changing literary aesthetics, one in which the marginal, overlooked medium of the comic book has provided opportunities and resources for artists working both inside and outside its precincts. Moore and Gibbons's series, alive to both the aesthetic achievements of superhero comics and their potential to be better, had and will continue to have an effect across various media not unlike the one that *Citizen Kane* had in the middle of the twentieth century. In *Kavalier & Clay* Chabon imagines the effect of Welles's film on his protagonist, Joe Kavalier, in a man-ner that resonates deeply with Chabon's own trajectory as a fiction writer: "All of the dissatisfactions he had felt in his practice of the art form he had stumbled across within a week of his arrival in America, the cheap conventions, the low expectations among publishers, readers, parents, and educators, the spatial constraints that he had been struggling against in the pages of *Luna Moth*, seemed capable of being completely overcome, exceeded, and escaped."[74] If in this passage the comic book is the cramped, constrained art form and post-*Kane* cinema the exciting new one, in Chabon's own work as it is implicitly analogized here it is the comic book that provides examples of how to overcome the conventions of literary fiction. *Watchmen*, like *Kane* in transcending the constraints of its medium, not only remade the world of comics but also helped transform the cognate medium of print fiction. It was and always will remain a comic book, but it also, we might say, becomes literature retroactively, by expanding our understanding of what literature can do and be.

NOTES

INTRODUCTION

1. "10 of *Time*'s Hundred Best Novels," *Time* 166.17 (24 October 2005): 110. The full list can be found online at "ALL-TIME 100 Novels," *Time*, 16 October 2005, accessed 24 January 2013, http://entertainment.time.com/2005/10/16/all-time-100-novels/slide/all/.
2. Both *Maus* and *Jimmy Corrigan* appeared on *Time*'s 2009 follow-up list of "Top 10 Graphic Novels," along with Alison Bechdel's *Fun Home: A Family Tragicomic*, the 2006 book which has mounted the strongest challenge to *Maus* for the title of most critically praised graphic novel of all time. See Lev Grossman, "Top 10 Graphic Novels," *Time*, 4 March 2009, accessed 5 December 2013, http://entertainment.time.com/2009/03/06/top-10-graphic-novels/slide/watchmen/.
3. "10 of *Time*'s Hundred Best Novels."
4. Hillary Chute, *Graphic Women: Life Narrative and Contemporary Comics* (New York: Columbia University Press, 2010), 2. I continue to use the term "graphic novel" when I am referring strictly to Moore and Gibbons's fictional *Watchmen*.
5. Bart Beaty, *Comics versus Art* (Toronto: University of Toronto Press, 2012), 12.
6. Ibid.
7. Charles Hatfield, "Indiscipline, or, The Condition of Comics Studies," *Transatlantica* 1 (2010), paragraphs 2, 24, 21, accessed 19 March 2013, http://transatlantica.revues.org/4933.
8. Jared Gardner, *Projections: Comics and the History of Twenty-First-Century Storytelling* (Stanford, CA: Stanford University Press, 2012).
9. Paul Lopes, *Demanding Respect: The Evolution of the American Comic Book* (Philadelphia: Temple University Press, 2009), 186.
10. For examples of the joint invocation of Moore, Miller, and Spiegelman's work

see Eric L. Berlatsky, "Introduction," in *Alan Moore: Conversations*, ed. Eric Berlatsky (Jackson: University Press of Mississippi, 2012), vii; and Sara J. Van Ness, *"Watchmen" as Literature: A Critical Study of the Graphic Novel* (Jefferson, NC: McFarland, 2010), 1.

11. Lopes, *Demanding Respect*, 186.
12. Douglas Wolk, *Reading Comics: How Graphic Novels Work and What They Mean* (New York: Da Capo, 2008), 11–12.
13. Ibid., 68.
14. Ibid., 27–28.
15. Cf. Wolk, *Reading Comics*, 19.
16. Chute, *Graphic Women*, 2; both these blind spots are less prominent now than they were in 2010, in large part thanks to Chute's work.
17. Ibid.
18. Ibid., 3.
19. Gardner, *Projections, 109.*
20. The closest it comes is Richard Walsh's piece on *Sandman*, the 1990s horror series written by Neil Gaiman and published by DC (after issue 47 in the company's more adult imprint Vertigo). See Walsh, "The Narrative Imagination across Media," *Modern Fiction Studies* 52.4 (Winter 2006): 855–868.
21. "The Top 100 (English-Language) Comics of the Century," *Comics Journal* 210 (February 1999): 34–108.
22. Richard Lacayo, "How We Picked the List," *Time*, 6 January 2010, accessed 17 September 2013, http://entertainment.time.com/2005/10/16/all-time-100-novels/.
23. Lev's brother Austin Grossman is a video-game designer and the author of the semirealist superhero novel *Soon I Will Be Invincible* (2007).
24. Lev Grossman, "Literary Revolution in the Supermarket Aisle: Genre Fiction Is Disruptive Technology," *Time*, 23 May 2012, accessed 24 January 2013, http://entertainment.time.com/2012/05/23/genre-fiction-is-disruptive-technology/.
25. "Junot Díaz: By the Book," *New York Times*, 30 August 2012, accessed 24 January 2013, http://www.nytimes.com/2012/09/02/books/review/junot-diaz-by-the-book.html?pagewanted=all&_r=0.
26. Junot Díaz, *The Brief Wondrous Life of Oscar Wao* (New York: Riverhead, 2007), 20.
27. Harvey notes this in a response, "The First What?," to Andrew D. Arnold's "A Graphic Literature Library," *Time*, 21 November 2003, accessed 10 September 2013, http://www.time.com/time/arts/article/0,8599,547796,00.html; see also Chute, *Graphic Women*, 15.
28. Chute, *Graphic Women*, 14.

29. Joe Queenan, "Drawing on the Dark Side," *New York Times,* 30 April 1989, sec. 6, 32.

30. Lopes, *Demanding Respect,* xvii–xviii, 99–101.

31. Joshua Lukin, "I'm Not Your Boss: The Paradox of the Anarchist Superhero," *Anarchist Studies* 5.2 (1997): 134–135; see also Lopes, *Demanding Respect,* 101–102.

32. Lopes, *Demanding Respect,* 103, 132.

33. This mode of serialization distinguishes *Watchmen* and *The Dark Knight* from *Maus,* which originally appeared in the upscale, experimental anthology *Raw* published by Spiegelman and his wife, Françoise Mouly.

34. Fredric Jameson, *The Political Unconscious* (Ithaca, NY: Cornell University Press, 1981), 25.

35. Lopes, *Demanding Respect,* 104. Queenan's 1989 piece cites a claim by DC "that the average reader of [its "Suggested for Mature Readers"] line is 23.9 years old," while Pamela Young, writing for the Canadian newsweekly *Maclean's* in 1987, cites "a recent survey at Canada's largest comic book shop, the Silver Snail in Toronto, [which] revealed that males over the age of 18 generated 80 per cent of the store's sales." Young, "The Comic Book's Quest for Maturity," *Maclean's,* 28 September 1987, 66. For a detailed account of the midcentury anti-comic-book movement see David Hadju's invaluable *The Ten-Cent Plague: The Great Comic-Book Scare and How It Changed America* (New York: Farrar, Straus and Giroux, 2008).

36. Peter S. Prescott with Ray Sawhill, "The Comic Book (Gulp!) Grows Up," *Newsweek,* 18 January 1988, 70.

37. Len Strazewski, "Comics Fantasyland Brought to Earth by Some Serious Issues," *Advertising Age,* 7 July 1986, 31.

38. Prescott with Sawhill, "Comic Book Grows Up," 71.

39. Queenan, "Drawing on the Dark Side."

40. Prescott with Sawhill, "Comic Book Grows Up," 70.

41. Ibid., 71.

42. Queenan, "Drawing on the Dark Side."

43. Mark Salisbury, *Artists on Comic Art* (London: Titan Books, 2000), 96.

44. Tasha Robinson, "Interview: Alan Moore," *A.V. Club,* 24 October 2001, accessed 10 September 2013, http://www.avclub.com/articles/alan-moore,13740/. Outtakes from this interview appear in Tasha Robinson, "Moore in *The Onion* Edits," in Berlatsky, *Alan Moore,* 95–107.

45. Craig Fischer, "Charmageddon! Or the Day Aleister Crowley Wrote Wonder Woman," *Iowa Journal of Cultural Studies* 6 (2005): 122–127.

46. Geoff Klock, *How to Read Superhero Comics and Why* (New York: Continuum, 2002), 3.

47. Ibid., 29–30.

48. Ibid., 65.

49. Ibid., 63.

50. Alan Moore, Stephen Bissette, and John Totleben, *Saga of the Swamp Thing: Book One* (1983–1984; New York: DC Comics, 2009), 18. In this passage I follow what will be my strategy with the characteristic formal tics of comic books' captions and dialogue balloons. First, although they are usually printed in all capital letters, I translate them into standard sentence case. Second, I reproduce the ellipses that comics frequently employ; where an ellipsis is my own, I will place it within brackets to indicate this. Finally, I represent the bold typeface within which comics regularly place some words by means of italics.

51. Ibid., 14.

52. Stan Lee and Jack Kirby, *Fantastic Four* 41 (August 1965): 2; reprinted in Lee and Kirby, *The Essential Fantastic Four*, vol. 3 (New York: Marvel, 2007), n.p.

53. Moore's first issue of the series bears a January 1984 cover date, although at the time comic book publishers followed a longstanding convention of employing cover dates two months later than the date on which the issue actually appeared.

54. David Roach, Andrew Jones, Simon Jowett, and Greg Hill, "Garry Leach and Alan Moore," in Berlatsky, *Alan Moore*, 13–14.

55. Ibid., 14.

56. Robinson, "Moore in *The Onion* Edits," 97.

57. Alan Moore, Dave Gibbons, and John Higgins, *Absolute Watchmen* (New York: DC Comics, 2005), III.1; hereafter cited as *AW*.

58. Clement Greenberg, "Modernist Painting," *Modern Art and Modernism: A Critical Anthology*, ed. Francis Frascina and Charles Harrison (New York: Westview, 1982), 5.

59. Ibid., 6.

60. Ibid., 7.

61. Ibid., 8.

62. Beaty argues that comics' combination of words and images places the form outside Greenberg's definition of (modernist) art: "The hybrid nature of comics, which is seen by its proponents as one of its principle strengths, serves to mitigate against the modernist purity that Greenberg and others identified in artists like the abstract expressionists" (21). Here Beaty treats the two elements of comics as artificially distinct, however, rather than locating their formal specificity in the interaction of the two, as Moore does.

63. Alan Moore, *Alan Moore's Writing for Comics*, vol. 1 (Rantoul, IL: Avatar, 2003), 3; Moore's emphasis.

64. Ibid., 3–4.

65. Queenan, "Drawing on the Dark Side."

66. "Watchmen: An Oral History," *Entertainment Weekly*, 21 October 2005, accessed 13 January 2013, http://www.ew.com/ew/article/0,,1120854,00.html.

67. As Craig Fischer has reminded me, two issues skipped a month.

68. Dave Itzkoff, "DC Plans Prequels to Watchmen Series," *New York Times*, 1 February 2012, accessed 21 December 2012, http://www.nytimes.com/2012/02/01/books/dc-comics-plans-prequels-to-watchmen-series.html.

69. On this tradition see Mark Lawson, "To Be Continued' . . . : The Grand Tradition of Prequels and Sequels," *Guardian*, 9 March 2012, accessed 25 December 2012, http://www.guardian.co.uk/books/2012/mar/09/prequels-sequels-books.

70. Noah Berlatsky, "Who Watches the *Watchmen*'s Watchers?," *Slate*, 31 May 2012, accessed 23 December 2012, http://www.slate.com/articles/arts/culturebox/2012/05/before_watchmen_controversy_alan_moore_is_right_.html; ellipsis in original.

71. Tom McCarthy, *Tintin and the Secret of Literature* (London: Granta Books, 2006), 9–10.

72. Ibid., 10.

73. Ibid., 32.

74. Ibid.

75. Wolk, *Reading Comics*, 238; Wolk's emphasis.

76. Ibid., 27–28.

77. Ibid., 31.

78. Beaty, *Comics versus Art*, 37–38.

79. *AW*, n.p.

80. See Jerome Christensen, *America's Corporate Art: The Studio Authorship of Hollywood Motion Pictures* (Stanford, CA: Stanford University Press, 2012); Derek Nystrom, *Hard Hats, Rednecks, and Macho Men: Class in 1970s American Cinema* (New York: Oxford University Press, 2009); J. D. Connor, "'The Projections': Allegories of Industrial Crisis in Neoclassical Hollywood," *Representations* 71 (Summer 2000): 48–76; and Connor, "The Biggest Independent Pictures Ever Made: Industrial Reflexivity Today," *The Wiley-Blackwell History of American Film*, vol. 4, *1976 to the Present*, ed. Cynthia Lucia, Roy Grundmann, and Art Simon, 517–541 (Hoboken, NJ: Wiley-Blackwell, 2011).

81. Klock, *How to Read Superhero Comics*, 16, 52–76.

82. Ibid., 11–15.

83. Ibid., 3.

84. "Wanted: Superheroes," *Forbes*, 12 November 2001, 120; qtd. in Lopes, *Demanding Respect*, 158.

85. Andrew Gamble, *The Free Economy and the Strong State: The Politics of Thatcherism*, 2nd ed. (London: Macmillan, 1994).

86. Lopes, *Demanding Respect*, 152–157, 122.

CHAPTER ONE

1. See Bart Beaty, *Comics versus Art* (Toronto: University of Toronto Press, 2012), 84–85.

2. Alan Moore, Stephen Bissette, and John Totleben, *Saga of the Swamp Thing: Book One* (1983–1984; New York: DC Comics, 2009), 111; cf. Guy Lawley and Steve Whitaker, "Alan Moore," in *Alan Moore: Conversations*, ed. Eric L. Berlatsky (Jackson: University Press of Mississippi, 2012), 42.

3. Ibid., 111.

4. Ibid. Moore's investment in this aspect of the Superman character already in 1984 indicates a strain of his writing that departed from the realism with which he became identified and on which I am focusing here. In 1986 DC relaunched Superman under the guidance of popular writer-artist John Byrne, giving the character a more realistic makeover: reducing his previously godlike powers, eliminating some of the more fanciful aspects of his mythos (his career as Superbaby, his superdog Krypto), transforming his main villain, Lex Luthor, from a mad scientist into a corrupt businessman, and so forth. Moore, given the opportunity to write the concluding chapter of the original continuity (a story I focus on later), took the opportunity instead to emphasize the mythic aspects of the character, including the power to crush coal into diamonds. He later made these aspects central to his loosely disguised homage to the Superman mythos in his run on the Image Comics series *Supreme* (1996–1998).

5. Lawley and Whitaker, "Alan Moore," 27.

6. Peter Y. Paik, *From Utopia to Apocalypse: Science Fiction and the Politics of Catastrophe* (Minneapolis: University of Minnesota Press, 2010), 27.

7. Ibid., 27–28.

8. Standard accounts of the genre's history locate the Golden Age in the late thirties and early forties period that saw the birth of the first superhero (Superman in 1938) along with such characters as Batman (1939), Captain Marvel (1940), and Captain America and Wonder Woman (both 1941), while the Silver Age is associated with DC's late-fifties revamping of its characters The Flash (1956) and Green Lantern (1959) and the early sixties creation by Stan Lee, Jack Kirby, and Steve Ditko of the Marvel superheroes including the Fantastic Four (1961), Spider-Man, and the Hulk (both 1962).

9. Geoff Klock, *How to Read Superhero Comics and Why* (New York: Continuum, 2002), 3–4.

10. Alan Moore, Dave Gibbons, and John Higgins, "The World," *Absolute Watchmen* (New York: DC Comics, 2005), n.p.; hereafter cited as *AW*.

11. Ibid. Here "Earth One" refers to the world on which DC comics were at the time imagined to take place, while "Earth Two" is the name the company gave the world that it cleverly made the home of its earlier, World War II–era

heroes after it revamped many of its characters. "Marvel Earth" here probably refers to the home of DC's competitor company, although it could also refer to the home world of Captain Marvel and his supporting characters, which DC established as another alternate time line when it licensed the Marvel Family from its original publisher, Fawcett, in 1972.

12. Erich Auerbach, *Mimesis: The Representation of Reality in Western Literature* (1946; Princeton, NJ: Princeton University Press, 1953).

13. Virginia Woolf, *Mr. Bennett and Mrs. Brown* (London: Hogarth, 1924), 4.

14. Ibid., 21.

15. Ibid., 9–10.

16. David Roach, Andrew Jones, Simon Jowett, and Greg Hill, "Garry Leach and Alan Moore," in Berlatsky, *Alan Moore*, 15.

17. Ibid., 14.

18. Woolf, *Mr. Bennett*, 11.

19. Ibid.

20. *AW*, "Captain Atom" n.p.

21. *AW*, "Captain Atom" n.p.

22. Auerbach, *Mimesis*, 535.

23. Virginia Woolf, *The Waves* (New York: Harcourt, 1931), 9.

24. *AW* IV.1.

25. *AW* IV.1; *AW* IV.10. In both these cases the suggestion that the images are subjective point-of-view shots is reinforced by reverse eye-line matching in the panels immediately following. In the first example the image of the photo is followed by one of Manhattan looking at the photo; in the second the image from below of Manhattan rematerializing precedes a high-angle shot of his colleagues looking up at the scene.

26. Auerbach, *Mimesis*, 536.

27. Sara J. Van Ness, *"Watchmen" as Literature: A Critical Study of the Graphic Novel* (Jefferson, NC: McFarland, 2010), 97.

28. Mark Bernard and James Bucky Carter, "Alan Moore and the Graphic Novel: Confronting the Fourth Dimension," *ImageText: Interdisciplinary Comics Studies* 1.2 (2004), paragraph 20, accessed 14 April 2013, http://www.english.ufl.edu/imagetext/archives/v1_2/carter/.

29. Bernard and Carter, "Alan Moore and the Graphic Novel," paragraph 2. Bernard and Carter discuss the sequence with Dr. Manhattan on Mars in paragraphs 12–20; see also Van Ness, *"Watchmen" as Literature*, 96–100.

30. *AW* IV.12.

31. *AW* IV.2.

32. *AW* IV.2.

33. *AW* IV.13.

34. Auerbach, *Mimesis,* 536–549.

35. Van Ness, *"Watchmen" as Literature,* 99.

36. Bernard and Carter, "Alan Moore and the Graphic Novel," paragraph 20.

37. Daniel Whiston, David Russell, and Andy Fruish, "The Craft: An Interview with Alan Moore," in Berlatsky, *Alan Moore,* 134–135.

38. Auerbach, *Mimesis,* 540.

39. In reality, *Time*'s 29 July 1985 Hiroshima issue featured a mushroom cloud on the cover flanked by the quote from Captain Robert Lewis (the commander of the *Enola Gay* mission), "My God, what have we done?"

40. *AW* IV.24.

41. *AW* IV.8.

42. Christopher Sharrett, "Alan Moore," in Berlatsky, *Alan Moore,* 53.

43. *AW* IV.5.

44. *AW* IV.16.

45. Sharrett, "Alan Moore," 51.

46. *AW,* "Thunderbolt" n.p.

47. Sharrett, "Alan Moore," 51.

48. *AW,* "The Question" n.p.

49. Ditko's biographer Blake Bell notes that as Ditko became increasingly committed to Objectivism, he "began moving Spider-Man away from Lee's initial paradigm of Peter Parker, the obsessive, neurotic teenager, and toward Rand's ideal of a young, romantic male hero." Bell, *Strange and Stranger: The World of Steve Ditko* (Seattle: Fantagraphics Books, 2008), 89.

50. Sharrett, "Alan Moore," 51.

51. *AW* VI.5.

52. *AW* VI.11.

53. Responding to Long's suggestion that he "decided to become *Rorschach*" following the Genovese murder, Kovacs replies, "Don't be stupid. I wasn't Rorschach *then.* Then I was just Kovacs. Kovacs pretending to be Rorschach" (*AW* VI.14).

54. *AW* VI.21.

55. *AW* VI.26.

56. *AW* VI.28.

57. Van Ness, *"Watchmen" as Literature,* 101–119; the Dr. Manhattan quote is from *AW* IV.19.

58. E. M. Forster, *Aspects of the Novel* (New York: Harcourt, 1927), 67–78.

59. Alan Wilde, *Middle Grounds: Studies in Contemporary American Fiction* (Philadelphia: University of Pennsylvania Press, 1987); Robert McLaughlin, "Post-Postmodern Discontent: Contemporary Fiction and the Social World," *symploke* 12.1–2 (2004): 53–68.

60. Forster, *Aspects of the Novel*, 71.
61. *AW*, "Blue Beetle" n.p.
62. *AW* I.13; *AW*, "Blue Beetle" n.p.
63. Van Ness, *"Watchmen" as Literature*, 108–109.
64. Auerbach, *Mimesis*, 552.
65. *AW* II.supplemental.
66. Steve Englehart and Sal Buscema, *Captain America* 180 (December 1974).
67. Klock, *How to Read Superhero Comics*, 65.
68. Chris Ware, *Jimmy Corrigan: The Smartest Kid on Earth* (2000; New York: Pantheon, 2003).
69. *AW* I.supplemental.
70. Pádraig Ó Méalóid, "Alan Moore and *Superfolks* Part 1: The Case for the Prosecution," *The Beat*, 25 October 2012, accessed 20 May 2013, http://comicsbeat.com/alan-moore-and-superfolks-part-1-the-case-for-the-prosecution/.
71. *AW*, "Nightshade" n.p.
72. *AW*, "The Blue Beetle" n.p.
73. *AW* XII.27.
74. *AW* XII.27.
75. *AW*, "The Nite-Owl" n.p.
76. Klock, *How to Read Superhero Comics*, 65–66.
77. *AW* IV.13; Moore notes in his character sketch for Captain Atom that "he is still the only super-hero with real, non-artificial powers, and his position in the super-hierarchy of this world is comparable to that of Superman" ("Captain Atom," *AW* n.p.).
78. Klock, *How to Read Superhero Comics*, 66.
79. *AW*, "The Nite-Owl" n.p.
80. *AW*, "Blue Beetle" n.p.
81. *AW*, "The Original Nite-Owl" n.p.
82. *AW* I.supplemental.
83. *AW* VII.4.
84. *AW* VII.5.
85. *AW* VII.5.
86. *AW* VII.8.
87. *AW* VII.8.
88. *AW* VII.8.
89. *AW* VII.8.
90. *AW* VII.4.
91. *AW* VII.7.
92. *AW* VII.9.
93. *AW* XII.30.

94. Beaty, *Comics versus Art*, 66.
95. Daniel Worden, "The Shameful Art: *McSweeney's Quarterly Concern*, Comics, and the Politics of Affect," *Modern Fiction Studies* 52.4 (Winter 2006): 907.
96. *AW* XII.29.
97. *AW* VI.supplemental, XII.24.
98. *AW* II.4.
99. *AW* II.8.
100. *AW* XII.29.
101. *AW* I.1.
102. *Watchmen*, dir. by Zack Snyder (Burbank, CA: Warner Home Video, 2009), DVD.
103. Gibbons's lettering for *Watchmen* was, famously, one of two influences (alongside John Costanza's lettering in *The Dark Knight Returns*) on the cursive font Comic Sans that Vincent Connare designed for Microsoft. See Simon Garfield, *Just My Type: A Book about Fonts* (New York: Gotham Books, 2011), 12–13.
104. *AW* V.6.
105. Junot Díaz, *The Brief Wondrous Life of Oscar Wao* (New York: Riverhead, 2007), 177.
106. Sharrett, "Alan Moore," 48.
107. Ibid.
108. *AW* VI.7.
109. See *AW* V.supplemental.
110. *AW* V.supplemental.
111. *AW* VII.13.
112. *AW* V.supplemental.
113. *AW* V.supplemental.
114. *AW* III.25.
115. *AW* V.supplemental.
116. Beaty, *Comics versus Art*, 107–117.
117. *AW* V.supplemental.
118. Beaty, *Comics versus Art*, 108.
119. *AW* VIII.3.
120. Beaty, *Comics versus Art*, 110.
121. Ibid., 79–82.

CHAPTER TWO

1. Christopher Sharrett, "Alan Moore," in *Alan Moore: Conversations*, ed. Eric L. Berlatsky (Jackson: University Press of Mississippi, 2012), 55.
2. Alan Moore, Dave Gibbons, and John Higgins, *Absolute Watchmen* (New York: DC Comics, 2005), XI.supplemental, 22; hereafter cited as *AW*.

3. *AW* I.17–18.

4. *AW* X.supplemental.

5. *AW* X.supplemental.

6. *AW* X.supplemental.

7. Blake Bell, *Strange and Stranger: The World of Steve Ditko* (Seattle: Fantagraphics Books, 2008), 57, 60.

8. Ibid., 57, 60, 61.

9. Ibid., 66.

10. Ibid., 65, 89.

11. Ibid., 93.

12. Ibid., 95.

13. Ibid., 40, 42–43.

14. Randy Duncan and Matthew J. Smith, "The Charlton Comics Story," *Power of Comics*, n.d., accessed 13 December 2012, http://www.powerofcomics.com/charlton.html. This essay is one of the "Additional Readings" posted on the website for Duncan and Smith's book *The Power of Comics: History, Form and Culture* (New York: Continuum, 2009). See also Bell, *Strange and Stranger*, 23.

15. Bell, *Strange and Stranger*, 24; Jon B. Cooke and Christopher Irving, "The Charlton Empire: A Brief History of the Derby, Connecticut Publisher," *Comic Book Artist* 9 (2000): 14.

16. Bell, *Strange and Stranger*, 24.

17. Ibid.

18. Steve Ditko (writing as D. C. Glanzman), "The Destroyer of Heroes," *Blue Beetle* 5 (November 1968): 18; reprinted in Ditko, *The Action Heroes Archives*, vol. 2 (New York: DC Comics, 2007), 322.

19. As Bell points out, this critic is directly modeled on the critic Ellsworth Toohey, the villain of *The Fountainhead*.

20. See Bell, *Strange and Stranger*, 111.

21. Bell reproduces this page of the Mr. A story on page 113 of his book.

22. See Steve Skeates (writing as Warren Savin) and Steve Ditko, "Kill Vic Sage!," *Blue Beetle* 4 (December 1967): 8; reprinted in Ditko, *Action Heroes Archives*, 276.

23. Bell, *Strange and Stranger*, 89.

24. Ayn Rand, *Atlas Shrugged* (1957; New York: Penguin, 1992), 88.

25. Sharrett, "Alan Moore," 49.

26. Ibid.

27. Jon B. Cooke, "Toasting Absent Heroes: Alan Moore Discusses the Charlton-Watchmen Connection," *Comic Book Artist* 9 (2000): 104–105; emphasis in original.

28. *In Search of Steve Ditko*, dir. Steven Boyd MacLean, *YouTube*, 10 January 2013, accessed 12 June 2013, http://www.youtube.com/watch?v=CwmfkclY1DI.

29. Eric L. Berlatsky, "Introduction," in Berlatsky, *Alan Moore*, xiii.

30. Ibid., ix.

31. Ibid.

32. Ibid.

33. Craig Fischer, "Charmageddon! Or the Day Aleister Crowley Wrote Wonder Woman," *Iowa Journal of Cultural Studies* 6 (2005): 123.

34. Alex Musson and Andrew O'Neill, "The *Mustard* Interview: Alan Moore," in Berlatsky, *Alan Moore*, 194.

35. Dave Itzkoff, "DC Plans Prequels to Watchmen Series," *New York Times*, 1 February 2012, accessed 21 December 2012, http://www.nytimes.com/2012/02/01/books/dc-comics-plans-prequels-to-watchmen-series.html; Noah Berlatsky, "Who Watches the *Watchmen*'s Watchers?," *Slate*, 31 May 2012, accessed 23 December 2012, http://www.slate.com/articles/arts/culturebox/2012/05/before_watchmen_controversy_alan_moore_is_right_.html. Berlatsky quotes one of the *Before Watchmen* writers, J. Michael Straczynski, as saying, "Did Alan Moore get screwed on his contract? Of course. Lots of people get screwed, but we still have Spider-Man and lots of other heroes"; he then notes, "Straczynski's contrast between Alan Moore (screwed!) and Spider-Man (still ours!) nicely sums up the fandom dynamics of superhero comics. Creators are there to churn out marketable, exploitable properties' . . . and then disappear. And because the comics companies own the characters, and because they have substantial marketing departments, they're in a position to make that disappearance stick."

36. Itzkoff, "DC Plans Prequels to Watchmen Series."

37. Kiel Phegley, "DC Comics to Publish 'Before Watchmen' Prequels," *Comic Book Resources*, 1 February 2012, accessed 23 December 2012, http://www.comicbookresources.com/?page=article&id=36724.

38. Brian Truitt, "'Watchmen' Prequels Stir a Debate," *USA Today*, 4 June 2012, accessed 23 December 2012, http://usatoday30.usatoday.com/life/comics/story/2012-06-05/Before-Watchmen-prequel-series/55386328/1.

39. Paul Lopes, *Demanding Respect: The Evolution of the American Comic Book* (Philadelphia: Temple University Press, 2009), 73.

40. Itzkoff, "DC Plans Prequels to Watchmen Series."

41. On this history see Mark Lawson, "To Be Continued' . . . : The Grand Tradition of Prequels and Sequels," *Guardian*, 9 March 2012, accessed 25 December 2012, http://www.guardian.co.uk/books/2012/mar/09/prequels-sequels-books.

42. Lawson, "To Be Continued."

43. See Caren Irr, "Literature as Proleptic Globalization, or a Prehistory of the

New Intellectual Property," *South Atlantic Quarterly* 100.3 (Summer 2001): 773–802. Irr's compelling essay argues that intellectual property law has, since its emergence in the eighteenth century, occupied a series of (temporally shifting) relationships to transformations in the nature of capitalism more generally: "In the early eighteenth century, the promotion of authors' (really booksellers') rights was homologous to protection of merchants' property rights against the ravages of piracy over long and dangerous trade routes" (798); in the nineteenth century "the economic incentives of the author (and publisher or bookseller) are balanced against those of the public at large, and in this sense the Romantic ideal of the artist synechdocally recalls the larger social world of early industrial capitalism" (792); while in the late twentieth century intellectual property law actually anticipates proleptically a new round of capitalist accumulation characterized by "the sudden and immensely profitable treatment of a vast array of existing relations as property relations" through the conversion of "existing cultural and natural resources into [ownable] texts" (797). This latest shift is characterized, Irr writes, by "the fetishistic substitution of the text for the author as the central concern of intellectual property disputes" (795).

44. As Lopes argues in his invaluable history of the industry, the rise of the direct market in the early 1980s transformed comic books from a mass-market product to one purchased almost exclusively by "a decidedly teen and adult male culture of fanboys" (104)—a niche market that nearly imploded around a speculative bubble in the 1990s, only to see comic book heroes (if not necessarily comic books themselves) return to mass consciousness in the early twenty-first century thanks to "Hollywood's financial success with mainstream comic book franchises" (158). See also Lopes, *Demanding Respect,* 116–117. As Jared Gardner notes in *Projections: Comics and the History of Twenty-First-Century Storytelling* (Stanford, CA: Stanford University Press, 2012), the comic strip syndicates pioneered transmedia cross-branding around popular strips such as *Mutt and Jeff* (44, 64), and "in many ways the comic book as it emerged in the 1940s can be understood as itself an attempt to reel in the more unruly aspects of serial comics, to create consistent markets independent of the newspaper syndicates with reliable readers whose appetites for the material could be satisfied in monthly installments in self-contained comics stories" (67).

45. See, for instance, Alison Flood and Subhajit Bannerjee, "Alan Moore Conjures Up Extraordinary Antichrist: Harry Potter," *Guardian,* 18 June 2012, accessed 11 January 2013, http://www.guardian.co.uk/books/2012/jun/18/alan-moore-extraordinary-antichrist-harry-potter.

46. Alan Moore and Kevin O'Neill, *The League of Extraordinary Gentlemen Cen-*

tury: 2009 (Marietta, GA: Top Shelf, 2012), n.p.

47. See "James Bond Film Franchise Turns Fifty," *CBC News*, 5 October 2012, accessed 12 January 2013, http://www.cbc.ca/news/arts/story/2012/10/05/james-bond-first-film-50th-anniversary.html.

48. See Joe Nocera, "Who Owns How Much of Harry Potter?," *New York Times*, 9 February 2008, accessed 12 January 2013, http://www.nytimes.com/2008/02/09/business/worldbusiness/09iht-wbj0e09.4.9893157.html?pagewanted=all. Vander Ark was eventually able to publish a version of his book as *The Lexicon: An Unauthorized Guide to Harry Potter Fiction and Related Materials* (Muskegon, MI: RDR Books, 2009).

49. In the case of Bond, Warner had been on the other side of the debate over corporate property rights, releasing the *Thunderball* adaptation *Never Say Never Again* (whose film rights had been awarded to the writer Kevin McClory following a legal dispute) in competition with MGM's official Bond release of the same year, *Octopussy*.

50. Warner Bros., "Dianne Nelson, President, DC Entertainment and President & Chief Content Officer, Warner Bros. Interactive Entertainment," WarnerBros.com, n.d., accessed 14 September 2013, http://www.warnerbros.com/studio/executives/divisional-executives/diane-nelson.html.

51. Vaneta Rogers, "Warner Bros. Creates DC ENTERTAINMENT to Maximize DC Brands," *Newsarama*, 9 September 2009, accessed 13 January 2013, http://www.newsarama.com/comics/090909-DC-Restructuring.html.

52. *AW*, "The World" n.p.

53. *AW*, "The World" n.p.

54. Nix, "D.C. Reveals Their Watchmen Comic Book Prequel Plans," *BeyondHollywood.com*, 1 February 2012, accessed 21 September 2013, http://www.beyondhollywood.com/d-c-reveals-their-watchmen-comic-book-prequel-plans/.

55. Alan Moore, "The Mark of Batman: An Introduction," *Batman: The Dark Knight Returns*, by Frank Miller, Klaus Janson, and Lynn Varley (New York: DC Comics, 1986), n.p.

56. "Grim and gritty" has become a stock phrase to describe the comics that appeared in the wake of *Watchmen* and *The Dark Knight Returns*. Besides Gibbons's use of it in his interview with Mark Salisbury (Salisbury, *Artists on Comic Art* [London: Titan Books, 2000], 96) see E. Berlatsky, introduction x (where Berlatsky places the phrase in scare quotes). For Moore's critique see Tasha Robinson, "Interview: Alan Moore," *A.V. Club*, 24 October 2001, accessed 10 September 2013, http://www.avclub.com/articles/alan-moore,13740/.

57. Moore, "Mark of Batman."

58. Ibid.

59. Ibid.; my emphasis.

60. Alan Moore and Curt Swan, *Superman: Whatever Happened to the Man of Tomorrow?* (New York: DC Comics, 2010), 11. Unlike the normal comic book lettering set in all caps, this font uses both uppercase and lowercase letters, making it clear that "IMAGINARY STORY" is capitalized.
61. As Colin Beineke has pointed out to me, this image mirrors the cover of *Watchmen* 8, which features an award statuette that was presented to the original Nite Owl at an award ceremony in May 1962 (as shown in issue 4) and will be used to kill him at the end of the issue.
62. *AW* XII.23–24.
63. *AW* XII.27.
64. Peter Y. Paik, *From Utopia to Apocalypse: Science Fiction and the Politics of Catastrophe* (Minneapolis: University of Minnesota Press, 2010), 36.
65. *AW* X.22.
66. *AW* XII.31.
67. *AW* XII.32.
68. Bryan D. Dietrich, "The Human Stain: Chaos and the Rage for Order in *Watchmen*," *Extrapolation* 50.1 (Spring 2009): 126–127, 128, 137, 121.
69. Barry Kavanagh, "The Alan Moore Interview," *blather.net*, 17 October 2000, accessed 6 January 2013, http://www.blather.net/articles/amoore/index.html; qtd. in Dietrich 137.
70. *AW* IX.27.
71. Dietrich, "The Human Stain," 137 mentions this epilogue in passing.
72. Gardner, *Projections*, 46.
73. Ibid.
74. Ibid., 33.
75. Ibid., 29–40.
76. Ibid., 33.
77. Gardner's account of the rise of the classical Hollywood narrative interestingly suggests that in the film medium at least the ideal of the autonomous work of art arose not as a countermodel to the industry's corporate nature but, in fact, out of "the desire of the producers to exercise greater control over the emerging economics of the industry": "The shift to the feature film was motivated at least as much by the desire on the part of producers for market control and product differentiation as by any demands from audiences. Studios such as Pathé and Biograph had been working to 'brand' their products, but they were struggling to convince exhibitors that the Pathé rooster or the circled 'AB' represented enough of a difference in quality and guaranteed profits to justify differential pricing. The exchanges continued to sell film by the foot, and as far as both distributors and exhibitors were concerned, it was a system that was working just fine" (31). Movie studios turned, that is, to the

discrete feature film as a way of asserting their brands over the interests of exhibitors who were happy to sell film per se in a purely quantitative manner, literally "by the foot."

78. Gardner, *Projections,* 47.

79. Ibid., 186–190 (quote on 188).

80. Daniel Worden, "On Modernism's Ruins: The Architecture of 'Building Stories' and *Lost Buildings*," *The Comics of Chris Ware: Drawing Is a Way of Thinking,* ed. David M. Ball and Martha B. Kuhlman (Jackson: University Press of Mississippi, 2010), 111.

81. Salisbury, *Artists on Comic Art,* 94–96.

82. Ibid., 80, 82.

83. Ibid., 82.

84. Tasha Robinson, "Moore in *The Onion* Edits," in Berlatsky, *Alan Moore,* 97.

85. Gardner, *Projections,* 47.

86. Ibid., 39.

87. Salisbury, *Artists on Comic Art,* 94. This echoes Moore's account of the difference between comics (which enable "complete control of the experience") and film (where "you're being dragged through the experience at twenty-four frames a second") that I cite in chapter 1 (Daniel Whiston, David Russell, and Andy Fruish, "The Craft: An Interview with Alan Moore," in Berlatsky, *Alan Moore,* 134).

88. Salisbury, *Artists on Comic Art,* 82.

89. Alan Moore and Kevin O'Neill, *The League of Extraordinary Gentlemen Century: 2009* (Marietta, GA: Top Shelf, 2012), n.p.

90. Robinson, "Interview: Alan Moore."

91. Irr, "Literature as Proleptic Globalization," 797–798.

92. Tom Lamont, "Alan Moore—Meet the Man behind the Protest Mask," *Observer,* 26 November 2011, accessed 15 January 2013, http://www.guardian.co.uk/books/2011/nov/27/alan-moore-v-vendetta-mask-protest; emphasis in original.

93. See Musson and O'Neill, "The *Mustard* Interview," 197–206.

94. Ibid., 204.

95. Ibid., 201.

96. Ibid., 197–198.

97. John Horn details the legal struggle over the franchise rights in "A Super Battle over 'Watchmen,'" *LA Times,* 16 November 2008, accessed 15 January 2009, http://www.latimes.com/entertainment/news/movies/la-ca-watchmen16-2008nov16,0,4972856,full.story. When the movie was released, bad word of mouth led to a steep drop-off in receipts following opening weekend. Its worldwide box office eventually totaled around $184 to $185 million (with

domestic receipts accounting for around $107 million) and grossed around $53 million on DVD rentals. But given its production price of $130 to $138 million (plus the additional 50 percent, or $65 million, we can estimate for marketing) and the fact that only about 55 percent of the gross was, in all probability, returned to the studio as rentals, we can estimate that its net of $132 million still fell well short of its $195 million cost. Even if the film did turn a slight profit on television sales and DVD rentals, the amount that Warner paid Fox probably means that Moore's curse was, in fact, successful. See the figures at http://www.boxofficemojo.com/movies/?id=watchmen.htm and http://www.the-numbers.com/movies/2009/WATCH.php; thanks to J. D. Connor for helping me sort out these numbers.

98. Musson and O'Neill, "The *Mustard* Interview," 199.

99. See ibid., 193–194.

100. Gerard Jones, *Men of Tomorrow: Geeks, Gangsters, and the Birth of the Comic Book* (New York: Basic Books, 2004), 44–45.

101. Ibid., 280.

102. See my *The Twilight of the Middle Class: Post–World War II American Fiction and White-Collar Work* (Princeton, NJ: Princeton University Press, 2005).

103. On these conditions see Lopes, *Demanding Respect,* 13–16.

104. Jones, *Men of Tomorrow,* 155–156.

105. Ibid., 125; see also Lopes, *Demanding Respect,* 15.

106. Moore mentions DC's retention of his non-*League* ABC titles and quotes Rick Veitch, another artist with whom he worked on *The Saga of the Swamp Thing,* as saying that Jones's account of the relationship between DC and organized crime "explains why everybody at DC acted so fucking weird" when the two worked there in the mideighties. This allows Moore to implicitly describe DC's rights to the ABC line and other of his creations as a form of theft, of course, but it problematically ignores the distinctions between these forms of appropriation, including the fact that DC's assertion of property rights functions totally within the law. See Musson and O'Neill, "The *Mustard* Interview," 193, 197.

107. Sharrett, "Alan Moore," 45.

108. Ibid., 46.

109. Ibid., 45; emphasis in original.

110. *AW* VIII.supplemental.

111. *AW* VIII.10.

112. *AW* VIII.supplemental.

113. *AW* XI.supplemental.

114. Asked by Sharrett about the name *Nova Express* and the other references to Burroughs in *Watchmen,* Moore replies, "If I had to single out one major

influence on my work, it would probably be Burroughs," but not at the level of Burroughs's "style of writing" so much as "his thinking, his theoretical work." Sharrett, "Alan Moore," 52–53.

115. Sharrett, "Alan Moore," 53.
116. William S. Burroughs, *Nova Express* (New York: Grove, 1964), 63.
117. Sharrett, "Alan Moore," 52.
118. *AW* XII.31–32.
119. Sharrett, "Alan Moore," 48.
120. *AW* V.14–15.
121. *AW* X.8.
122. *AW* X.supplemental.
123. *AW* XII.32.
124. *AW* XII.31.
125. Gardner, *Projections,* 64; see also David Hadju, *The Ten-Cent Plague: The Great Comic-Book Scare and How It Changed America* (New York: Farrar, Straus and Giroux, 2008), 21.
126. Gardner, *Projections,* 64.
127. Sharrett, "Alan Moore," 48.
128. Ibid.
129. Jones, *Men of Tomorrow,* 185.
130. Salisbury, *Artists on Comic Art,* 77, 80.
131. Clement Greenberg at one point in his essay "Modernist Painting" suggests as much, only to ultimately fall back on and thereby reinscribe the adherence to convention as a form of aesthetic failure: "The essential norms or conventions of painting are also the limiting conditions with which a marked-up surface must comply in order to be experienced as a picture. Modernism has found that these limiting conditions can be pushed back indefinitely before a picture stops being a picture and turns into an arbitrary object; but it has also found that the further back these limits are pushed the more explicitly they have to be observed. The intersecting black lines and colored rectangles of a Mondrian may seem hardly enough to make a picture out of, yet by echoing the picture's enclosing shape so self-evidently they impose that shape as a regulating norm with a new force and a new completeness. Far from incurring the danger of arbitrariness in the absence of a model in nature, Mondrian's art proves, with the passing of time, almost too disciplined, too convention-bound in certain respects; once we have become used to its utter abstractness we realize that it is more traditional in its color, as well as in its subservience to the frame, than the last paintings of Monet are." Greenberg, "Modernist Painting," *Modern Art and Modernism: A Critical Anthology,* ed. Francis Frascina and Charles Harrison (New York: Westview, 1982), 8.

CHAPTER THREE

1. For a detailed account of the administration's prosecution of the Cold War see Odd Arne Westad's chapter "The 1980s: the Reagan offensive" in *The Global Cold War: Third World Interventions and the Making of Our Times* (2005; New York: Cambridge University Press, 2007), 331–363. Westad notes that "the administration was divided between moderates and radicals in the debate over how far the United States could go in confronting the Soviet Union without the risk of war" but that "from day one it was the radicals' . . . who created the administration's agenda, even though they were mostly dependent on establishment figures' . . . to implement it," and that "Reagan's own occasional involvement with policy making also seemed to confirm that he supported the radical options over the more moderate ones" (337–338).

2. See Will Bunch, *Tear Down This Myth: The Right-Wing Distortion of the Reagan Legacy* (New York: Free Press, 2009), 71–75.

3. Peter Y. Paik, *From Utopia to Apocalypse: Science Fiction and the Politics of Catastrophe* (Minneapolis: University of Minnesota Press, 2010), 26.

4. See Westad, *Global Cold War*, 332–333.

5. Eric L. Berlatsky, "Introduction," in *Alan Moore: Conversations*, ed. Berlatsky (Jackson: University Press of Mississippi, 2012), xxi–xxvi.

6. Mark Salisbury, *Artists on Comic Art* (London: Titan Books, 2000), 75. In "Watchmen: An Oral History" (*Entertainment Weekly*, 21 October 2005, accessed 13 January 2013, http://www.ew.com/ew/article/0,,1120854,00.html), Gibbons notes that because "there weren't fax machines back then," Moore would send the pages via a taxi to Gibbons's home fifty miles away. He also tells a version of this story in his interview with Salisbury (94).

7. Paik, *From Utopia to Apocalypse*, 4.

8. Ibid., 6. Paik offers an intriguing reading of Stalinist socialist realism and the Western superhero narrative as genres whose heroes "share superhuman capabilities and engage their no less extraordinary adversaries in struggles with cosmic significance" (6) but which at the same time seek to provide "a reassuring and identifiable face to essentially godlike personages, that is to say, to humanize the inhuman" (17).

9. Ibid., 19.

10. Ibid.

11. Ibid., 26.

12. Alan Moore, Dave Gibbons, and John Higgins, *Absolute Watchmen* (New York: DC Comics, 2005), XII.20; hereafter cited as *AW*.

13. *AW* XII.27.

14. *AW* XII.27.

15. Paik, *From Utopia to Apocalypse*, 50.

16. Ibid, 35.
17. Ibid., 59.
18. Ibid.
19. Ibid., 63.
20. Ibid.
21. *AW* XI.28.
22. *AW* XII.1–6.
23. Paik, *From Utopia to Apocalypse*, 69.
24. Hannah Arendt, *The Origins of Totalitarianism* (1951; New York: Harcourt, 1968), 475.
25. Ann Douglas, "Punching a Hole in the Big Lie: The Achievement of William S. Burroughs," *Word Virus: The William S. Burroughs Reader*, ed. James Grauerholz and Ira Silverberg (New York: Grove, 1998), xxiii.
26. Ibid., xxiii–xxiv.
27. Christopher Sharrett, "Alan Moore," *Alan Moore: Conversations*, ed. Eric Berlatsky (Jackson: University Press of Mississippi, 2012), 53.
28. Timothy Melley, *Empire of Conspiracy: The Culture of Paranoia in Postwar America* (Ithaca, NY: Cornell University Press, 2000), 172, 165. In *The Twilight of the Middle Class: Post–World War II American Fiction and White-Collar Work* (Princeton, NJ: Princeton University Press, 2005) I offer a different genealogy of this absolute individualism, one related not to explicit politics but to the trajectory of the middle class under advanced capitalism. This formation is clearly overdetermined, in ways that help to explain the continuities between Cold War (political) rhetoric and neoliberal (economic) rhetoric.
29. David Harvey, *A Brief History of Neoliberalism* (New York: Oxford University Press, 2005), 23.
30. Ibid., 57.
31. *AW* X.supplemental.
32. *AW* XI.supplemental.
33. Sharrett, "Alan Moore," 44–45.
34. *AW* XI.supplemental.8.
35. *AW* XII.31–32.
36. *AW* XI.supplemental.7.
37. Sharrett, "Alan Moore," 48.
38. *AW* XII.27.
39. *AW* X.3.
40. *AW* XI.10.
41. *AW* XI.supplemental.10.
42. *AW* IV.22.
43. *AW* IX.27.

44. *AW* XII.18.
45. *AW* XII.27.
46. *AW* IX.27.
47. *AW* IX.28.
48. *AW* XII.20, XII.24.
49. *AW* XII.30.
50. *AW* XII.30.
51. *AW* VI.10.
52. *AW* VI.18.
53. *AW* VI.18.
54. See *AW* VI.26.
55. *AW* XII.29.
56. Paik, *From Utopia to Apocalypse*, 60.
57. Harvey, *Brief History of Neoliberalism,* 80–81.
58. "Interview for *Woman's Own* ('No Such Thing as Society')," Margaret Thatcher Foundation, n.d., accessed 8 February 2013, http://www.margaretthatcher.org/document/106689.
59. "Interview for *Woman's Own.*"
60. Andrew Gamble, *The Free Economy and the Strong State: The Politics of Thatcherism,* 2nd ed. (London: Macmillan, 1994), 243–244. Gamble argues that this process "was a trend made necessary by budget cuts rather than specific legislation" (244) but that it was "approved by Conservatives and nothing was done to arrest it" (244).
61. Ibid., 239.
62. Ibid., 241.
63. Ibid., 242.
64. *AW* III.11–14.
65. *AW* VIII.25–28.
66. *AW* II.16–18.
67. *AW* II.17.
68. Sharrett, "Alan Moore," 48.
69. Paik, *From Utopia to Apocalypse*, 41.
70. Moore's period with the Arts Lab began in 1970. See E. Berlatsky, introduction, xxi.
71. Maggie Gray, "Alan Moore's Underground: The Formation of a Cultural Dissident Practice," *Studies in Comics* 2.1 (2011): 24.
72. Ibid., 31; Gray is here discussing the Oxford-based *Backstreet Bugle*, but she makes a similar point about Northampton's *anon.* (28).
73. Ibid., 25.
74. Ibid., 27–28.

75. Ibid., 33.
76. Ibid., 35.
77. Matthew De Abaitua, "Alan Moore Interview," in Berlatsky, *Alan Moore* 77–78.
78. Ibid., 78.
79. Ibid.
80. *AW* X.supplemental.
81. *AW* III.7, VII.13–14, VIII.1, IX.23–24.
82. *AW* IX.24.
83. Gray too, despite her focus on the institutions of the underground through which Moore circulated, shows the impress of such thinking. At one point she refers to the original Arts Lab in London as "one of a number of' . . . 'anti-institutions' that attempted to reconfigure cultural and pedagogic relations on a more direct democratic basis, including the London Anti-University and the London Free School in Notting Hill"—as though these were not alternative institutions but, generalizing from the Anti-University's name, something else entirely. Gray, "Alan Moore's Underground," 24.
84. George Khoury, *The Extraordinary Works of Alan Moore* (Raleigh, NC: TwoMorrows, 2003), 42.
85. Chris Richards, "Alan Moore," *The Art of Dismantling*, March 2011, accessed 16 February 2013, http://www.theartofdismantling.com/2011/03/17/alan-moore-2/.
86. See Gray, "Alan Moore's Underground," 35.
87. Richards, "Alan Moore."
88. Ibid.
89. Gray, "Alan Moore's Underground," 33, 35.
90. Ibid., 35.
91. Elsewhere in the interview in which Moore discusses the Northampton Arts Lab he declares, "Capitalism and communism felt like they were always going to be around, but it turns out they were just two ways of ordering an industrial society. If you were looking for more fundamental human politics poles, you'd take anarchy and fascism, for my money. Which are not dependent upon economic trends because they are both a bit mad. One of them is complete abdication of individual responsibility into the collective, and one of them is absolute responsibility for the individual." De Abaitua, "Moore Interview," 76.
92. Gray, "Alan Moore's Underground," 35.
93. Chin-tao Wu, *Privatising Culture: Corporate Art Intervention since the 1980s* (2002; New York: Verso, 2003), 33–40.
94. Andrew Sinclair, *Arts and Cultures: The History of the 50 Years of the Arts Council of Great Britain* (London: Sinclair-Stevenson, 1995), 112.

95. Wu, *Privatising Culture,* 47; see also Sinclair.

96. Ibid., 53–63 (quote on 56).

97. *AW* XI.20; see Sara J. Van Ness, *"Watchmen" as Literature: A Critical Study of the Graphic Novel* (Jefferson, NC: McFarland, 2010), 140.

98. "Interview for *Woman's Own.*"

99. *AW* XII.25.

100. Gamble, *Free Economy,* 242.

101. Alan Moore and David Lloyd, *V for Vendetta* (New York: DC Comics, 1990), 6.

102. *AARGH (Artists Against Rampant Government Homophobia)* (Northampton, UK: Mad Love, October 1988), an anthology comic produced by Mad Love, the publishing company Moore founded with his then-wife, Phyllis, and their joint lover, Deborah Delano, when he left DC in 1988, provides some vital context for this critique of looming British totalitarianism. Featuring contributions by a virtual who's who of British and American creators (including Gibbons, Harvey Pekar, Art Spiegelman, Neil Gaiman, and the Hernandez brothers), *AARGH* was designed to protest Clause (or Section) 28 of the Local Government Act of 1988, a Thatcher government initiative which responded to the AIDS epidemic by prohibiting local authorities from "intentionally promot[ing] homosexuality or publish[ing] material with the intention of promoting homosexuality" and from "promot[ing] the teaching in any maintained school of the acceptability of homosexuality as a pretended family relationship." "Local Government Act 1988: Section 28," legislation.gov.uk, n.d., accessed 24 September 2013, http://www.legislation.gov.uk/ukpga/1988/9/section/28. While Clause 28 had no legal teeth, its language and intent were obviously chilling, and many of the contributors to *AARGH,* Moore included, depict it as the first step toward a fascist Britain. Moore's story, a history of homosexuality and the fight against homophobia, asks near its end, "As we approach the future, will utopia's spires hove into view, or death-camp chimney stacks?" (9); Gibbons's brilliant one-page cartoon shows a double-decker bus (number 28) pulling away from a stop, its occupants being beaten by baton-wielding policemen while another policeman hanging off its side tells the members of various other minorities waiting at the stop that another will be along soon (19). See also E. Berlatsky, "Introduction," xxiii.

103. Gamble, *Free Economy,* 242.

104. Torin Douglas, "Forty Years of *The Sun,*" *BBC News,* 14 September 2004, accessed 16 May 2013, http://news.bbc.co.uk/2/hi/uk_news/magazine/3654446.stm.

105. Sharrett, "Alan Moore," 48.

106. Melley, *Empire of Conspiracy,* 172.

107. Sharrett, "Alan Moore," 48.

108. Melley, *Empire of Conspiracy,*172.

109. Ibid.; Melley's emphasis.

110. Michael Clune, *American Literature and the Free Market, 1945–2000* (New York: Cambridge University Press, 2010), 7.

111. Ibid., 15.

112. Ibid., 25.

113. Ibid., 79.

114. Ibid., 87.

115. Ibid., 101.

116. Ibid., 90–92.

117. Ibid., 92.

118. Ibid., 94.

119. Ibid., 101, 102; Clune's emphasis.

120. Richards, "Alan Moore."

121. Alex Musson and Andrew O'Neill, "The *Mustard* Interview: Alan Moore," in Berlatsky, *Alan Moore,* 201, 204.

122. Sharrett, "Alan Moore," 48.

123. Clune, *American Literature and the Free Market,* 163.

124. Fredric Jameson, *The Political Unconscious: Narrative as a Socially Symbolic Act* (Ithaca, NY: Cornell University Press, 1981), 48.

125. *AW* XII.21.

126. *AW* XII.10.

127. *AW* X.20–21.

128. *AW* X.20.

129. *AW* XI.10.

130. *AW* XI.11.

131. *AW* XI.22.

132. Percy Bysshe Shelley, "Ozymandias," *Ode to the West Wind and Other Poems* (Mineola, NY: Dover, 1993), 5.

133. Joshua Lukin, "I'm Not Your Boss: The Paradox of the Anarchist Superhero," *Anarchist Studies* 5.2 (1997): 143.

134. Ibid., 153.

135. Ibid., 143.

136. Ibid., 143.

137. Francis Fukuyama, "The End of History?," *National Interest* 16 (Summer 1989): 3.

138. Ibid., 5.

139. *AW* XII.31–32.

140. Fukuyama, "End of History?," 3, 8.

141. See Phillip E. Wegner, *Life between Two Deaths, 1989–2001: U.S. Culture in the Long Nineties* (Durham, NC: Duke University Press, 2009), 139–140. In addition to Fukuyama's essay's status as a neoliberal rallying cry he participated, as a member of the Project for the American Century, in the buildup to the 2003 Iraq War—a role he later recanted, seeking to disentangle his ideas from Bush administration policy. See, for instance, Fukuyama, "The History at the End of History?," *Guardian*, 3 April 2007, accessed 24 February 2013, http://www.guardian.co.uk/commentisfree/2007/apr/03/thehistoryattheendofhist.
142. *AW* XII.20.
143. Gray, "Alan Moore's Underground," 35.
144. As Veidt outlines the reasons for his decision to Nite Owl and Rorschach, "*Other* factors emerged: *arms expenditures* boosted international *lending* rates. To repay soaring *debt interest*, nations like *Brazil* leveled their *forests*. Nuclear *power*, providing vital weapons-grade *waste*, became *mandatory*. War *aside*, atomic deadlock was guiding us downhill towards environmental *ruin*." *AW* XI.22.
145. Scott Thill, "Alan Moore: Comics Won't Save You, But *Dodgem Logic* Might," *Wired*, 31 December 2009, accessed 1 June 2013, http://www.wired.com/underwire/2009/12/alan-moore-dodgem-logic/.
146. Thill, "Alan Moore."
147. Adolph Reed, "*Django Unchained*, or, *The Help*: How 'Cultural Politics' Is Worse Than No Politics at All, and Why," *nonsite*, 25 February 2013, accessed 28 February 2013, http://nonsite.org/editorial/django-unchained-or-the-help-how-cultural-politics-is-worse-than-no-politics-at-all-and-why.
148. See *AW* II.9–11, IV.17, VI.15, XI.19.
149. *AW* II.18.
150. Juvenal, *The Satires*, trans. Niall Rudd (New York: Oxford University Press, 1991), 49–50.

CODA

1. Pádraig Ó Méalóid, "Alan Moore and *Superfolks* Part 1: The Case for the Prosecution," *The Beat*, 25 October 2012, accessed 28 May 2013, http://comicsbeat.com/alan-moore-and-superfolks-part-1-the-case-for-the-prosecution/; "Alan Moore and *Superfolks* Part 2: The Case for the Defense," *The Beat*, 11 November 2012, accessed 28 May 2013, http://comicsbeat.com/alan-moore-and-superfolks-part-2-the-case-for-the-defence/; and "Alan Moore and *Superfolks* Part 3: The Strange Case of Grant Morrison and Alan Moore," *The Beat*, 18 November 2012, accessed 28 May 2013, http://comicsbeat.com/alan-moore-and-superfolks-part-3-the-strange-case-of-grant-morrison-and-alan-moore/.

2. Geoff Klock, *How to Read Superhero Comics and Why* (New York: Continuum, 2002), 3.

3. Robert Mayer, *Superfolks* (1977; New York: St. Martin's, 2005), 51.

4. Ó Méalóid, "Moore and *Superfolks* Part 1."

5. Mayer, *Superfolks*, 12.

6. Guy Lawley and Steve Whitaker, "Alan Moore," in *Alan Moore: Conversations*, ed. Eric L. Berlatsky (Jackson: University Press of Mississippi, 2012), 27. The actual line from Patten's poem reads that the World War II flying ace "has now gone off to commit suicide in the disused Hangars of Innocence." Brian Patten, "Where Are You Now, Batman?," *The Mersey Sound: Adrian Henri, Roger McGough, Brian Patten* (1967; Baltimore: Penguin, 1974), 113.

7. T. H. White, *The Once and Future King* (1958; New York: Ace, 1987), 339.

8. Michael Chabon, *Maps and Legends: Writing and Reading along the Borderlands* (2008; New York: Harper Perennial, 2009), 77. At the inaugural Eisner Awards in 1988 Moore won Best Writer, and Moore and Gibbons won Best Writer/Artist for *Watchmen*, which itself won Best Finite Series and Best Graphic Album. In 2004, when Chabon delivered his keynote, Moore won Best Writer again for *League of Extraordinary Gentlemen* and his other ABC comics.

9. Chabon, *Maps and Legends*, 75.

10. Ibid., 6.

11. Ibid., 12.

12. Chris Talbott, "Chabon Ties It All Together in 'Telegraph Avenue,'" *Seattle Times*, 13 December 2012, accessed 31 May 2012, http://seattletimes.com/html/entertainment/2019895605_apusbooksmichaelchabon.html.

13. Michael Chabon, *The Amazing Adventures of Kavalier & Clay* (New York: Picador, 2000), 74–78.

14. In a 1996 interview with Peter DePree, Eisner notes that he "was very much aware of Welles in 1940" and would "be much surprised" if he "wasn't influenced by him." Peter DePree, "Night of the Paper Noir," *Will Eisner: Conversations*, ed. M. Thomas Inge (Jackson: University Press of Mississippi, 2011), 154.

15. See Mark McGurl, *The Program Era: Postwar Fiction and the Rise of Creative Writing* (Cambridge, MA: Harvard University Press, 2009), 273–320.

16. Chabon graduated in 1987 with *Mysteries of Pittsburgh* as his thesis—a book he has claimed in interviews to have written there in order to get feedback, since his early attempts to workshop "SF of a kind" were "met with, if not hostility then incomprehension." See Charlie Jane Anders, "The Grad Students Who Mocked Michael Chabon's Fiction," *io9*, 16 May 2008, accessed 3 June 2013, http://io9.com/391013/the-grad-students-who-mocked-michael-chabons-science-fiction.

17. See McGurl, *The Program Era*, 294–296.

18. Chabon, *Kavalier & Clay,* 6–7.

19. Ibid., 123–154.

20. Ibid., 269, 267–274. The librarian, Judy Dark, is granted her powers by the Cimmerian moth goddess Lo, who created a group of female champions to assist her people when a "shrivel-hearted malcontent" named Nanok overthrew the Cimmerians' matriarchal society (272). Luna Moth's origin story demonstrates the wide-ranging appropriation of comics history underlying Chabon's focus on the Golden Age: her origin a feminist inversion of Robert E. Howard's pulp fantasy character Conan (Nanok spelled backward) and the 1970s Marvel comic book series about him, Luna Moth's character also contains elements of Wonder Woman (the matriarchal utopia) and Captain Marvel (the visit to a mystical figure searching for a champion), while the character's powers and Chabon's descriptions of them suggest Winsor McCay's early twentieth-century newspaper strip *Little Nemo in Slumberland,* Jerome Siegel and Bernard Baily's creation the Spectre, and Stan Lee and Steve Ditko's Doctor Strange.

21. Chabon, *Kavalier & Clay,* 631; Chabon's emphasis.

22. Ibid., 271.

23. Ibid., 131.

24. Ibid., 130.

25. Ibid.

26. Ibid., 575–576.

27. Ibid., 601.

28. See Carrie Tirado Bramen's brilliant account of "Jamesian realism" as "an aesthetic that emerges from an understanding of the world as fundamentally hostile, constituted by limits and constraints of all kinds, beginning with those established by our own mortality," in "James, Pragmatism, and the Realist Ideal," *The Cambridge History of the American Novel,* ed. Leonard Cassuto, Clare Virginia Eby, and Benjamin Reiss (New York: Cambridge University Press, 2011), 304–321 (quote on 304).

29. Chabon, *Kavalier & Clay,* 636.

30. Ibid., 328.

31. Ibid., 329.

32. Ibid., 330.

33. Ibid., 333.

34. Jonathan Lethem, *The Fortress of Solitude* (2003; New York: Vintage, 2004), 163; Lethem's emphasis.

35. Florence Dore, "The Rock Novel and Jonathan Lethem's *The Fortress of Solitude,*" *nonsite,* 20 January 2013, accessed 7 June 2013, http://nonsite.org/article/the-rock-novel-and-jonathan-lethems-the-fortress-of-solitude.

36. Lethem, *Fortress of Solitude,* 97; Lethem's emphasis.

37. Ibid.,179.

38. Ibid., 180.

39. Ibid.

40. Junot Díaz, *The Brief Wondrous Life of Oscar Wao* (New York: Riverhead, 2007), 11.

41. Ibid., 32.

42. Ibid., 45.

43. Ibid., 331.

44. Ibid., 333–334.

45. Daniel Bautista, "Comic Book Realism: Form and Genre in Junot Díaz's *The Brief Wondrous Life of Oscar Wao,*" *Journal of the Fantastic in the Arts* 21.1 (2010): 50, 45. As Bautista points out (53n. 5), Díaz alludes in *Oscar Wao* to the Chilean writer Alberto Fuguet's declaration of his own break with magical realism.

46. Díaz, *Oscar Wao,* 94.

47. Bautista, "Comic Book Realism," 46.

48. Díaz, *Oscar Wao,* 2.

49. Bautista, "Comic Book Realism," 46.

50. Díaz, *Oscar Wao,* 321–322.

51. Anne Garland Mahler, "The Writer as Superhero: Fighting the Colonial Curse in Junot Díaz's *The Brief Wondrous Life of Oscar Wao,*" *Journal of Latin American Cultural Studies* 19.2 (2010): 120.

52. Ibid., 121.

53. Díaz, *Oscar Wao,* 97; Díaz's emphasis.

54. Cf. Mahler, "Writer as Superhero," 129–130.

55. Ibid.,134. This dynamic is driven home, I would argue, in a section of the novel that Mahler does not discuss, in which Yunior with ever growing abusiveness seeks to make his then college roommate Oscar exercise—tyrannizing Oscar, like the United States might tyrannize a Caribbean nation, under the guise of promoting Oscar's own good. Yunior tellingly refers to this plan as the diplomatic-sounding "Oscar Redemption Program" (Díaz, *Oscar Wao,* 179).

56. Mahler, "Writer as Superhero," 134.

57. See Gina Frangello, "The Sunday Rumpus Interview: Junot Díaz," *The Rumpus,* 30 September 2012, accessed 11 June 2013, http://therumpus.net/2012/09/the-sunday-rumpus-interview-junot-diaz/.

58. See Virginia Vitzhum, "Junot Díaz's Pro-Woman Agenda," *Elle,* 18 September 2012, accessed 11 June 2013, http://www.elle.com/pop-culture/reviews/junot-diaz-interview.

59. Paul Lopes, *Demanding Respect: The Evolution of the American Comic Book* (Philadelphia: Temple University Press, 2009), 104.
60. Aimee Bender, *The Particular Sadness of Lemon Cake* (New York: Anchor, 2010), 3.
61. Ibid., 6.
62. Ibid., 281.
63. Ibid., 10.
64. Ibid., 195.
65. Ibid., 272.
66. Rainbow Rowell, *Eleanor & Park* (New York: St. Martin's, 2013), 39.
67. Ibid., 64. When Park objects that Shadowcat's power is actually intangibility, Eleanor replies, "It's still something you could do in the middle of a tea party" (64). At the same time Rowell cleverly points out the covertly gender-bending generic makeup of Marvel's books in this period: "The *X-Men* were worse than *General Hospital*," Eleanor thinks (39).
68. She tells Park, "They all sound the same when they're yelling at me" (230).
69. The fact that she does so as much out of economic necessity as aesthetic choice (see, for instance, 81) does not, of course, blunt the association with punk.
70. Rowell, *Eleanor & Park*, 162.
71. Ibid., 215.
72. Ibid., 325.
73. Ibid., 322.
74. Chabon, *Kavalier & Clay*, 361.

WORKS CITED

AARGH (Artists Against Rampant Government Homophobia). Northampton, UK: Mad Love, October, 1988.

"ALL-TIME 100 Novels." *Time*, October 16, 2005. http://entertainment.time.com/2005/10/16/all-time-100-novels/slide/all/.

Anders, Charlie Jane. "The Grad Students Who Mocked Michael Chabon's Fiction." *io9*, May 16, 2008. http://io9.com/391013/the-grad-students-who-mocked-michael-chabons-science-fiction.

Arendt, Hannah. *The Origins of Totalitarianism*. 1951. Reprint, New York: Harcourt, 1968.

Auerbach, Erich. *Mimesis: The Representation of Reality in Western Literature*. 1946. Reprint, Princeton, NJ: Princeton University Press, 1953.

Barthelme, Donald. "The Joker's Greatest Triumph." *The Teachings of Don B.: Satires, Parodies, Fables, Illustrated Stories, and Plays of Donald Barthelme*. Edited by Kim Herzinger, 37–44. Berkeley, CA: Counterpoint, 1992.

Bautista, Daniel. "Comic Book Realism: Form and Genre in Junot Díaz's *The Brief Wondrous Life of Oscar Wao*." *Journal of the Fantastic in the Arts* 21.1 (2010): 41–53.

Beaty, Bart. *Comics versus Art*. Toronto: University of Toronto Press, 2012.

Bell, Blake. *Strange and Stranger: The World of Steve Ditko*. Seattle: Fantagraphics Books, 2008.

Bender, Amy. *The Particular Sadness of Lemon Cake*. New York: Anchor, 2010.

Berlatsky, Eric L., ed. *Alan Moore: Conversations*. Jackson: University Press of Mississippi, 2012.

———. Introduction to Berlatsky ed., *Alan Moore*, vii–xix.

Berlatsky, Noah. "Who Watches the *Watchmen*'s Watchers?" *Slate*, May 31, 2012. http://www.slate.com/articles/arts/culturebox/2012/05/before_watchmen_controversy_alan_moore_is_right_.html.

Bernard, Mark, and James Bucky Carter. "Alan Moore and the Graphic Novel: Confronting the Fourth Dimension." *ImageText: Interdisciplinary Comics Studies* 1.2 (2004). http://www.english.ufl.edu/imagetext/archives/v1_2/carter/.

Bramen, Carrie Tirado. "James, Pragmatism, and the Realist Ideal." *The Cambridge History of the American Novel.* Edited by Leonard Cassuto, 304–321. Clare Virginia Eby, and Benjamin Reiss. New York: Cambridge University Press, 2011.

Bukatman, Scott. *Matters of Gravity: Special Effects and Supermen in the 20th Century.* Durham, NC: Duke University Press, 2003.

Bunch, Will. *Tear Down This Myth: The Right-Wing Distortion of the Reagan Legacy.* New York: Free Press, 2009.

Burroughs, William. *Nova Express.* New York: Grove, 1964.

Chabon, Michael. *The Amazing Adventures of Kavalier & Clay.* New York: Picador, 2000.

———. *Maps and Legends: Writing and Reading along the Borderlands.* 2008. Reprint, New York: HarperPerennial, 2009.

Christensen, Jerome. *America's Corporate Art: The Studio Authorship of Hollywood Motion Pictures.* Stanford, CA: Stanford University Press, 2012.

Chute, Hillary. *Graphic Women: Life Narrative and Contemporary Comics.* New York: Columbia University Press, 2010.

Clune, Michael. *American Literature and the Free Market, 1945–2000.* New York: Cambridge University Press, 2010.

Connor, J. D. "The Biggest Independent Pictures Ever Made: Industrial Reflexivity Today." *The Wiley-Blackwell History of American Film,* vol. 4, *1976 to the Present.* Edited by Cynthia Lucia, Roy Grundmann, and Art Simon, 517–541. Hoboken, NJ: Wiley-Blackwell, 2011.

———. "'The Projections': Allegories of Industrial Crisis in Neoclassical Hollywood." *Representations* 71 (Summer 2000): 48–76.

Cooke, Jon B. "Toasting Absent Heroes: Alan Moore Discusses the Charlton-Watchmen Connection." *Comic Book Artist* 9 (2000): 104–110.

Cooke, Jon B., and Christopher Irving. "The Charlton Empire: A Brief History of the Derby, Connecticut Publisher." *Comic Book Artist* 9 (2000): 14–21.

Coover, Robert. *The Public Burning.* 1977. Reprint, New York: Grove, 1998.

De Abaitua, Matthew. "Alan Moore Interview." In Berlatsky, ed., *Alan Moore,* 61–94.

DePree, Peter. "Night of the Paper Noir." *Will Eisner: Conversations.* Edited by M. Thomas Inge. 131–175. Jackson: University Press of Mississippi, 2011.

Díaz, Junot. *The Brief Wondrous Life of Oscar Wao.* New York: Riverhead, 2007.

Dietrich, Bryan D. "The Human Stain: Chaos and the Rage for Order in *Watchmen.*" *Extrapolation* 50.1 (Spring 2009): 120–144.

Ditko, Steve. *The Action Heroes Archives.* Vol. 2. New York: DC Comics, 2007.

Dore, Florence. "The Rock Novel and Jonathan Lethem's *The Fortress of Solitude*." *nonsite*, January 20, 2013. http://nonsite.org/article/the-rock-novel-and-jona-than-lethems-the-fortress-of-solitude.

Douglas, Ann. "Punching a Hole in the Big Lie: The Achievement of William S. Burroughs." *Word Virus: The William S. Burroughs Reader*. Edited by James Grauerholz and Ira Silverberg, xv–xxx. New York: Grove, 1998.

Douglas, Torin. "Forty Years of *The Sun*." *BBC News*, September 14, 2004. http://news.bbc.co.uk/2/hi/uk_news/magazine/3654446.stm.

Duncan, Randy, and Matthew J. Smith. "The Charlton Comics Story." *Power of Comics*. n.d. Accessed 13 December 2012. http://www.powerofcomics.com/charlton.html.

———. *The Power of Comics: History, Form and Culture*. New York: Continuum, 2009.

Englehart, Steve, and Sal Buscema. *Captain America* 180 (December 1974).

Fischer, Craig. "Charmageddon! Or the Day Aleister Crowley Wrote Wonder Woman." *Iowa Journal of Cultural Studies* 6 (2005): 122–127.

Flood, Alison, and Subhajit Bannerjee. "Alan Moore Conjures up Extraordinary Antichrist: Harry Potter." *Guardian*, June 18, 2012. http://www.guardian.co.uk/books/2012/jun/18/alan-moore-extraordinary-antichrist-harry-potter.

Forster, E. M. *Aspects of the Novel*. New York: Harcourt, 1927.

Frangello, Gina. "The Sunday Rumpus Interview: Junot Díaz." *The Rumpus*, 30 September 2012. Accessed 11 June 2013. http://therumpus.net/2012/09/the-sunday-rumpus-interview-junot-diaz/.

Fukuyama, Francis. "The End of History?" *National Interest* 16 (Summer 1989): 3–18.

———. "The History at the End of History." *Guardian*, April 3 2007. http://www.guardian.co.uk/commentisfree/2007/apr/03/thehistoryattheendofhist.

Gamble, Andrew. *The Free Economy and the Strong State: The Politics of Thatcher-ism*. 2nd ed. London: Macmillan, 1994.

Gardner, Jared. *Projections: Comics and the History of Twenty-First-Century Story-telling*. Stanford, CA: Stanford University Press, 2012.

Garfield, Simon. *Just My Type: A Book about Fonts*. New York: Gotham Books, 2011.

Gray, Maggie. "Alan Moore's Underground: The Formation of a Cultural Dissident Practice." *Studies in Comics* 2.1 (2011): 21–37.

Greenberg, Clement. "Modernist Painting." *Modern Art and Modernism: A Critical Anthology*. Edited by Francis Frascina and Charles Harrison, 5-10. New York: Westview, 1982.

Grossman, Lev. "Literary Revolution in the Supermarket Aisle: Genre Fiction Is Disruptive Technology." *Time*, May 23, 2012. http://entertainment.time.com/2012/05/23/genre-fiction-is-disruptive-technology/.

———. "Top 10 Graphic Novels." *Time*, March 4, 2009. http://entertainment.time. com/2009/03/06/top-10-graphic-novels/slide/watchmen/.

Hadju, David. *The Ten-Cent Plague: The Great Comic-Book Scare and How It Changed America*. New York: Farrar, Straus and Giroux, 2008.

Harvey, David. *A Brief History of Neoliberalism*. New York: Oxford University Press, 2005.

Harvey, R. C. "The First What?" Response to Andrew D. Arnold's "A Graphic Literature Library." *Time*, November 21, 2003. http://www.time.com/time/arts/ article/0,8599,547796,00.html.

Hatfield, Charles. *Hand of Fire: The Comics Art of Jack Kirby*. Jackson: University Press of Mississippi, 2012.

———. "Indiscipline, or, The Condition of Comics Studies." *Transatlantica* 1 (2010). http://transatlantica.revues.org/4933.

Hoberek, Andrew. *The Twilight of the Middle Class: Post–World War II American Fiction and White-Collar Work*. Princeton, NJ: Princeton University Press, 2005.

Horn, John. "A Super Battle over 'Watchmen.'" *LA Times*, November 16, 2008. http://www.latimes.com/entertainment/news/movies/la-ca-watchmen16-2008nov16,0,4972856,full.story.

In Search of Steve Ditko. Directed by Steven Boyd MacLean. *YouTube*, January 10, 2013. http://www.youtube.com/watch?v=CwmfkclY1DI.

"Interview for *Woman's Own* ('No Such Thing as Society')." Margaret Thatcher Foundation, n.d. http://www.margaretthatcher.org/document/106689.

Irr, Caren. "Literature as Proleptic Globalization, or a Prehistory of the New Intellectual Property." *South Atlantic Quarterly* 100.3 (Summer 2001): 773–802.

Itzkoff, Dave. "DC Plans Prequels to Watchmen Series." *New York Times*, February 1, 2012. http://www.nytimes.com/2012/02/01/books/dc-comics-plans-prequels-to-watchmen-series.html.

"James Bond Film Franchise Turns Fifty." *CBC News*, October 5, 2012. http://www. cbc.ca/news/arts/story/2012/10/05/james-bond-first-film-50th-anniversary. html.

Jameson, Fredric. *The Political Unconscious: Narrative as a Socially Symbolic Act*. Ithaca, NY: Cornell University Press, 1981.

Jones, Gerard. *Men of Tomorrow: Geeks, Gangsters, and the Birth of the Comic Books*. New York: Basic Books, 2004.

"Junot Díaz: By the Book." *New York Times*, August 30, 2012. http://www. nytimes.com/2012/09/02/books/review/junot-diaz-by-the-book. html?pagewanted=all&_r=0.

Juvenal. *The Satires*. Translated by Niall Rudd. New York: Oxford University Press, 1991.

Kavanagh, Barry. "The Alan Moore Interview." *blather.net*, October 17, 2000. http://www.blather.net/articles/amoore/index.html.

Khoury, George. *The Extraordinary Works of Alan Moore*. Raleigh, NC: TwoMorrows, 2003.

Klock, Geoff. *How to Read Superhero Comics and Why*. New York: Continuum, 2002.

Lacayo, Richard. "How We Picked the List." *Time*, January 6, 2010. http://entertainment.time.com/2005/10/16/all-time-100-novels/.

Lamont, Tom. "Alan Moore—Meet the Man behind the Protest Mask." *Observer*, November 26, 2011. http://www.guardian.co.uk/books/2011/nov/27/alan-moore-v-vendetta-mask-protest.

Lawley, Guy, and Steve Whitaker. "Alan Moore." In Berlatsky ed., *Alan Moore*, 26–43.

Lawson, Mark. "To Be Continued' . . . : The Grand Tradition of Prequels and Sequels." *Guardian*, March 9, 2012. December 25, 2012. http://www.guardian.co.uk/books/2012/mar/09/prequels-sequels-books.

Lee, Stan, and Jack Kirby. *The Essential Fantastic Four*. Vol. 3. New York: Marvel, 2007.

Lethem, Jonathan. *The Fortress of Solitude*. 2003. Reprint, New York: Vintage, 2004.

"Local Government Act 1988: Section 28." *legislation.gov.uk*, n.d. http://www.legislation.gov.uk/ukpga/1988/9/section/28.

Lopes, Paul. *Demanding Respect: The Evolution of the American Comic Book*. Philadelphia: Temple University Press, 2009.

Lukin, Joshua. "I'm Not Your Boss: The Paradox of the Anarchist Superhero." *Anarchist Studies* 5.2 (1997): 131–155.

Mahler, Anne Garland. "The Writer as Superhero: Fighting the Colonial Curse in Junot Díaz's *The Brief Wondrous Life of Oscar Wao.*" *Journal of Latin American Cultural Studies* 19.2 (2010): 119–140.

Mayer, Robert. *Superfolks*. 1977. Reprint, New York: St. Martin's, 2005.

McCarthy, Tom. *Tintin and the Secret of Literature*. London: Granta Books, 2006.

McGurl, Mark. *The Program Era: Postwar Fiction and the Rise of Creative Writing*. Cambridge, MA: Harvard University Press, 2009.

McLaughlin, Robert. "Post-Postmodern Discontent: Contemporary Fiction and the Social World." *symploke* 12.1–2 (2004): 53–68.

Melley, Timothy. *Empire of Conspiracy: The Culture of Paranoia in Postwar America*. Ithaca, NY: Cornell University Press, 2000.

Moore, Alan. *Alan Moore's Writing for Comics*. Vol. 1. Rantoul, IL: Avatar, 2003.

———. "The Mark of Batman," Introduction to *Batman: The Dark Knight Returns*. By Frank Miller, Klaus Janson, and Lynn Varley, n.p., New York: DC Comics, 1986.

Moore, Alan, Stephen Bissette, and John Totleben. *Saga of the Swamp Thing: Book One*. 1983–1984. New York: DC Comics, 1987.

Moore, Alan, Dave Gibbons, and John Higgins. *Absolute Watchmen*. New York: DC Comics, 2005.

Moore, Alan, and David Lloyd. *V for Vendetta*. New York: DC Comics, 1990.

Moore, Alan, and Kevin O'Neill. *The League of Extraordinary Gentlemen Century: 2009*. Marietta, GA: Top Shelf, 2012.

Moore, Alan, and Curt Swan. *Superman: Whatever Happened to the Man of Tomorrow?* New York: DC Comics, 2010.

Musson, Alex, and Andrew O'Neill. "The *Mustard* Interview: Alan Moore." In Berlatsky ed., *Alan Moore*, 182–206.

Nix. "D.C. Reveals Their Watchmen Comic Book Prequel Plans." *BeyondHollywood.com*, February 1, 2012. http://www.beyondhollywood.com/d-c-reveals-their-watchmen-comic-book-prequel-plans/.

Nocera, Joe. "Who Owns How Much of Harry Potter?" *New York Times*, February 9, 2008. http://www.nytimes.com/2008/02/09/business/worldbusiness/09iht-wbjoe09.4.9893157.html?pagewanted=all.

Nystrom, Derek. *Hard Hats, Rednecks, and Macho Men: Class in 1970s American Cinema*. New York: Oxford University Press, 2009.

Ó Méalóid, Pádraig. "Alan Moore and *Superfolks* Part 1: The Case for the Prosecution." *The Beat*, 25 October 2012. Accessed 28 May 2013. http://comicsbeat.com/alan-moore-and-superfolks-part-1-the-case-for-the-prosecution/.

———. "Alan Moore and *Superfolks* Part 2: The Case for the Defense." *The Beat*, November 11, 2012. http://comicsbeat.com/alan-moore-and-superfolks-part-2-the-case-for-the-defence/.

———. "Alan Moore and *Superfolks* Part 3: The Strange Case of Grant Morrison and Alan Moore." *The Beat*, November 18, 2012. http://comicsbeat.com/alan-moore-and-superfolks-part-3-the-strange-case-of-grant-morrison-and-alan-moore/.

Paik, Peter Y. *From Utopia to Apocalypse: Science Fiction and the Politics of Catastrophe*. Minneapolis: University of Minnesota Press, 2010.

Patten, Brian. "Where Are You Now, Batman?" *The Mersey Sound*. By Adrian Henri, Roger McGough, and Brian Patten. 1967. 113, Revised, Baltimore: Penguin, 1974. 113.

Phegley, Kiel. "DC Comics to Publish 'Before Watchmen' Prequels." *Comic Book Resources*, February 1, 2012. http://www.comicbookresources.com/?page=article&id=36724.

Prescott, Peter S., with Ray Sawhill. "The Comic Book (Gulp!) Grows Up." *Newsweek*, January 18, 1988, 70–71.

Queenan, Joe. "Drawing on the Dark Side." *New York Times*, April 30, 1989, sec. 6, 32.

Rand, Ayn. *Atlas Shrugged*. 1957. Reprint, New York: Penguin, 1992.

Reed, Adolph. "*Django Unchained*, or, *The Help*: How 'Cultural Politics' Is Worse than No Politics at All, and Why." *nonsite*, February 25 2013. http://nonsite.org/editorial/django-unchained-or-the-help-how-cultural-politics-is-worse-than-no-politics-at-all-and-why.

Richards, Chris. "Alan Moore." *The Art of Dismantling*, March, 2011. http://www.theartofdismantling.com/2011/03/17/alan-moore-2/.

Roach, David, Andrew Jones, Simon Jowett, and Greg Hill. "Garry Leach and Alan Moore." In Berlatsky, ed., *Alan Moore*, 8–25.

Robinson, Tasha. "Interview: Alan Moore." *A.V. Club*, October 24, 2001. http://www.avclub.com/articles/alan-moore,13740/.

———. "Moore in *The Onion* Edits." In Berlatsky, ed., *Alan Moore*, 95–107.

Rogers, Vaneta. "Warner Bros. Creates dc entertainment to Maximize DC Brands." *Newsarama*, September 9, 2009. http://www.newsarama.com/comics/090909-DC-Restructuring.html.

Rowell, Rainbow. *Eleanor & Park*. New York: St. Martin's, 2013.

Salisbury, Mark. *Artists on Comic Art*. London: Titan Books, 2000.

Sharrett, Christopher. "Alan Moore." In Berlatsky, ed., *Alan Moore*, 44–60.

Shelley, Percy Bysshe. "Ozymandias." *Ode to the West Wind and Other Poems*. 5. Mineola, NY: Dover, 1993.

Sinclair, Andrew. *Arts and Cultures: The History of the 50 Years of the Arts Council of Great Britain*. London: Sinclair-Stevenson, 1995.

Strazewski, Len. "Comics Fantasyland Brought to Earth by Some Serious Issues." *Advertising Age*, July 7, 1986, 31.

Talbott, Chris. "Chabon Ties It All Together in 'Telegraph Avenue.'" *Seattle Times*, December 13, 2012. http://seattletimes.com/html/entertainment/2019895605_apusbooksmichaelchabon.html.

"10 of *Time's* Hundred Best Novels." *Time* 166.17 (24 October 2005): 110.

Thill, Scott. "Alan Moore: Comics Won't Save You, but *Dodgem Logic* Might." *Wired*, December 31, 2009. http://www.wired.com/underwire/2009/12/alan-moore-dodgem-logic/.

"Top 100 (English-Language) Comics of the Century, The." *Comics Journal* 210 (February 1999): 34–108.

Truitt, Brian. "'Watchmen' Prequels Stir a Debate." *USA Today*, June 4, 2012. http://usatoday30.usatoday.com/life/comics/story/2012-06-05/Before-Watchmen-prequel-series/55386328/1.

Vander Ark, Steven. *The Lexicon: An Unauthorized Guide to Harry Potter Fiction and Related Materials*. Muskegon, MI: RDR Books, 2009.

Van Ness, Sara J. *"Watchmen" as Literature: A Critical Study of the Graphic Novel*. Jefferson, NC: McFarland, 2010.

Vitzhum, Virginia. "Junot Díaz's Pro-Woman Agenda." *Elle*, September 18, 2012. http://www.elle.com/pop-culture/reviews/junot-diaz-interview.

Walsh, Richard. "The Narrative Imagination across Media." *Modern Fiction Studies* 52.4 (Winter 2006): 855–868.

"Wanted: Superheroes." *Forbes*, November 12, 2001. 120.

Ware, Chris. *Jimmy Corrigan: The Smartest Kid on Earth*. 2000. New York: Pantheon, 2003.

Warner Bros. "Dianne Nelson, President, DC Entertainment and President & Chief Content Officer, Warner Bros. Interactive Entertainment." WarnerBros. com, n.d. http://www.warnerbros.com/studio/executives/divisional-executives/diane-nelson.html.

Watchmen. Directed by Zack Snyder. Burbank, CA: Warner Home Video, 2009.

"Watchmen: An Oral History." *Entertainment Weekly*, October 21, 2005. http://www.ew.com/ew/article/0,,1120854,00.html.

Wegner, Phillip E. *Life between Two Deaths, 1989–2001: U.S. Culture in the Long Nineties*. Durham, NC: Duke University Press, 2009.

Wertham, Fredric. *Seduction of the Innocent*. New York: Rinehart, 1954.

Westad, Odd Arne. *The Global Cold War: Third World Interventions and the Making of Our Times*. 2005. Reprint, New York: Cambridge University Press, 2007.

Whiston, Daniel, David Russell, and Andy Fruish. "The Craft: An Interview with Alan Moore." In Berlatsky, ed., *Alan Moore*, 108–135.

White, T. H. *The Once and Future King*. 1958. Reprint, New York: Ace, 1987.

Wilde, Alan. *Middle Grounds: Studies in Contemporary American Fiction*. Philadelphia: University of Pennsylvania Press, 1987.

Wolk, Douglas. *Reading Comics: How Graphic Novels Work and What They Mean*. New York: Da Capo, 2008.

Woolf, Virginia. *Mr. Bennett and Mrs. Brown*. London: Hogarth, 1924.

———. *The Waves*. New York: Harcourt, 1931.

Worden, Daniel. "On Modernism's Ruins: The Architecture of 'Building Stories' and *Lost Buildings*." *The Comics of Chris Ware: Drawing Is a Way of Thinking*. Edited by David M. Ball and Martha B. Kuhlman, 107-120. Jackson: University Press of Mississippi, 2010.

———. "The Shameful Art: *McSweeney's Quarterly Concern*, Comics, and the Politics of Affect." *Modern Fiction Studies* 52.4 (Winter 2006): 891–917.

Wu, Chin-tao. *Privatising Culture: Corporate Art Intervention since the 1980s*. 2002. New York: Verso, 2003.

Young, Pamela. "The Comic Book's Quest for Maturity." *Maclean's*, 28 September 1987, 66.

INDEX

ABOUT THE AUTHOR

Andrew Hoberek is an associate professor of English at the University of Missouri, where he teaches courses in twentieth- and twenty-first-century literature and other arts. In addition to his book *The Twilight of the Middle Class: Post–World War II American Fiction and White-Collar Work* (2005) he has published articles and book chapters on works from the 1940s through the present. He is past president of the Association for the Study of the Arts of the Present (ASAP), a group devoted to the investigation of the contemporary moment across the arts.